LOOK NORTH

Suffolk

Wormingford
Dedham
Lawford
Wix
Harwich

Colchester
Elmstead
Tendring
Frinton

Birch
Fingringhoe
Wivenhoe
Clacton

Tollesbury
Mersea

KING COLE'S COUNTRY

Bradwell

Burnham

Foulness

LAND OF THE RIVERS

Key to sections and chapters

IN SEARCH OF ESSEX

IN SEARCH OF ESSEX

A TRAVELLER'S COMPANION TO THE COUNTY

by
STANLEY M. JARVIS, F.L.A.
and COLIN T. HARRISON, A.L.A.

Published by
ESSEX COUNTRYSIDE
LETCHWORTH PRINTERS LTD., NORTON WAY NORTH
LETCHWORTH, HERTS

Letchworth Printers Ltd., Norton Way North, Letchworth, Herts

DEDICATED
TO
HAZEL
AND PAT
BUT FOR WHOM...

CONTENTS

Foreword by Col. Sir John Ruggles-Brise

Introduction

List of illustrations

SECTION ONE—THE HEART OF THE COUNTY

SECTION TWO—LAND OF THE RIVERS

SECTION THREE—AWAY TO THE WEST

LIST OF ILLUSTRATIONS

FOREWORD

by

COL. SIR JOHN RUGGLES-BRISE, BT., C.B., O.B.E., T.D., J.P.
Her Majesty's Lieutenant for the County of Essex

Those who read this book cannot fail to get the " feel " of what surely is one of the most fascinating and charming counties in the country, for it is written by two librarians who live, work and play in our county. It is relevant, up to date, intimate and personal. The authors have spent most of their spare time at weekends and in the evenings during the last year out " in the field," thereby steeping themselves in the grass roots and ensuring that their words are not only historical but fascinating and first hand. This brought out an immediate response from me as a reader not only while sitting in my armchair but also when getting around in my car.

This book, in my opinion, is one not to be missed, for I am sure that its readers' appetites will be whetted afresh as mine was. Indeed, I found it the most comprehensive and up-to-date book in this format that I know of.

Spains Hall,
Finchingfield,
Essex.

INTRODUCTION

Essex is all things to all men. Its beauty occupied the brush of no less a painter than Constable. From its very heart were first beamed Marconi's magical wireless waves which have since circled the world and changed its way of life. The southern boundary is the bank of the Thames, the busiest waterway in the world, and its eastern shore has been a bastion against the North Sea and the threat of invasion through the ages.

Our book reflects these areas in its arrangement, covering the whole county in six sections which make natural divisions and at the same time allow for easier reference. Within each section towns and villages are arranged in smaller groups and the name of the place by which the area can best be identified is taken as the key-word in an alphabetical arrangement.

Where possible road numbers are quoted, but the charm of Essex lies in its unspoilt villages down narrow side roads. It is a pleasure to lose oneself down such winding lanes, but time is a tyrant, so we recommend the consultation of the one-inch Ordnance Survey maps for full directions.

Over the broad expanse of Essex shores, under the wide skies and long horizons which give a never-to-be-forgotten luminosity to the Essex scene, there has flowed from prehistoric times a flood of men who came to love their Essex homes and in their turn were dispossessed by following waves of settlers. Essex in its history and its culture has been marked and moulded by Ancient Britons, Romans, Vikings, Danes, Saxons and Normans. Village after village, in its ancient church, its earth entrenchments, its inns and its folklore, testifies to the variety of men who have passed its way.

In our book we invite you to follow in their footsteps.

SECTION ONE

THE HEART OF THE COUNTY

THE HEART OF THE COUNTY

CHELMSFORD

WHY is it the county town? One of the most obvious reasons is its position—twenty-nine miles from London, twenty-two from Colchester, ten from Maldon, thirty-eight from Ipswich and fifty-six from Bury St. Edmunds. Every place in Essex is within easy reach.

There are indications of a settlement before the advent of the Romans, though it was they who first bridged the rivers to bring the place they called Cæsaromagus in direct contact with London and Colchester. Chelmsford probably sprang up as a half-way house, where Romans and later travellers might rest after a hard day's march.

The town's present name comes from the ford over the River Chelmer made by the Saxons after the decay of the Roman bridge; but the town actually stands at the confluence of three rivers, the Chelmer, the Wid and the Can, and it is the last-named which passes through the centre of the town and under the High Street.

If the development of Chelmsford can be put to the credit of any one man it is Maurice, Bishop of London and owner, under the Church, of the land around Chelmsford. He saw the possibilities of the place, provided the rivers were bridged, as a flourishing centre of trade. His bridges, built about the year 1100, have long since disappeared, but his judgment has proved right to this very day.

By 1226, perhaps through the influence of the Church, the town was recognized as the centre for the assize court in the county. This important function led to a great deal of business being done in the town, which was by then of settled importance.

The Peasants' Revolt of 1381 caused King Richard to march into Chelmsford with a great army, and the town has been visited on less warlike occasions by royalty ever since.

Henry VII stayed here in 1489, when he summoned the gentlemen of Essex to meet him, telling them to be " well appointed, so that Lancashire men might see that there were gentlemen of so great substance in Essex that they could buy all Lancashire."

Under Henry VIII the friary established in 1222 was dissolved and its lands, which included half the town, were granted to Thomas

Mildmay, a local man who rose from standing behind a stall in the market to become a knight and one of the king's right-hand men in the disposal of monastery land and property. By 1563 the other half of the town became his and the family ruled as lords of the manor for nearly 300 years. A survey of the Mildmay property drawn up in 1591 is itself a survey of the town. It says: " This towne is called the Shire towne, not only by the statute of XI of King Henry the VIIth for the custodye of weightes and measures, but soe reputed and taken longe time before, by the keeping of all assizes and sessions of the peace, and many other certificacons and Inquisitions there. It is alsoe a greate thorowefare, and markett towne weekly upon the fryday."

It must be one of the few towns that do not boast a bullet hole from the civil war, but the fine east window in the church was smashed by a rampaging mob in 1641. Attention may have been diverted from the war by the great local witch scare. After hangings at Chelmsford in the sixteenth century the hunt was revived with a great trial here in this town in 1645, when twenty-five unfortunate women were sent to the gallows as evil-doing witches.

Visitors ask " Where are all the old buildings? " Most of them are gone, sad to say, but not all through the neglect of the present generation. The interesting old sessions house which stood in the middle of the High Street was allowed to fall down in the eighteenth century. In fact, the late eighteenth century was as busy a time of rebuilding and replanning as today.

The Shire Hall, which replaced the sessions house in 1791, was built to the design of John Johnson, the county surveyor. He had also designed the stone bridge at the foot of the High Street which replaced an earlier one in 1787. Both remain, with the cathedral, as prime objects of historical interest.

When looking at the cathedral remember that it was first built as, and for 500 years served the purposes of, a parish church. It was extensively restored in 1424, but in 1800 " Chelmsford church and Writtle steeple fell down one day, but killed no people " as the children of the day chanted. A vault dug in the church floor weakened a pillar so that overnight the whole nave collapsed. It was John Johnson who was responsible for the rebuilding, including the design of the roof of the nave, now beautifully restored in original colours.

A full guide which can be had for a small sum in the cathedral does the place the justice that cannot be afforded it in this short account. The Mildmay or north chapel must be mentioned; the restoration of the tomb of Thomas Mildmay in all its gilt and colour is very impressive. An unusual feature which often goes unnoticed is the two wooden cupboards built into a couple of pillars. Prosaic enough in themselves, these cupboards date from pre-Elizabethan days when plays were performed in the church, to instruct as much as to entertain. Few people know that Chelmsford was a very important centre for the production of these plays, but old records show that all the costumes and props were kept in these cupboards.

The south porch is an instance of old beauty revivified. In 1953 this " graceful example of Perpendicular work " was restored and embellished as a memorial to all those American airmen stationed in Essex during World War II. Above the porch is the library, presented to the town in 1679 by Dr. Knightbridge and constantly added to, which can be seen on application. For the record book, the tower is ninety feet high, excluding the spirelet. Under its parapet can be seen modern carvings by Huxley-Jones, symbolic of Chelmsford and Essex personalities and products. They were added during restoration in 1959.

Chelmsford is such a busy centre that a complicated system of one-way traffic flow is necessary. To make a little tour of the town it is best to put your car in one of the several car parks available and do some walking. From a westerly point the Civic Centre would make a good beginning. The block of administrative offices was built in 1962 to harmonize with the library building erected in 1935. Behind it stands the Assembly Hall, which combines a fully equipped theatre with a hall which can be let to private parties. The bus station adjoins the Civic Centre and is followed, on the other side of the road, by the railway station.

Under the bridge and down on the right stands County Hall. Its murals in the hall and in the grand council chamber show scenes from Essex history, portraits of Essex personages and two maps, of ancient and modern Essex. It has been extended between Duke Street and King Edward VII Avenue in an impressive new skyscraper block.

Almost opposite is the entrance to the cathedral, and just ahead is Tindal Square, so called from the statue which adorns it, put up in 1852 to celebrate a son of Chelmsford, Sir Nicholas Conyngham Tindal (1776-1846), who became Lord Chief Justice of the Court of Common Pleas.

On the left of the square is Shire Hall, an impressive building with three plaques high on its façade denoting wisdom, justice and mercy—the great qualities required in the serious business of the assizes which is carried out in the courtrooms within. The great ballroom, or county room, upstairs is practically in its original state, dating from 1791, with an interesting, elaborate ceiling and frieze. The picture room has copies of well-known canvases and some local originals.

New Street, so called from the fourteenth century, leaves the square by the Shire Hall, and has in it an interesting house called Guy Harlings—a name which appears in the 1591 survey. There is still some pleasant linenfold panelling of the sixteenth century to be seen in its hall.

Below the Shire Hall on the left of the High Street is the Saracen's Head hotel, where Trollope is said to have written parts of his novels, and below this in turn is the old Mansion House, or judge's lodging, now the offices of the *Essex Weekly News*, which has been preserved almost entirely in its outward appearance.

On the left-hand side again is Springfield Road, an exit from the town to the A12 and Colchester. A short distance up this road is situated Rivers House, a bright new building on stilts, which houses the headquarters of the Essex Rivers Board.

At the foot of the High Street the old stone bridge of 1787 still accommodates the flow of modern traffic, but most of Chelmsford past has vanished almost as rapidly as the stream which flows beneath. However, the Chelmsford and Essex Museum in Oaklands Park, Moulsham Street, offers a number of collections which help in recalling the history of the locality, as well as other very interesting collections such as those of old drinking glasses, coins, and local industries. It is open from 10 a.m. to 5 p.m. daily and from 2 to 5 p.m. on Sundays, and admission is entirely free.

Oaklands Park itself is a very pleasant place in which to stroll, with swings and other things to amuse the children, but if you just want to sit at peace or walk through a wide expanse of unspoilt countryside try Hylands Park. The entrance is some way out of Chelmsford, through Writtle, turning left by the Cock and Bell and following the signs. This 400-acre park with mansion (not open to the public) was bought by the townspeople of Chelmsford, though really not within the borough boundary, as a perpetual open space for the enjoyment of everybody in the area. It includes one of the biggest of the nine heronries in the county—worth a visit in itself.

Chelmsford is a focal point for entertainment of a more energetic nature—swimming. Its new heated indoor pool is very spacious, and is a popular centre in the county. You will find it down Waterloo Lane, off New Street.

Some people find markets entertaining. The market has always been an important aspect of Chelmsford's prosperity. It continues so, to the degree that in 1963 a new market was opened on a site in Victoria Road to cope with growing trade in up-to-date conditions. The stallage market, where the housewife hunts her bargains, still opens on Friday and Saturday on the old site just off Tindal Square.

Chelmsford today is noted for the many-sided activities of the Marconi and associated companies in and about the town, for the big Hoffmann ball-bearing works and for the English Electric Valve Company's products.

A well-planned, rapidly developing industrial estate has been laid out on the Widford side of the town, which now includes important new editorial offices and printing plant for the *Essex Chronicle* series of newspapers and general printing.

Widford itself is a parish which has become identified with the county town. Its village street has been bisected by the roaring A12, isolating the church and pub, the White Horse. It used to be called the Silent Woman and its sign (now in the museum of rural life at Reading) shows a woman with her head cut off! The place has been reorganized recently and offers good meals in comfortable surroundings.

Round the other side of the town two other villages have been more or less swallowed in its expansion. The road to Broomfield is now continuously built up. Philip Morant, the great Essex historian, was vicar here for five years from 1733. The church is much restored after being bombed in World War II, but boasts one of the half-dozen round towers to exist in the county and owns a Bible which belonged to Charles I.

The tower of Springfield church bears the inscription " Prayse God for al the Good Benefactors ano 1586 " on its south side, as a record of an early repair. Fragments of Roman bricks and tiles can still be seen in the original fabric of the nave and chancel walls. The font is a good 800 years old—proof of Norman foundation. Goldsmith is reputed to have stayed in a cottage here, where he wrote parts of *The Deserted Village*. Part of the village was absorbed into Chelmsford as far back as 1907 and recent building has brought a rash of housing estates in this area, so that its rural aspect is fast vanishing. The old Springfield mill, which stands in Victoria Road in what is now Chelmsford, is of clapboard construction in typical Essex style. Its work done, it seems to brood above the stream which once was its life-blood.

Great Baddow, in like manner, can hardly be differentiated from the ever-spreading county town. What nucleus of village remained has been given an air of nightmare fantasy by the erection of a great concrete-and-glass office block which looms and leers above the humble cottages and modest villas. It has been quoted by one authority as a good example of bad development. The old Baddow Hall has been swept away in favour of this and other development, but the church, with its interesting sixteenth-century brickwork, still stands to give the place a sense of its history.

COGGESHALL and its approaches

THE three spans of Stephen's Bridge, one of the oldest brick-built bridges in the country, join together the two villages of Great and Little Coggeshall. Although the distinction is of no great importance today, Little Coggeshall is on the southern side of the bridge, and was the site of an old abbey, parts of which can still be seen.

It is possible to approach Coggeshall from any direction with equal ease, for the B1024 runs north to south and the A120 east to west, both passing through open farmland, much of which is a blaze of colour during the flowering season, for this is a well-known seed-growing area.

Let us start a tour round this region from the south on the B1024. About a mile north of Kelvedon, on the right, stands the home of the de Coggeshall family, who were lords of the manor during the reign of King Stephen. Having passed through Coggeshall hamlet look out for Abbey Lane, again on the right, for along this lane stand the church of St. Nicholas and the abbey mill. The church, used by the monks as an additional chapel, was used as a barn for many centuries after the dissolution, but in 1897 was restored and is now returned to its former use. Notice the small pinkish bricks used in some parts of this small church, for they are probably the first bricks made in England after the Romans left. Farther along the lane the farm buildings contain parts of the fabric of the old abbey. At the end of the lane, where a bridge crosses the river, stand the wooden buildings of the mill. To provide a head of water for the mill the industrious monks diverted the river into an artificial bed, and it is this line that the river still follows. This is a most relaxing sight, with the large area of water, the wooden buildings and the occasional visits from wild birds.

Returning to the B1024 and travelling on towards Great Cogges-hall look for Grange Farm on the left, with its tithe barn dating from 1500. The barn has a king-post roof support and is covered in tiles. Crossing the young River Blackwater by way of Stephen's Bridge the road runs up into the main town centre. To the right of the bridge is the Rood House, which was probably the site of a cross or rood marking the entrance to the abbey.

There is much for the eye to feast on in Coggeshall. Particularly attractive is the way the shops and houses seem to fight each other for a place on the street fronts, the victors standing proud, the vanquished being pushed back a few feet. In an age of huge glass-fronted supermarkets it is good to see small shops of varying archi-tectural style still open for trade.

While in the town three things must not be missed. The first of these is in West Road and is the famous merchant's house of Pay-cocke's. Little need be said about this house, so well known is it, but the description given in *Historic Houses* will serve to refresh the memory: " A merchant's house dating from about 1500, with unusually rich panelling and wood carving." It is open on Wednes-day, Thursday and Sunday from 2 to 5.30 p.m., and admission is 2/6. Paycocke was one of the Flemish weavers who settled in this part of the country and helped to make " Coggeshall whites," one of the most famous cloths in England.

The other two places of interest stand close together in the northern part of the town. These are the parish church of St. Peter ad Vincula (St. Peter in chains) and the Woolpack inn. When you look at the fine fifteenth-century Perpendicular church it is difficult to believe that much of it was reconstructed as recently as 1956 after being bombed during World War II. The loving care of the modern builders has indeed matched that of the original craftsmen. Contained within the church are the memorial brasses to the Paycocke family. Next to the church is the timber-and-plaster

Woolpack inn; in 1450 it was a priest's house and was only later converted into an inn.

Before leaving Coggeshall mention must be made of the almost forgotten insult of the " Coggeshall job." This was used when, by some mischance, a person did a job in such a way that it became ludicrous. Typical of the many stories is the following one quoted by E. Tyrell-Green in his guide to Coggeshall. " Far-fetched is the story attaching to the Coggeshall town clock, which tells how one day the clock struck eleven at twelve noon. Word came from Lexden, near Colchester, that the clock there had struck twelve at eleven, so the Coggeshall people sent off one of their number in a pony and trap to bring back the missing stroke."

A couple of miles north of Coggeshall is the strange but attractive village of Markshall. This village gets smaller each decade; in 1932 the church was demolished—the monument to Mary Honeywood, who died in 1620 leaving 367 descendants, is now housed in St. Peter's, Coggeshall—and in 1951 the Hall was taken down. Surrounding the village are many woods, and nearby Robin's brook flows down to join and swell the Blackwater.

West of Coggeshall, along the A120 Roman road, called Stane Street, lies Bradwell-juxta-Coggeshall. This is a lovely country village, with cottages and trees vying with the eleventh-century church for your attention. If you drive around this part of the county take care, for the lanes are narrow and designed for horse and cart rather than for fast cars. In many places two cars cannot pass each other, so be ready to back up and be a good neighbour.

CRESSING

CRESSING lies half-way between Witham and Braintree just off the B1018. The big feature of the place is a couple of miles out of the village on the Witham side, and is easily spotted from the road. It is the two great tithe barns—the only remains of Cressing Temple, a manor granted to the Knights Templars in 1136 which passed in the fourteenth century to the Knights of St. John of Jerusalem.

The barns have weathered all the storms of time over 600 years and stand as a monument to the patient skill of medieval craftsmen. Their intricate construction must be seen from the interior, where the dimensions (around 150ft. by 40ft.) of each barn make the great oak beams seem almost delicate in the fretwork of the roof.

From Cressing there is a view across the River Brain to Black and White Notley, villages connected by a road running parallel with the B1018. To the south White Notley can show an early Tudor manor house and a Norman church with later additions. Going north on the winding road we pass The Green, a tiny hamlet, and see on our left the extensive buildings and grounds of Black Notley hospital. The village spreads from here to a triangular road junction, on the base of which sit the Hall and the church of St. Peter.

Once upon a time the villages were one, but the land was divided at the Conquest between de Mandeville, Earl of Essex, and Bigod, Earl of Norfolk, and each set about building his own church on his own land for the use of himself and his serfs and villeins.

The countryside is pleasantly undulating, with views of some fine estates and old inns and houses, but Black Notley's claim to fame lies in the fact that John Ray (1628-1706) was born here, son of the village blacksmith. He became a celebrated naturalist, writing to authorities all over the world, but still died in his native village, where he is buried under a monument in the churchyard with a long Latin inscription.

DANBURY and the villages round the hill

DANBURY tops one of the highest hills in Essex. The ascent is sharper on the Chelmsford side, where the road runs over the Sandford brook to the foot of the hill. On the left-hand side going up there is evidence of one of the county's greatest assets— gravel. Thousands of tons have been removed from this area, and half-way up the hill the gravel works, still in operation, are hidden behind St. Clere's Hall, an attractive house with Tudor associations and the name of an ancient family.

On the other side of the road run the grounds of Danbury Palace, an unashamed mock-Tudor brick building splendidly conceived in 1834 by the Round family and so called because it was later lived in by the bishop of this diocese. Today its chief function is as a centre for Civil Defence and it is not open to the public, though part of the grounds is, and the lakes in particular are very popular for picnics and fishing. That part of the park above the palace and fronting the road is reserved for youth camping; details can be had from County Hall.

At the top of the hill, the church, the crowning glory, mostly 600 years old, stands within the protective ramparts of a fortification said to have been thrown up by the Danes, from which the village gets its name. You will see that the spire has been partly renewed. It has been struck by lightning on several occasions. Look inside for the memorials to the St. Clere family—three oaken effigies in low recesses in the wall. All are of the turn of the thirteenth century, beautifully executed in poses of stiff heraldic significance.

Round about the village there are any number of interesting buildings. The Griffin inn, sixteenth-century, timber-framed, is actually mentioned in the preface to the Waverley novels by Sir Walter Scott. All round the hill there are little roads to a variety of pleasures. To the south Danbury Common, National Trust property, draws picnickers and walkers to its furzy acres. We might add here that Lingwood Common, to the north across the A414, is also held by the National Trust, and in both areas, we are told, car owners should park in the authorized car parks or on the roadside verges only.

To the south-west past Horne Row and on, the Sandon road runs parallel with the A414, entering Sandon at the crossroads by the church. In Tudor days the famous Cardinal Wolsey was lord of the manor of Sandon. Some of the great elms by the church must have been saplings in his time, while more than one of the cottages across the green is old enough to have housed his tenants.

How solid and dependable St. Andrew's looks, with its massive sixteenth-century tower and stair turret in mellow red brick. Inside, the octagonal pulpit is even older, and unusually all-of-a-piece, for it was carved of English oak in the 1400s.

From the crossroads go north and turn on to the A414, then the very next turning on the right will take you down a narrow road to Little Baddow. Look out on the right for a tree-lined track called Grace's Walk, said to be haunted, which goes up to Great Graces, home of the Mildmays in the sixteenth century and still beautiful with its old brick buildings and weatherboarded barn. The road runs past the old Independent chapel of 1708 and on to a meeting with the Chelmer by an old watermill, now a pleasant residence, and a bridge popular with fishermen for miles around.

The church of St. Mary is just up the road on the right away from the river. Stop and, as a traveller, admire the fifteenth-century wall painting of St. Christopher—the patron saint of travellers. Wonder, too, at the fifteenth-century craftsmanship which produced the stained glass of St. Michael and the dragon. There is a splendid Mildmay monument here, dated 1639, and a memorial 300 years older than this shows oaken effigies of a man and his wife which are tenderly realized.

The climb up the hill back to Danbury now begins, and a number of side roads offer opportunities for exploration. Houses of interest like Riffhams, overlooking Lingwood Common, stand in old-world gardens which are open on certain days in aid of charity. Round the hill, by narrow roads, you will come to Woodham Walter, where the most striking building is the half-timbered Bell inn, dating from around 1600. The church is a strange contradiction; though built as late as 1563, and remarkable for this very fact because so few churches were built at this time, in its architectural style it harks back 300 years to the Perpendicular, carried out in red brick. To the natural pleasures offered here we can add the man-made holes and hazards of the Warren Golf Club.

To get to the associated village of Woodham Mortimer (both villages are named after their first Norman lords) it is necessary to go back to Danbury and head towards Maldon on the A414. A sharp bend to the left where it meets the B1010 and we are on the long, straight road to the church. On the right we pass Woodham Mortimer Place, the home of Mr. A. J. Brush, a man who made a million from gravel excavation. He set out his own racecourse in the grounds. The Hall and church stand together farther up the road. The church was restored 100 years ago and only a Norman window in the south aisle testifies to an earlier existence. A church-yard stone records the death in 1683 of Dr. Peter Chamberlen, physician to three kings.

The Hall, with its seventeenth-century Dutch-gabled brick front, is interesting today as the headquarters of a sugar-beet growing firm. Sugar production is, believe it or not, a thriving Essex industry. In the field opposite there is a monument which puzzles passers-by. It is an obelisk put up by the Coopers Company in 1825 to the memory of William Alexander, lord of the manor.

FAULKBOURNE

WHEN people talk about a wishing well they usually think of one of those things with a tiny roof and a bucket on a rope, but the belief is much older than that, going back beyond the time of our religion to the days when men believed in spirits of the wood and water; so a well may be a spring, as at Faulkbourne, where the water wells up to make a large, shallow, reed-fringed pond. The wishing pond is near the road, yet almost hidden from it by the lush growth of grass and nettle.

The footpath to the church is just beyond it, and once you are standing by the lich-gate you are in another world. The church is small and humble-looking, but of great age. Across the parkland through the trees one can catch glimpses of Faulkbourne Hall, remarkable for its brickwork of all ages from medieval to Victorian times. Even the lodge in its planned, picturesque wilderness has a fairy-tale air when seen through the summer verdure.

The village itself lines the road around the corner, with more than one pink- or white-plastered house to catch the eye. Notice the little window in the side wall of the post office. That dates back to the mail-coach days. The postmaster put his bed beneath it so that he could take in the mail bags in the early hours of the morning without going to the trouble of getting dressed!

MALDON

OVERLOOKING the sparkling waters of the Blackwater, Maldon is a town to excite all our senses. The eye can run down the hill, following the line of the streets down to the cobbled quayside, and out on to the river with its changing pattern of ships and birds. The nose is assailed by the fresh tang of the sea air and the timber stacked along the water's edge. One's hands can follow the contours of buildings dating from almost every age, while the imagination can conjecture with the historic events that have occurred in the town.

Maldon owes its name to its Saxon founders, who called it Maeldun (hill of assembly); and a more modern building, the Moot Hall, in name and character continues the Saxon tradition of a meeting place. The town has always been a prize worth having, and many battles must have taken place for the control of the hill on which the present town stands, for he who controlled the hill controlled the rich land surrounding it.

The most famous of these battles took place in A.D. 991 between the Saxons, under Brihtnoth, and the invading Danes. With the death of their leader, the Saxons fled the field and the Danes took possession of the town. The tale of this battle is recorded in the contemporary Saxon poem, which says in the translation by Kevin Crossby-Holland:

> " Bryhtnoth drew out his sword from its sheath,
>> Broad-faced and gleaming, and made to slash at the sea-
>> farer's corselet,
>
> But his enemy stopped him all too soon
> Then the heathens hewed him down
> And the two men who stood there supporting him."

The scene of the battle is about one and a quarter miles south-east of Maldon along the B1018.

It was as a result of this battle that the king, Ethelred (the Unready), started to pay Danegeld to buy off the Danes. Some of the coins minted at Maldon have been discovered in Scandinavia.

Maldon retains many of its old houses and inns and the visitor will not have to look far to find them, for they are round every corner. A figure-of-eight walk will show the visitor many of the historic buildings in the town and perhaps whet the appetite for a more detailed private search. In Gate Street a fine five-bayed Georgian house looks down to the High Street. In the High Street there are several eighteenth-century houses and opposite All Saints' church, which has a triangular tower, is the King's Head, with its eighteenth-century porch. The church stands at the corner of Silver Street, and in this street is the Blue Boar hotel, dating from about 1390. The stabling at the rear is quite impressive. Across from the Blue Boar and behind the church is the vicarage, a timber-framed fifteenth-century house with two gables, one at either end of the building.

Just round the corner from All Saints, in the High Street again, is the Moot Hall, dating from 1440 and now used as law courts and council chamber. Its great clock is a landmark in the street, for it projects out over the pavement. Past the entrance to Market Hill is the tower—and all that remains—of St. Peter's church. Climb the tower steps to the Plume library, which is over the county branch library. This was founded by Dr. Plume in 1704 and contains many rare books. Visitors wishing to see the fine collection and the rich surroundings are welcome on Tuesday and Saturday mornings and Wednesday and Thursday afternoons.

For recreation the visitor can do no better than follow the High Street down to its junction with Mill Road. Here a footpath leads out to the recreation ground, with its marine lake, swimming pool and boating pool. Along the edge of the river is a broad tree-lined walk where deck-chairs are available, as are boat trips on the river, and where you can very often obtain shrimps fresh from the baskets of wayside sellers. Looking out over the waters of the Blackwater, the old sailing barges *Marjorie* and *Memory* may still be seen performing useful tasks.

At this end of the town St. Mary's church can be seen. This church, whose history dates back to Saxon times, was used as a navigation mark by sailors using the harbour.

No visit to Maldon would be complete without seeing Beeleigh Abbey, which was founded in 1180 by Robert Mantell. It was restored about thirty-five years ago and visitors are welcome on Wednesdays between 2 and 5 p.m. There is a small charge. Finding the Abbey is not difficult; a short walk from the end of Beeleigh Road off High Street, or from Abbey Turning off London Road, will soon get you there.

Just north of Beeleigh are Beeleigh waterfalls and lock. Here a ruined mill, a pretty pathway leading to Weir Bridge, and the golf course may be seen.

Across the river from Maldon is its sister town of Heybridge. The route is over Full Bridge and down the Causeway into Heybridge Street. To the right of the junction is the church of St. Andrew, which is almost completely Norman. At the end of Heybridge Street/Hall Road is the timber-framed and plastered Heybridge Hall, built in the 1700s. At the opposite end of the road and along Anchor Lane the miller's small red-brick house can be seen, with its attendant weatherboarded mill.

These are the parts of the town which are of architectural interest, but it is to the hundreds of small boats that Heybridge owes its fame. To find the heart of this boatman's paradise cross Wave Bridge and follow Goldhanger Road, B1026, to Basin Road, at the end of which you will find Heybridge Basin. This is where the boats are and the visitor can look over the masts and spars to the towers of Maldon across the river and the fields.

Returning along the B1026 for about two miles, the village of Langford is reached. With the River Blackwater flowing across the west end of the village, the golf course to the north and the reservoirs to the south, this is a pleasant place to drive through on a summer's day. While in Langford the connoisseur of churches must not miss St. Giles's, for it is the only church in England to have preserved its western apse. The church is certainly Norman, and may even date from before the Conquest. Looking to the south, the merging of the River Chelmer with the Blackwater makes an attractive sight.

Onwards with the B1026 again, the last village to see in this group is Ulting. For the scenic route turn left for Ulting Wick about three-quarters of a mile after leaving Langford. This road runs along the line of the River Chelmer and into the large orchards that surround Ulting Wick. Standing on the banks of the river is the tiny church of All Saints, which dates from the fifteenth century. Here you can stand by the church gate and look round the Essex countryside, with its trees and streams and fields, and, on those magic days that sometimes occur in rural England, watch the mole push his way up to the sunlight from the darkness of the earth.

PLESHEY

LET us take a run from Chelmsford through the Chignals to Pleshey. The road off the A414 on the Roxwell side of the town runs up through housing estates, to emerge in gently rising open country. The next left turn takes us through Chignal St. James, past Brickbarns Farm, where the brick barn has an unusual dovecote built into its end gable, and on to the little church, which, except for a couple of cottages, stands in its own little wilderness, an island in rich Essex farmland. In the churchyard, almost forgotten, lies Miller Christy, a great Essex antiquarian and naturalist of the first years of this century.

Passing Chignal Hall on our left we go on to Chignal Smealy, where the church was built entirely of brick in Elizabethan days and stands so today. Go inside and see the font, which is also, and very unusually, made of the same bricks! A name, perhaps of the builder, can be seen deeply carved.

Farther on the road bends back to Chelmsford, passing the Three Elms, which must surely rank among the smallest of Essex pubs. But we shall retrace our route to the road to Mashbury and go all round the houses, as they say, by Good Easter and High Easter to arrive at last at Pleshey.

Mashbury, with Sparrow End, has evidence of Roman occupation with Roman bricks in the Norman walls of the church, which owns a great chest worth looking at. It represents the equivalent of our town hall strong-room today, for it held all the legal and other papers concerning the running of the village. As we go by, one or two white-walled thatched cottages peep out over their thick hedges. Mashbury Hall, down the cul-de-sac by the church, shows bits of building through the ages, while Baileys, almost due north, retains its Tudor features.

People have been known in the past to travel to Good Easter to get the postmark on their Easter greeting cards. The village includes Tye Green, Farmbridge End, and Clatterford End. The church was partly burnt down in 1885, but its stout thirteenth-century walls defied the flames and, phœnix-like, it rose again with a timbered spire over 100 feet high. Nearby note the village whipping post still in position.

There are any number of interesting cottages and farmhouses tucked away down narrow lanes. To give one example, Great Newarks, a seventeenth-century house in excellent preservation with part of an earlier moat, is down a long cul-de-sac on the banks of the Can. It is best to walk!

High Easter has the remains of that symbol of Essex industry the windmill, and a church with an entrance between two old gabled houses which go back to the fifteenth century.

There is something about prehistoric encampments and earthworks that causes admiration and wonder. The vast amounts of earth moved, the primitive tools used, the imagination of their creators and the dogged persistence of those who laboured are brought to mind when one views remains like those of the Mount at Pleshey. Here a rampart and ditch a mile in circumference enclose a prehistoric dwelling site which has been turned to good account by succeeding generations of Romans, Saxons and Normans.

Geoffrey de Mandeville, Norman lord of vast estates, made the 12,000 acres round Pleshey his headquarters and built a castle on the old mound, surrounding it with a moat. The bridge which crosses it today dates from the fifteenth century, though it has been lovingly restored by the present owner. Of the castle only the foundations remain, but it has a high place in English history. In 1397 Richard II believed its then owner, his uncle, the Duke of Gloucester, was plotting against him. He therefore came to Pleshey, tricked his uncle into arrest and had him taken to Calais, where he was murdered. The duke's body was brought back to Pleshey as proof that the deed was done before it was buried in Westminster Abbey.

The man who planned it all was the Duke of Exeter, Richard's half-brother. When Richard was deposed the mob seized Exeter and brought him to Pleshey, where he was beheaded. So Pleshey achieved especial fame by having its name and these stirring times immortalized in Shakespeare's *Richard II*.

Though the Mount is private it can be seen from various points in the village. At the White Horse you can refresh yourself in a fifteenth-century inn which has seen kings and corpses pass.

The church is a comparatively recent building, incorporating older fabric including an interesting stone thought to have come from Pleshey castle and which has Latin letters and " Richard II " inscribed on it.

TERLING

FROM the fabulously busy A12 it is doubly refreshing to turn off into the country road which runs to Terling. It is possible to take a route which loops out to the village and back to the A12 a mile farther on, and in that short time and distance you will have stepped into an Essex of another age.

Down the road the pheasants scuttle in front of the car and a rabbit bobs away along the bank, while through the trees which roof the road you get glimpses of well-tilled farmland and lush green parkland.

If you are approaching from the south you cross the River Ter and climb a hill, to come suddenly upon the ideal view of an English village—the fifteenth-century Manor House on the one side and a wide green on the other, where the church raises its tower of warm red brick against a backcloth of elm and oak. It is a church well worth a visit, with a number of brasses going back to 1490.

As the road bends round further views delight the eye. Pink-washed cottages and the village shop cluster round the junction where the road runs down to the ford and the windmill. Children

love to splash through the ford, which is long and shallow, but
brakes do need drying out before proceeding. The windmill's bold,
black shape pushes up against the sky, but its sails are rotting in
the nettles at its foot. The arms are left, pointing like accusing
fingers.

Almost hidden behind the church is Terling Place, home of the
Rayleigh family. The present mansion dates from the eighteenth
century, but the previous house here was visited by Henry VIII.

Fairstead takes you farther into the hinterland of Essex agriculture. Called " fair " when it was first settled in Saxon times it
remains so today. Warley Hall was a fortified dwelling then, now
it is a farmhouse, but it still keeps its moat. Do not miss the church,
St. Mary's, because it has mural paintings actually dated 1275 and
other interesting evidences of Fairstead's history.

GREAT WALTHAM

ESSEX is full of villages prefixed Great and Little, and it is
not always possible to tell from their size today which is
which; but Great Waltham still retains its superiority over its
Little neighbour. It is an ancient place, deriving its name from
Wealdam, the settlement in the wood; for the great Essex forest
pressed in on it in Saxon times. Today it is one of the largest parishes
in the county, including the hamlets of North End, Howe Street,
Broads Green, Littley Green, Ford End, Ringtail Green and Minor
End.

The church of St. Mary and St. Lawrence makes the road bend
right round it, and care is needed. It was an early building of the
Norman invaders, who used the odd Roman bricks they found
still lying about. What to look for? The very old carved benches,
the brasses of 1580 and 1617, the peal of eight bells—one of the
oldest in the county, with one bell made in 1336—and the monument of 1614 to Sir Anthony Everard of Langleys.

Langleys has been in the Tufnell family since 1711, and was
built to the design of Samuel Tufnell, including in it part of the
existing house, already 100 years old. Later additions and restora-
tions have been faithful to the Jacobean splendour of the interior
and today the estate is still beautifully maintained. The heraldic
decoration of the lodge (a miniature of the house itself) in recent
years proves this. The gardens are sometimes open to the public,

when the amazing variety of trees and shrubs can be enjoyed, together with a view of the Chelmer, which flows through the grounds.

The Royal Commission on Historical Monuments lists more than eighty buildings in this village which are of great interest, so it is impossible to cover them all in this work. Best to go there and let the scene speak for itself. There are houses of all periods to be seen. One good example of a large gabled house is now the Six Bells inn, while Waltham House is a Georgian gem. Hyde Hall still shows part of its moat, though the existing house is only 300 years old. The Green Man at Howe Street goes back to the fourteenth century.

While Great Waltham lies on the Dunmow road (A130), Little Waltham is on the Braintree road (A131). A sharp turn in the village combined with a bridge over the Chelmer requires careful driving.

Despite the bungalows spreading on the Braintree side this is a pretty, homogeneous village. Its church is down a side road. A recent visit showed its fabric to be in a poor state, but there are treasures to be seen here—a big " dug-out " chest all of 500 years old and a three-foot-long brass of 1447 depicting an armoured knight. You can find a pleasant walk here down by the river to an old clapboard mill which soars above the locks. A bridge takes the footpath over to connect up with the Broomfield road.

From Little Waltham our way lies conveniently towards Braintree and Great and Little Leighs. Little Leighs does not show on the main road, but it is worth branching off to visit it. The church, largely of twelfth-century construction, has one really unusual item, the memorial figure of a priest carved in oak at least 700 years ago, and one of only ten such figures in the whole of Essex. If you want to know what linenfold panelling looks like inspect the Tudor pews. Leighs Hall, farther up the road, is a sixteenth-century building.

One and three-quarter miles (and a couple of turnings) north-west are the remains of Leez Priory. Little of the Austin priory is left, for Lord Rich acquired the property at the Reformation and built himself a fabulous residence. That in its turn was largely pulled down when the place was bought in 1735 by Guy's Hospital. But the huge gatehouse in red Tudor brick patterned with blue still stands and has been carefully restored in a setting of beautiful gardens.

Great Leighs is on the A131 nearer Braintree, lining the main road for a mile between two crossroads. Standing at one of these is St. Anne's Castle, said to be the oldest licensed public-house in England, which was in medieval times a hermitage and developed into an inn by the resting of pilgrims here on their way to the shrine of St. Thomas à Becket at Canterbury.

The church has a Norman round tower, but the spire is recent. There is an old barrel-organ here, the first signs of automation in the church! The crossroads beckon with encouraging names like Willows Green and Molehill Green to the north-west and Gubbions Green and Ranks Green to the south-east. On the way to Willows Green stands Moulsham Hall, where the Court Oak is remarkable for its twenty-five-foot girth and its corresponding age.

WICKHAM BISHOPS

NOT far from the madding crowd that races along the A12 Witham by-pass lie five villages that can give the visitor solace from the hurry and bustle of trunk-road travel. Around these villages are large woods, orchards, an ornamental park, and a fine mountain view. This region is a maze of country roads with their finger-posts pointing to the various habitations: Great and Little Braxted, Great and Little Totham, and of course the name place of this chapter, Wickham Bishops. If you miss a turning as you drive round regard it as a bonus, look at the landscape, and press on a few hundred yards to the next crossroads and pick up another signposted route.

Wickham Bishops is best approached from the now strangely quiet Witham town centre and down the B1018 (Maldon road) until just after it goes under the new by-pass, then turn left down Wickham Hill. This road runs through Chantry Wood, a cool place on a summer's day, before entering the village centre. The " Bishops " part of its name comes from the connection with the Bishops of London, the moated remains of whose residence can still be seen today.

To the right of the crossroads in the village stands the " new " church, built only just over 100 years ago. Along this lane, as it runs down to the railway station, there are fine views over the rich farmland, orchards and small woods that are features of this hilly region. Just beyond the railway station the road crosses the River Blackwater, and from the bridge the visitor can see the old water-mill with its early-Georgian house next door. The river here is little more than a stream and is lined by banks of trees.

Travelling in the opposite direction, the lane climbs Beacon Hill towards Great Totham. From Beacon Hill there is a wonderful eagle's-eye view in every direction: to the east the coastline is displayed like a relief map before you; at the foot of the hill the cottages, houses and pub are clustered together in a gay jumble so untypical of our modern planned estates.

A mile or so east lies the other Totham—the Little one. This village is built on more leisurely sloping land than the other villages hereabouts and is enclosed by many farms. South of the village is the 500-year-old Hall, and near this is the church of All Saints, set in the centre of a cluster of trees. This church is one of the few in the county to escape having some of its registers destroyed, and these date back to 1558. Within the church is a marble monument to Sir John Samms and his wife. He is shown in Stuart armour and his wife is wearing a dress that is typical of the Stuart fashion for ladies of importance.

Looping north-west and crossing the B1022 just south of Tiptree Heath we reach Great Braxted. To the north lies the large Braxted Park, with its ornamental gardens and serpentine lake. This was the home of the Du Cane family in the seventeenth century. In more recent years it housed the headquarters of the large Plessey company, although it is now once more under private ownership. Tucked away in the corner of the park is the parish church of All Saints, which stands on the edge of a small wood with fine views of the lake. South of the road is a fairly large orchard—one of the many that feed the Witham fruit-packing station.

On the other side of this orchard, but a long U-loop by road, is Little Braxted. Near the road, where it crosses the river, is the sixteenth-century Hall, with its original chimney still standing. Across the road from the Hall is the church of St. Nicholas, which has parts dating from Norman times and has one of those apses that only the Normans could build so perfectly. A little farther on is a mill with a Georgian miller's house. The scenery here is most attractive, being made perhaps more lush by the Blackwater running along this end of the parish and feeding the willow trees that are a feature of the landscape.

WITHAM and the long straight road

THAT old long straight road of the Romans, our A12, which runs between Chelmsford and Colchester is becoming as curved and crooked as Harry Lauder's stick, and all to the good, for it means that one Essex village after another is being by-passed to save it from the tyranny of through traffic.

Boreham awaits the pleasure of just such a by-pass, and the village is divided completely by the main road. If you are approaching from the Chelmsford side the first clue to its history is the gatehouse in red brick on the left, which guards the entrance to New Hall. What a history this place has!

It was first built about 1500, and owned at some time by Sir Thomas Boleyn, father of one of Henry VIII's ill-fated queens. It is quite likely that Henry visited the place to court Anne. He liked it so much that he became its owner in 1517 or thereabouts, called it Beaulieu and restored and extended it. His daughter Queen Mary, and after her Queen Elizabeth, stayed here and added to the buildings. For a long time the Elizabethan coat of arms could be seen over the entrance door.

After having various owners it was sold to George Villiers, Duke of Buckingham, for £30,000 in 1620; but when Parliamentarian forces seized it in 1650 they sold it to Oliver Cromwell—for five shillings! From royal magnificence it has dwindled in stature and in size to its present function as a convent school. During the war it was further humbled by a German bomb aimed at the American-made aerodrome which it overlooked.

As the road continues to the brow of the rise there is a pleasing view away to the right of rich farmland rising to the hill crowned by Danbury church spire. Then the view is blocked by Boreham House. It stands away from the road at the farther end of a lake which runs the length of the quarter-mile drive. This elegant eighteenth-century house, said to have been built of material from demolitions at New Hall, now houses a tractor and equipment training centre run by the Ford organization. Two rooms, the saloon and the entrance hall, reflect the original splendour of the place.

Farther along, a right-hand turn by the Red Lion takes you down to the village, where some sixteenth-century houses, a couple recently lovingly restored, still stand in the lee of the church. St. Andrew's cannot be classed as beautiful, but it does have interesting features, including a three-figure monument to successive Earls of Sussex, and in the ancient registers there is the record of the burial of a witch after being hanged.

All around the old village there is springing up a whole series of estates to suit the needs of commuters in both directions along the A12; there is nothing to explore there, so we can go back to the main road and on past the Cock. Down the left-hand turn by the inn stands Porters, the oldest house in the village, under threat of demolition as work on the by-pass develops.

The relief that a by-pass brings can be seen very clearly in the next village—Hatfield Peverel, so called from the name of its Norman lord. Now it is possible to drive slowly down the street, admiring the buildings ranging in date from the first Elizabeth to the second, a picture of the ceaseless development of an Essex village. Though the high road brought the houses huddling round it, the village began long before down the other road, the B1019 on the Maldon side, where the church stands on the site of, and is actually part of, an ancient Benedictine priory. The view from the churchyard across the meadow to the old priory fishponds is still rustic and refreshing.

It is a couple of years now since Witham was by-passed, and the residents are just about getting used to the novelty of easy parking and easier street crossing. There is no doubt that the Georgian aspect of the main street can be better appreciated without the interruption of massive, fume-belching lorries. Witham is largely Georgian because a chalybeate spring discovered locally raised hopes that a kind of Bath or Cheltenham might be established.

The hope faded, but the town lived on, changing its industries to suit the age, so that today it is as important industrially as it was in medieval days when its cloth market was well known.

The site of its ancient importance is off to the north-west of the present main street, at Chipping Hill. A cheaping or chipping was a Saxon market, an important gathering place. If you stand on the spot today, by the church, and look out over green fields with just a hint of houses spreading over the crest of the hill, and with the River Brain running in its age-old bed under the humped-back bridge, it is hard to realize that this was once the busy town centre.

Yet it was a fortified place as early as 913, when Edward the Elder was trying to keep the Danes in order. Roman bricks in the tower testify to even earlier importance, but the main fabric is of the four-

teenth century. It grew, no doubt, with the cloth trade, and pros-
pered with it. The rood screen still has its cross in position, all finely
carved in wood, while the blocked stairway which may have given
access to the rood loft can still be detected. The Southcotte monument, two reclining figures in fine attire, shows clearly the costume
of the late sixteenth century. There is a lot to be seen at St.
Nicholas's, right down to the little golden dove which hovers on its
chain above the font.

The memory of the cloth trade and the market is preserved in
the name of the inn next the churchyard, the Woolpack. When we
dropped in the widowed landlady proved to be a mine of interesting
information on things Essex, from Waltham Abbey to Brightlingsea. The Woolpack is a rambling place which has outgrown itself
several times, so that upstairs an old Tudor window is now in-
corporated in the bedroom itself. Round about the church there are
several old timber-framed and plastered houses to delight the eye.
One opposite the church has a curious finial to the great chimney
stack recently revealed—so decorative that first thoughts were that
it was a wayside shrine.

From the medieval atmosphere around the church it is but a step
down the road to the Georgian façades of the High Street. There
are too many interesting old places to be detailed here, but the inns,
the Spread Eagle and the White Hart, must be noted. Witham is
aware of its responsibilities in the modern world as well. It is co-
operating with London in the redeployment of population and
industry, so that its industrial estate is recent, well planned and
booming, though not exactly the route for an afternoon's drive!

To the north of the town, reached via the A12 or through Cut
Throat Lane and Rectory Lane, lies Rivenhall, now part of the
urban district though still " truly rural." Here, as at Witham, much
of the record of the past, in the form of Roman remains, still awaits
excavation and interpretation by the archæologist. The church of
St. Mary and All Saints is not old, yet it has some of the oldest
stained glass in the county, rescued by a former incumbent from a
decaying church at La Chenu in France and brought here to be
reset in all its thirteenth-century glory.

The " big house," Rivenhall Place, has grounds planned by
Repton, the landscape architect, in the late eighteenth-century.
Hogarth is said to have been a frequent visitor here while he painted
portraits of the Western family, lords of the manor. All around you

will see Essex farming at its best, which is not surprising, since it was here in 1523 that Thomas Tusser, author of the celebrated *Five Hundred Points of Good Husbandry*, was born.

The road runs on through the countryside to Silver End, a factory in the country where Crittall set up his metal window business in ideal surroundings for his workers. He was a social reformer who helped his workers to buy their own houses in pleasant surroundings near the factory, and who was the first employer (despite Henry Ford's claim) to introduce a five-day working week.

From Witham the A12 runs north-east, passing Rivenhall End and Durwards Hall, an old manor house which is today a kind of clearing house for antique dealers, so that it is not uncommon to see two or three old coaches in the yard, figureheads outside the door and statuary in the grounds.

Kelvedon is the next stop. It is a mystery how the Roman road got such a kink in it as it passed through the village, but the zigzag is there and the corner house on the Chelmsford side bears the marks of thoughtless drivers, who crowded the road until the recent completion of the by-pass. There is architecture here of all periods, with some particularly fine half-timbered houses and old coaching inns. The church is much restored, though sympathetically, and the tower remains as a fourteenth-century structure. It stands on the side road leading down to the manor house, Felix Hall.

This place is supposed to be the site of the Roman settlement Canonium. Excavations show that a Belgic tribe was settled here before the Roman occupation.

The bridge over the Blackwater here could serve as the dividing line between Kelvedon and Feering, for the two seem to merge together now. Feering does not seem much of a place from the main road, though you can get an interesting meal in congenial surroundings at the Sun. But take the turning almost opposite the B1023 and go under the railway bridge (a narrow road here) and you will come to a very pleasing view of old Feering, where across a little green the village street runs up to the church, which has a very decorative porch in Tudor brick, while on the other hand the river meanders in its valley.

The road to the north-west runs on to Coggeshall past Feeringbury, a large fifteenth-century house that stands beside the Blackwater.

A corner of the pretty village of Great Waltham.

" Overlooking the sparkling waters of the Blackwater, Maldon is a town to excite all our senses."

Great Leighs church, between Chelmsford and Braintree.

Little Coggeshall. "Farther along the lane the farm buildings contain parts of the fabric of the old abbey."

WRITTLE

TWO village greens and a duck-pond—that is what they say Writtle is famous for. It seems little on which to build a reputation, but wait until you see what stands around them and overlooks them.

St. John's Green, at the lower end of the village, is not as fashionable as Finchingfield, but it is very natural—a group of houses and a couple of shops which span the centuries, and the cottages still lived in by cottagers.

The old trees and the plaster walls, the mellow brick and tiles stand humbly enough before the entrance to the works which put Writtle on the map in the eyes of the world. For it is here that the Marconi Company built its research department at the beginning of the century; the flat flood plain of the River Wid gave a good field for the aerials used in its experiments. An aerial on a pylon still dominates the skyline to testify to the continuing interest of the company in these village premises.

The upper green, just called the Green, has the pond keeping its feet wet—a pond made all the more attractive in recent years with the introduction of a variety of waterfowl. Round this green the village gathers like a crowd of well-disposed friendly neighbours. Architecture of every period is represented in a juxtaposition which is a pleasure to the eye. Georgian fronts hide Tudor timbers and jostle with Victorian schoolroom and modernized shop-fronts. There are even two houses built from the ruins of the church tower, which fell down in a high wind in 1802.

That year the chant in the school playground was " Chelmsford church and Writtle steeple fell down one day but killed no people," for both events occurred about the same time.

The church of All Saints, which almost seems to hide itself behind the houses in the far corner of the Green, has a number of interesting points which reflect the history of the whole community. A well-produced guide is available at a small charge, but it might be mentioned that the vicar has become used to the pilgrimage of brass-rubbers from near and far to the interesting brasses.

Some people find in the name of the village—which, by the way, is the largest parish in the county—two Celtic words denoting a settlement in a valley by a ford, but I prefer the derivation from Writtolaburna, the name of the river running through it, now called the Wid, which charmingly means " the babbling, purling stream."

Any keen map-reader who rises to a challenge should look for Bedeman's Berg, " hill of the man of prayer," nearly four miles south-west of the church. A lone hermitage up in the woods, of which only a low wall still stands, was founded in the time of Henry I. It is not much to see, but the walk in the wood of a mile or so is still as beautiful as the day the hermit first closed his door on the world.

On the other side of Writtle, flanking the A1091 before its junction with the A414, is the Writtle Institute of Agriculture, which runs a model farm with excellent teaching premises and is built on the very site of King John's hunting lodge, built in 1211 for use by the king when he hunted in the vast forests which stretched up here from Epping. The outline of the defensive moat is still visible in the grounds.

Along the A122 on the Chelmsford side the river course near the road has been completely altered to suit a scheme of flood relief for the area, and an old watermill, with its rusting wheel, has been left high and dry. Opposite it is the old mill house belonging to the windmill, built higher up in the fields. Both are buildings of tragedy. The mill blew down in the early years of this century and a foul murder which has gone unsolved to this day was committed at the mill house in 1958.

Round the side road by the Cock and Bell one can follow the signposts to Hylands, a big mansion standing in its own extensive grounds which has been bought for use as a park by the borough of Chelmsford. The house cannot be looked over, but it is no great loss architecturally, though the Palladian entrance is impressive. The grounds, however, are to be kept in their natural state. Once the car has been left in the car park there are acres of parkland in which to wander; gardens and pools to be seen; even the graves, in their own garden sanctuary, of the last owners of the place; and interesting glimpses of wild life like the heronry in one of the copses just a few minutes from the house. It is open in summer until an hour after sunset. All this is within sight and sound of the bustling A12, but there is no access from that road.

SECTION TWO

LAND OF THE RIVERS
South Essex

LAND OF THE RIVERS
South Essex

ASHINGDON

CAUGHT between the claws of the Crouch and Roach rivers is a slice of historic Essex. In spite of the modernization of many of the shopping centres and the new housing, the area retains much of its rural freshness. Relying upon agriculture for its survival, the rivers and streams that cut the land make it rich enough to support quite intensive methods. While in the main the landscape is level the twisting lanes and farm hedges save it from being monotonous. Car drivers should take care, for some of these lanes have a surface that is rather hard on modern springs.

The principal historic event in this part of the county was in 1016, when the famous Danish king Canute and his army met Edmund Ironside in battle, the stake being the eastern part of England. The battle took place on the plains of Ashingdon, which are overlooked by the hill on which Canewdon now stands. The result of the fight was victory for Canute and his men, and in memory of this event he founded St. Andrew's church in Ashingdon.

Ashingdon is the main town in the group and is gradually building up into a small township of about 3,000 people. Surrounded by farmlands, it is a pleasant place to approach from any direction. The visitor will see little at first glance to indicate the history of the town, but a short walk up a dirt pathway will soon put that right.

At the top of this pathway stands the Saxon and Norman church of St. Andrew that was founded by Canute in 1016 and opened in 1020. Among the many things to see, a replica of a Viking ship that hangs from the roof beams must not be missed. There is also a diptych of carved oak showing Canute ordering back the waves. The church has also been the object of pilgrimages in its time. An image of the Virgin Mary was said to cure barrenness, and pilgrims crawled from Golden Cross to the church hoping for a cure. In 1931 a silver Canute penny was found in the churchyard. In other parts of the town there are remains of entrenchments said to have been used in the battle of 1016.

Canewdon, standing on its hill overlooking Ashingdon and the fertile fields on the banks of the River Crouch, is another growing village. Once an important market town, its population fell for many years, but with new housing things are on the mend.

The village is surrounded by an ancient defensive moat, but little can now be seen of it because of the years of farming that have gone on over it. The village was the site of a Roman camp before Canute made his on the north side of the village. The church of St. Nicholas stands atop the village and its huge square tower is a landmark for miles around. Inside the church there are a fine oak pulpit, a number of curios that include a deed signed by Elizabeth I, and the vertebra of a whale. In 1937 electricians discovered that there were oaken beams under the plaster of the roof of the north aisle. They are now visible in all their glory.

While in Canewdon be on your best behaviour—the village lock-up and stocks have been put back into working order by the parish council and are now on view!

To the north and south of the Ashingdon-Canewdon line are the villages of Fambridge and Stambridge. Fambridge is a tiny place on the banks of the River Crouch and consists of a few cottages and a white brick church. Stambridge is on the banks of the other river, the Roach. A larger place than Fambridge, it was the home of Captain John Harriott, founder of the Thames police, the force that was the inspiration for John Peel. The mill at Stambridge is mentioned in the Domesday Book and part of it is still in use today. In 1552 the churchwardens mended the road to the mill for a little over £3. I wonder how much this would cost today. The church of St. Mary and All Saints still has a great amount of the original Saxon stonework in its fabric. How many of our present-day walls will be supporting their roofs in 900 years' time?

Moving towards the sea, our next port of call is the village of Paglesham, which stands on the marshy land opposite Wallasea Island. For many years its chief source of income, apart from agriculture, has been from the oyster-fishing industry. Like many remote villages, it has been the home of smugglers, and a clump of trees known as Smugglers Trees marks the place where they used to hide their goods. Outside the village at East End is a pub, the Plough and Sail, that has changed little over the last three centuries.

Finally we arrive at Wallasea Island, a very flat and marshy place but with a yachting centre opposite the more famous one at Burnham-on-Crouch. During the summer months a passenger ferry service is usually available to get you across the Crouch to Burn ham. For those who prefer to stay on the island there is a grassy bank on the river's edge and a large cafe supplies snacks and drinks.

BASILDON

BASILDON is the keystone to an area of the county that more than any other shows the sharp contrast between the ultra-modern and the traditional. Even the approaches to the town offer a wide choice, from the fast A127, A13 and A130 trunk roads to the more attractive twisting lanes that cross the country-side. This part of the county demands that the narrow B roads are used, for it is along them that the true beauty of the countryside can be seen.

Basildon new town had its first house completed in 1951, Since then it has grown into a town of over 31,000 dwellings, and in doing so has become one of the famous new towns of England. For the visitor the great attraction is the shopping centre with its colourful murals and its freedom from traffic. Designed as the focal point of the new development, it has become the shopping centre for people from a wide area of south Essex.

Perhaps the oldest part remaining of the " original " Basildon is the church of the Holy Cross. This has a 500-year-old porch with a carving of a dragon and a boar.

At the time of writing the future of Basildon is causing as much controversy as its initial planning did. Under the south-east develop-ment plan Basildon is one of the growth towns, and the people living nearby are afraid that they will have their villages spoilt by the growth of the concrete giant. We must hope that in the construc-tion of the new a space is set apart to preserve the old.

Nearby is the village of Nevendon, a quiet corner of Essex next to the busy Southend road. The church of St. Peter is 700 years old and is situated at the bend of a wooded lane, a wonderful sight when the leaves are changing colour in the early autumn.

BILLERICAY

SOME two and a half miles away from Basildon is Billericay, which stands on a hill overlooking the London green belt. This town is as old as Basildon is new and traces of Bronze and Iron Age occupation have been found. Romans and Saxons both built here and at Great Burstead, the village from which Billericay grew, the Saxons built a stockade. Great Burstead houses the parish church that used to serve both villages in days gone by. This church, St. Mary Magdalen, is worth a visit if only to see the huge 800-year-old dug-out chest. The chest was used to collect money to pay for the crusades, and is still used to collect for the modern crusade that the church is conducting. Buried in the churchyard, at least by repute, is Sebert, king of the East Saxons, who was converted to Christianity during his stay in the area.

A chartered market town since the fourteenth century, Billericay is connected with many nationally important events. In 1381 it was the focal point for the Essex section in the famous (or infamous!) Peasants' Revolt. A battle took place at Norsey Wood between the peasants and the king's troops. It is said that nearly 500 peasants were killed in this battle, many to find their last resting place in Great Burstead churchyard.

The United States of America also owes a debt to Billericay, for the treasurer of the *Mayflower*, Christopher Martin, hailed from here. Together with his wife and a group of friends he sailed to the new land and helped found Billerica in Massachusetts—the old spelling being retained to this day. Flour for the *Mayflower* was probably milled on Mill Hill, where the remains of the old mill are still just visible.

Of less importance, but no less interesting, is the story of the " ghastly miller "—Thomas Wood. Born in 1719 with an appetite that was said to be enormous, he fed it until he reached twenty-five stone, whereupon he fell ill and started his now famous diet. His simple meal was a pudding made of one pound of flour boiled in one and a half pints of milk. Strange to say it worked, and he lived to become a medical legend until he died at the age of sixty-three.

Modern Billericay has taken pains to preserve as much of its past as possible, and the wide High Street has many buildings scheduled as having historic interest—Chantry House and the Georgian Burghsted Lodge are two examples. The history of the town can be seen through the exhibits in the Cater Museum.

Billericay is a town rapidly expanding to meet modern conditions but mindful of preserving its proud past.

BRADWELL-ON-SEA

STANDING along the southern bank of the river Blackwater is a strip of Essex that will put to shame all who say the county is uninteresting. Running from Latchingdon in the west to Bradwell in the east are mile after mile of beautiful country lanes, with banks of trees interspersed with wide views over the farmland that stretches away on either side of the road.

Latchingdon (which incorporates Snoreham) is the portal to this rich meadowland country. It stands at the junction of the B1010 and B1012, and drivers should beware, for the junction is not well marked. The village covers nearly six square miles, but most of this is farmland and the village centre stands along the main road. This is a pleasant mixture of the old and the new—thatch and weatherboard standing next to brick bungalows. The northern part of the area stands on the Blackwater and is a popular yachting centre; nearby are caravan sites. The present village church was built in 1857 of Kentish ragstone, and it stands on a corner with roads running either side of it. Keep left here and follow the signs for Steeple and Bradwell.

The road now runs towards Mayland and offers broad views over the open countryside. The village is taken up by the many nurseries that have made their home here. Most of the houses are of recent construction, and one called Bonanza on the right-hand side is particularly eye-catching with its bright colours and wagon wheels.

Steeple is marked by two silver domes standing in a farmyard— evidence of increasing technology in agriculture. The village, just round the bend in the road, is packed with weatherboarded houses, many of them thatched. On the left is the rebuilt church (1884), which incorporates parts of an older building, the doorways and font being of particular interest. In among the farm buildings of Stansgate, which lies north of Steeple and is on the banks of the river, the remains of an old Cluniac priory can still be seen. Founded in the twelfth century, it was dissolved in 1525 to pay for Cardinal Wolsey's university endowment.

After leaving Steeple watch for the first views over the Blackwater. The river is wide here and there are usually some boats to be seen—on a lucky day even sailing barges can still be spotted. It is a shock after such an unchanging scene to see the great block of the Bradwell nuclear power station towering in the distance.

There are many parts to Bradwell-on-Sea, most of them having something of interest to offer to the visitor. The first place to visit is Bradwell Waterside; but park your car back in the town, for parking is restricted near the quay. On the water's edge there is a

Basildon new town. " For the visitor the great attraction is the shopping centre."

Looking towards Stow Maries from the village church. " Its old cottages . . . stand on the rising village street."

" You cannot, however, go home without saying that you have been to
Audley End."

Epping Forest. " The very name conjures up a picture of a land of space and air, of trees and shrubs, of grass and water, sunlight and shade."

fine view of the river and the power station, and you can watch boats being run into the water to sail away across the estuary. The pub on the waterfront, the Green Man inn, is worth a visit if only to see the collection of " things " that hang from every available bit of roof space, and in the tap-room is a large fireplace. Around the quay are several old farmhouses. Westwick is a half-timbered building and Delamere's is Georgian in construction.

Talking of things Georgian brings us to Bradwell Lodge, now the home of Mr. Tom Driberg, M.P., and his wife. To find it turn first right after the Queen's Head in the village. It is open to the public on Wednesdays and Saturdays from 3 to 6 p.m. from Easter to mid-September, and on bank holidays at other times. Admission is 2/- for adults. Apart from its main building, the house has an Adam wing which was added in 1781, a belvedere, an octagon room, and a collection of modern paintings. From the house you can, as *Historic Houses* puts it, " look out over the sail-flecked Blackwater from the belvedere in which Gainsborough sketched Mrs. Siddons."

While in Bradwell the church of St. Peter-on-the-Wall should not be missed. Follow the many signposts and go down the no through road until you come to the farm buildings at the end—then walk! It is a walk of nearly half a mile to the church, which was the first cathedral in Essex and is one of the oldest churches in England. Built about 650 out of reclaimed Roman brick, it stands facing the North Sea, a gaunt, barn-like building. The church is now open to the public at all reasonable times.

A short walk from St. Peter's will bring you to the remains of a Roman fort. Built at Sales Point, it was designed to protect the area from the invasions of the Saxons. Much of the brickwork was used by St. Cedd in the construction of St. Peter's.

Back in the village centre there are plenty of old cottages to be seen, and Bradwell Rectory, which is Tudor and Georgian, is worth looking at.

Leaving Bradwell by the B1021, the next village to visit is Tillingham. This is an attractive road, winding downhill, with vast banks of trees giving way to open aspects. It is not uncommon to find pheasants wandering about on the road and in the grass verges, so drive slowly and you may get a close-up view of them. The village nestles most pleasantly at the foot of the hill, with old cottages and houses clustering round the small village green. The church of St.

Nicholas stands back from the green and still has the part of its thirteenth-century tower that remained after being struck by lightning in 1888. The doorway is Norman and inside are several brasses, one dating from 1526. East of Tillingham a duck decoy pond can be seen, and this is still in use.

Dengie is the last village on the tour and is south of Tillingham. In Saxon times it gave its name to the local hundred, but is far less important these days. The village is on low-lying ground with plenty of gorse and broom growing round it. Another duck decoy pond can be seen just outside it, while the church of St. James is a strange mixture of old and new. Mostly it is built of stone, flint and re-used Roman bricks, but the east face is of modern red brick. Inside the church this mixture of old and new is continued, with an old rood staircase and a modern altar screen. The latter was carved by a former rector of the church.

From Dengie follow the signposts for Asheldham, then Latchingdon, and we are back at the beginning again. For another, and most attractive, route back see the chapter on Burnham-on-Crouch.

BRENTWOOD and all around

BRENTWOOD—the burnt wood—takes its name from the forest clearing made some time in the twelfth century by burning off the timber to form a settlement to serve the needs of pilgrims from the north and east on their way to the shrines of St. Thomas à Becket at Canterbury. Today it is a bustling little town situated " in the heart of the metropolitan green belt," but in early days it was no more than a hamlet to the village of South Weald.

Its first church was a chapel erected about 1220 in honour of St. Thomas and for the convenience of passing pilgrims. The ruins of this ancient edifice still stand in a little garden in the grounds of the Odeon cinema. The story of how, in the sixteenth century, the women of Brentwood gathered in the chapel to prevent its desecration and demolition is a saga too long to be told here, but it is all the more reason for the careful preservation of what is left of the place.

The recent completion of the A12 by-pass round the town has eased congestion, though travellers to the Purfleet—Dartford tunnel still have to pass through the town centre. Night drivers on the by-pass run an unusual risk. Several accidents have been reported in which deer, leaping into the road and across the central reservation, have collided with cars.

There is night life in Brentwood. A club and several restaurants offer entertainment, while one or two attractive early coaching inns still stand to give atmosphere to your refreshment. The White Hart in the High Street is a classic example, for its windowed gallery over the old courtyard is still in use. During the day the open-air swimming pool in North Road and the public golf course in Ingrave Road are but two of the many amenities provided by the urban district council.

In Ingrave Road, too, stands the old school house (now a minor part of a complex of buildings), dating from 1568, founded by Sir Anthony Browne; but, to quote the South Weald parish guide, " his benevolence is somewhat overshadowed by the part he took in the burning of the Brentwood boy martyr, William Hunter, in 1555." This young man of nineteen had taught himself to read and, being of some independence of mind, was reading the church Bible when he was challenged by the vicar. He even argued the correct reading of some passages. This was too much for the vicar, who had him brought before Sir Anthony, who in turn referred the crime to the bishop and the boy's fate was sealed. After imprisonment he was burned at the stake in Ingrave Road near the present site of the Brentwood school chapel, under a tree of which a piece is still kept in the school museum. Gallows Green, where the Doddinghurst and Ongar roads meet, celebrates the site of the gibbet. Brentwood has had its fun, too. In 1600, on February 14, William Kemp, an actor, came to the town in the course of his famous dance all the way from London to Norwich. He rested a day here while a couple of pickpockets were dealt with. The railway " navvies " swelled the population in 1843 and the town spread rapidly as a result of their work.

Just one note of industrial interest. Should you have a vacuum flask with you on your journey it is ten to one that it was made here in Brentwood at the big Thermos works.

If you go roaring round the by-pass you will miss South Weald, and that would be a pity, for it is such a peaceful place. An eighty-year-old guide book tells us this is " a picturesquely wooded and undulating parish, situated upon a hill-top, and containing various good mansions "—a description that still rings true today despite much development.

The church dates from 1150, with additions over the years until the erection of the tower in 1500. Here you can see some very interesting old brasses, which are so useful in their depiction of the costume worn way back in medieval times. One is to a man with his wife and twelve children who actually married three times and fathered twenty-one offspring. The altar looks very beautiful with its alabaster reredos, permanently illuminated, representing the entombment of Christ. There is a guide you can buy in the church to tell you the whole story. Sir Anthony Browne was buried here in 1567. Some people say that his many benefactions stemmed from his remorse for his part in the martyrdom of William Hunter.

He was the owner of Weald Hall, but had no heirs, so it descended to Sir William Scroggs, Lord Chief Justice of England, who was buried in the churchyard in 1683. The longest ownership was that of the Tower family, who lived here from 1750 to 1939, when the Hall was commandeered by the Army. Damage and subsequent fire led to its complete demolition in 1948. The family is still remembered in the church, where you can see memorials to seven generations with the same name, Christopher Tower, from 1657 onwards.

The parish registers go back to 1538 and have all been carefully kept to show over 400 years of family history in this village, including Wright's Bridge, a farm on which the ancestors of the Wright brothers of aeroplane fame lived and died.

On the right-hand side of the Brentwood—South Weald road, called Weald Road, you will find a green belt car park where you can leave your car while you do a little exploring on foot.

The footpath across Weald Park takes you by the lake and on out to the Coxtie Green Road, which on the right hand leads to Pilgrim's Hatch, so called from the gateway which formerly guarded the road along which the pilgrims passed. Here the Black Horse shows its age in timber and plaster, for it was, in a much cruder form, a hospice for the pilgrims.

Shenfield might be called the northern suburb of Brentwood; so connected is it now by residential development that it hardly retains its individuality. To see the best of it turn off the A1023 to the north up Hall Lane, a steep little side road. Here is the nucleus the of old village. The happy noise of schoolchildren at play-time comes distantly to your ears as you walk up the church path—an absolute delight in June, for standard roses border its entire length.

The verger is a good-hearted man who will take you round and show you the treasures. His first comment will probably be on the number of very unusual specimens of trees growing in and about the churchyard. They were planted by a tree-loving incumbent long since dead. In the church there is a very unusual feature; the aisle has pillars and arches made of solid oak in delicate style, a great tribute to an unknown fifteenth-century workman. The carved rood beam may be by the same master craftsman, and the tower too has heavy timber work to support the belfry, which is amazing even by modern methods of construction. Shenfield Place, south of the church, and Shenfield Hall to the north with the Victorian turreted school house and the school itself to one side combine to give you a flavour of village life in calmer times.

But time passes and progress is adamant. As far back as 1833 the great McAdam himself was working on the improvement of the road from here to Chelmsford, and more traffic meant a greater spread of the village. Shenfield came up to date with its railway station, which formed a new centre for expansion, where today's buildings of note, like the county branch library designed by the county architect, can be seen.

Shenfield shares its station with Hutton, a village which has become a residential area for commuters, with London County Council and local housing estates. The church is a modern building with a backbone of fourteenth-century work in the pillars and arches of the nave, the chancel arch and the nave roof. Apart from the fifteenth-century bell turret the rest of the work is barely 100 years old. The Hall is on the opposite side of Church Lane, an eighteenth-century building with some interesting panelling.

The A128 runs north-west to south-east through Brentwood and is the easiest access to Ingrave and Herongate on the south-eastern side.

Two and a half miles down the road on the left-hand side you will see the most unusual eighteenth-century church in the whole county. It was commissioned by Lord Petre in 1735. The architect is unknown, but Pevsner rates him with Hawksmoor. It is all in red brick with a great tower with turrets. It replaced the churches of West Horndon and Ingrave, and preserves some very old brasses from the former, including John Fitz-Lewis (c. 1500) with his four wives, all in heraldic dress.

On the other side of the road Thorndon Park, part of West Horndon, runs all the way down to the arterial road. It was the estate of Thorndon Hall; now it is given over to a golf course, with public footpaths to the lake and right across to Childerditch, a small parish whose only claim to fame is its part of this estate combined with the lovely Thamesward views which can be obtained from the hill. Thorndon Hall was one of Lord Petre's places, built by James Paine from 1764 onwards, with an outstanding feature in the great six-column portico on the garden side. A hundred years later it was half burned to the ground. Another fire recently finally put paid to one wing, while the other, the headquarters of the golf club, stands even now under threat of demolition. Soon it will be gone and forgotten, but the grounds remain, and they were laid out by the famous Capability Brown, a landscape designer who in an age of artificial formality in gardens turned back to natural layouts. He got his name from his constant use to potential patrons of the phrase " This spot has great capabilities." When completed in the 1770s the work cost no less than £5,000.

Herongate stands opposite the entrance to the park. It got its name from Heron Hall, way off the main road where Heron House stands to day. The " Heron " is not the bird, but Old English for a nook or corner, showing how the estate stuck into Ingrave like a wedge.

Heron Hall and the whole parish of East Horndon was the home and happy hunting ground of the famous Tyrell family. In the church there is a monument of 1482 to Lady Tyrell, and other memorials to the family go down through hundreds of years. From the arterial road, just past the junction with the A128 on the Southend side, there is a picturesque view of the church, its brick mellowed with time and the squat tower and thick buttresses looking immensely strong as it tops a little hill. At the road junction the inn perpetuates the memory of the Tyrells in its sign, the Boar's Head, which was their crest.

Below East Horndon on the map lies Dunton, situated on a spur of the Laindon Hills. Its church was rebuilt less than 100 years ago, and today the whole place is losing its identity as it is slowly absorbed into Basildon new town.

As we continue to circle round Brentwood in a clockwise direction West Horndon and Childerditch are the next parishes; but as they are of little interest apart from their connection with Thorndon Park we can pass on to Little Warley.

The Halls and churches of Great and Little Warley lie within half a mile of each other just south of the arterial road between Great Warley Street and Little Warley Hall Lane. At Little Warley the Hall is a 400-year-old building with a characteristic chimney of huge dimensions. The church of St. Peter has a brick tower in chequered pattern, dating from 1718, and some rather interesting seventeenth-century monuments.

The place was well known for its barracks, originally built for the East India Company in 1805, but they have been declared surplus to War Office requirements and, so valuable is land today, their end was swift and unheralded. The great Ford company now has its vast new central offices on their site in Eagle Way, but the headquarters of the old Essex Regiment is still maintained. The garrison church stands serene and the nearby Essex Regiment museum continues to attract visitors with its mementoes of all the wars in which Essex men made their proud contribution.

Great Warley has a surprising number of interesting historical associations. John Evelyn, the famous diarist, bought the manor house, but sold it in 1655 because " the taxes are so intolerable." Pepys also had connections, visiting Brentwood on a number of occasions. Dr. Johnson came to see the great camp of soldiers assembled there in 1778 and later George III and his queen came up to review the troops. There is a ruined church here which might look old at first sight but was in fact built only in 1855. The present church of St. Mary was built in 1904 and is worth a visit, because it represents the standard of taste in building and furnishing churches at the beginning of the present century. Nikolaus Pevsner does not like it. He writes: " The inside is an orgy of the English arts-and-crafts variety of the international art nouveau."

Farther round to the west lies Harold Wood, in the London borough of Havering, under which it is dealt with, and then to the west itself lies South Weald, and so our round-the-clock tour of Brentwood is complete.

BURNHAM-ON-CROUCH

WIND whistling through rigging, boats bobbing on a blue sea, the slap of sails, the tang of salt air, the cry of seagulls— these are the sights and sounds that greet the visitor to Burnham-on-Crouch.

The approach to this corner of Essex, where the river and sea meet, is equally entertaining whether you come from the A130, A127, A12 or A414. Final entry to the region is from the B1010, a road which turns and twists its way through the heart of rich agricultural land before entering Burnham from the north.

A most pleasant tour of the area can be made by following the unclassified road to Asheldham shortly after passing through Latchingdon.

Asheldham is a small village about five miles north of Burnham and is remarkable for two sets of earthworks. On a plateau overlooking the Dengie marshes is a prehistoric camp site of the Ancient Britons. The other feature is an oval earthwork that encloses the village church, pond and Hall within its confines. The church (St. Lawrence's) is almost a fortress in its own right, the very thick walls containing re-used Roman bricks. Inside the church there is a beautiful Elizabethan altar table, its fat rounded legs typical of that age.

Leaving Asheldham via the B1021 we head south towards Southminster, a country market town. Tuesday is market day and there are always plenty of animals to be seen and sold. The long main street is always tidy, and the narrow streets that flow from it are made interesting by the juxtaposition of old and new houses that stand along them. Although surrounded by rich marshland, Southminster is near enough to the sea for the air to be filled with the tang of sea breezes. Like so many places in Essex, the village church contains some of the most exciting things in the vicinity. It was to the village church of St. Leonard that Dr. Alexander Scott came as vicar after the death of Nelson at Trafalgar. Scott had been Nelson's chaplain and was with him when he uttered his famous last words, " Thank God I have done my duty." Among several relics that Scott brought from the *Victory* and gave to St. Leonard's is the map table from the famous battle, which is still in use. Lucky are the brides who sign the marriage register over so famous a table. While in the church look for the old font and the many brasses—try finding the one dating from the 1550s.

Heading south again along the B1021, and covering three miles of country lanes, we arrive at Burnham. This is the yachting centre of Essex and calls the enthusiasts from many other parts of the nation. It is a brave sight to watch yachts of all sizes beating to windward, with the surface of the wide Crouch broken by white-topped waves. To cater for the yachtsmen Burnham has five clubs and extensive boatyards. The visitor can spend a pleasant half-hour watching the construction of ships on the quayside. It was from this quay that during the Black Death the sailors of Burnham carried grain to London. Together with those from Bradwell, they were the only mariners who would risk infection by making the journey, and as a mark of respect for their courage they were granted the privilege, in perpetuity, of landing corn in London free of duties.

There is a small pebble beach near to the restaurants and cafes, but to get the true beauty of the place a walk along the banks of the Crouch is called for. Eastwards is the sea, while inland on this walk are the marshes with their teeming wild life. To the west the river walk goes towards Creeksea, whose church stands 100 feet higher than the river. The view across the estuary from the church tower is worthy of note. A mile away is Creeksea Place, built in 1569.

The oyster beds that provided Burnham with this delicious sea food were badly damaged by frost a few years ago, but these are now being restocked in conjunction with fattening beds in the Roach, so that local oysters can again be bought in the town.

The two highlights of the year at Burnham are the carnival held on the last Saturday in October, when anything goes and a grand time is had by everyone, and the regatta, held during the first week in September; nearly 3,000 craft take part in this last meeting of the yachting season.

Leaving Burnham via the B1010, we head north-west for Althorne. This is a small village that has just started to develop, with the old and the new standing side by side. The flintstone church of St. Andrew is interesting for its Latin inscription over the west door, a scratch dial on an exterior buttress, and brasses dating from 1500.

For a magnificent country drive back to the B1012 follow the unclassified road posted North Fambridge. This road follows the line of the Crouch and offers fine views over the river and surrounding countryside. A short excursion from this road down the no through road to North Fambridge is well worth while for a closer look at the river. Watch the end of this road at high tide, for the river washes over the last few yards! The local pub, the Ferry Boat inn, stands on the edge of the river but is protected by a sea wall, so if it is open you can park in safety and pop in for a drink while you look at the surrounding river with its yachts and marshland. The tiny village church dates from the fifteenth century and has a wooden tower above its brick walls. For many years a ferry service operated across the river to South Fambridge, but this no longer runs, so if the view across the river tempts you the only answer is to drive to Battlesbridge and on to the south side of the Crouch.

CANVEY ISLAND

WILL it ever float away? The question has hung over the future of Canvey for many centuries and must have been in the forefront of the mind of anyone who saw the island during the terrible floods that struck Essex in the winter of 1953. We are happy to say that the visitor will still find it safely anchored off the mainland at Benfleet on the B1004. During most of the year the visitor has no choice but to approach the island from Benfleet, for the only bridge to it crosses the creek here. In the summer season an alternative route is often open, since when the tides permit boat trips are run from Southend. This offers a more traditional way to approach an island.

Romans, Danes, Saxons and Dutch have all lived from time to time on the island, and many Roman remains have been discovered here. They also had a signalling post here, but the exact location of this has yet to be proved. On Canvey are some of the "red hill" mounds. These were used in pre-Roman and Roman times in the extraction of salt from the sea. The heat used in boiling the water turned the soil red—hence the name.

As one might guess, much of the history of Canvey is connected with its fight against invasion from the sea. Many were the times when only a few parts of the land were above water. We have the Dutch to thank for the first effective sea walls. They were built by Cornelius Vermuyden on the orders of Joaz Croppenburg. This was no act of charity, for Joaz was given one-third of the island for his investment. Once the walls were built and the water was drained away it was quite an investment. Following on from this many Dutchmen came to live on the island and for a time there was some ill feeling between them and the natives, but the Dutch who stayed were soon absorbed into the general population.

Two major disasters have beset Canvey since this first sea defence was built, one in 1897 and the other in 1953. On both occasions further work was put in on the wall. On this last occasion, however, the rebuilding was on the largest scale since the original walls were erected. Over £1,000,000 was spent to secure the future of Canvey.

It is difficult to imagine that anything could again breach these walls, and the inhabitants sleep soundly in this knowledge.

For the visitor to modern Canvey there is much to see and do. The beach is long and is composed of sand and small shells, and the swimming is safe. For the less energetic sunbathing is a pleasure on the grass or the sea wall. When the inner man demands attention there are plenty of restaurants to choose from or you can take a picnic snack to one of the many parks that dot the place. There are, of course, all the other amenities that one would expect of a busy holiday centre, including the amusement arcades. Of the old buildings only a few now remain and they are to be found in the original village centre. An exception to this is the Dutch cottage on the Benfleet road. This is a fine example of local government and local society enterprise, for between them they have restored this ancient cottage to all its former glory, even to rethatching the roof. It was opened in 1962 as a museum and is now open to the public every weekend during the holiday season. Another old building is the Lobster Smack inn, which was mentioned in *Great Expectations*. It still has its weatherboard walls. Looking to the future, plans are going ahead for a seven-acre pedestrian-only shopping centre.

One final word to lovers of nature: keep a weather eye open when going around the island, for the creeks and streams abound with wild bird life and the saltings are covered with sea plant life.

FOULNESS

WAR and islands seem to be the overriding words to describe this corner of Essex. Surrounded by sea and river, the villages of Foulness, Wakering, Barling and Shopland have been unwillingly connected with war-like activities for most of their history, starting with the Romans and coming up to date with the War Department.

The landscape is open, rather flat and crossed by streams and drainage channels—in fact ideal for the farming and market gardening industries that thrive in this area. Because of the many waterways few of the roads run in anything like a straight line, and in fact only two come to mind. One is the road built by the War Department from Great Wakering to Foulness and the testing grounds there, and the other is the Broomway. Beware of the Broomway; it is half a mile off shore and must only be used at low tide. It runs from Wakering Stairs to Fisherman's Head on Foulness Island, but there are a few connecting hards back to the shore along its length. Although used for centuries by the locals it really came into its own in the Essex floods of 1953, for then it was the only way open to Foulness.

Most of the villages lie in a line north-west to south-east across the entrance to this tongue of land. The strangest of these is Shopland—the vanished village. Once a thriving place, it has slowly disappeared until even the church has now gone. The only remains are a few houses and the churchyard.

Barling, which stands opposite Potton island, shows no such signs of disintegration as yet. Even though the village is small, with a few cottages along its main street, it is still seeing to the fabric of the church. This church is 800 years old but has been enlarged and much rebuilt over the years. Of interest are the Jacobean sounding board of the pulpit and the communion plate dated 1562.

Little Wakering is part of the parish of Barling and lies about one mile south of it. This is an old village with a row of 300-year-old cottages standing along the main street and a fifteenth-century Hall and church. Although restored, the church of St. Mary still has traces of its Norman builders, chiefly the font and a window. The tower was built by John de Wakering, Bishop of Norwich, to commemorate his safe return from Agincourt. Inside the church are wall paintings, which were restored in 1936.

Great Wakering is about two miles south and east of its little sister and has a rather straight main street with the church standing at the head of it. Apart from the usual farming of the area Great Wakering has a brick field, which has yielded many remains of the Roman occupation of the area. The parish church of St. Nicholas has what is thought to be a unique priest's chamber in the west side of its tower, entry to it being from a stairway in a projecting wing of the church.

Foulness, the name place of this chapter, has been left till last for the very good reason that you just cannot go there! That is unless you have a pass from the War Department, for it owns the island and has patrols to keep out people. Not to worry, for our spies report that the land is rather flat and uninteresting anyway, so perhaps you have not missed much. In the past the local pub, the King's Head, and the church were the stage for smuggling and prizefighting, but these days are long since gone.

GRAYS THURROCK

LIKE an arrow, the busy A13 road cuts the largest urban district in the county into two neat pieces. Stretching from the edge of London in the west to Fobbing in the east and from Grays in the south to Bulphan in the north, it covers sixty-seven square miles of the county and needs three of our chapters to deal with it. This chapter takes in the western portion, from Purfleet to the "capital," Grays; the rest of the district is covered in the chapters on Stanford-le-Hope and Tilbury.

A few years ago the visitor might have been excused for thinking Grays an old-fashioned place, but modern building, particularly of the shopping area, is now changing that image for ever. Even so, Grays is still very much "two towns"—the old dockland along the edge of the Thames and the modern suburban town a little inland. The visitor leaving the A13 via Bradleigh Avenue and Orsett Road will enter the new part of the town and see much of the modern housing and shops that make up this busy place. In the middle of the town are the police station and the courts; nearby is the public library—soon to lose its old-fashioned appearance and be replaced by a large new building to meet the growing demands of the population. Going down the High Street towards the railway station the greatest change can be seen, with old shop-fronts giving way to those of the new style. On Saturday a stall market is held along the next part of the High Street from the railway station south to the Thames. This is the old town, with its terraced houses crowding the edge of the pavement. Do not be tempted to give up here, for a surprise awaits the intrepid explorer—Grays beach! Yes, follow the High Street round its sharp left turn and there on the right is a field with a pathway leading to the sea wall. Along the wall to the left, and behold a small holiday beach, complete with cafe, boating pool and playground, and benches that look out over the greatest river of them all—the Thames. It was just off this beach, in 1875, that the old wooden training ship *Goliath* caught fire and sank with many still on board. A plaque commemorates this in the church of St. Peter and St. Paul, which stands near the railway station. This church is attractive from the outside but dates only from 1846 in the main, although parts remain from the twelfth century and in the vestry there are some medieval tiles to be seen.

Heading west from Grays along the A126 London road, we

see the famous cement works that turn the roofs of nearby houses white. Much of the chalk used in the manufacture of the cement is taken from local sources, and many quarries can be seen in the area. Passing through South Stifford and its works, the road runs through West Thurrock. The casual driver might be forgiven for thinking the two places were one, for from the road the appearance changes little, but watch on the left for signs of the marshes. On these marshlands is the interesting St. Clement's church. The church now stands in the shadow of the large Hedley's soap factory —locals say it was built to wash away the cement dust! Looking at the church, one wonders how it came to be built so far from the village, but what a grand position it has, with the marshes surrounding it like some huge garden and with the Thames running along the bottom of it for good measure. The present church stands on the site of an older building, foundations of which can still be seen under the massive tower at the west end. Parts of the church are in the lancet style, but much of the building is supposed to have been erected by local fishermen before the Conquest of 1066. The church was enlarged after the murder of Thomas à Becket and was used as a rest station by pilgrims going to Canterbury. Inside the church, notice the chalk font and the Purbeck marble coffin lid.

Continuing along the road, the next town is Purfleet, but before coming to the town itself the new roadway to the Purfleet—Dartford tunnel will be seen. This starts two and a half miles east of Purfleet on the A13 and runs south and into the mouth of the tunnel, the latest connection between Essex and Kent. There is a fee payable by all who use the tunnel, but the saving in time and trouble more than compensates for the half-crown a private car driver must pay. A word of advice: the road passes another cement factory and if the wind is in the right direction your car will end up white with dust—so close the windows for a moment and save your lungs! For the town of Purfleet, leave the A126 and join the A1090, which runs through the main part of the town, kisses the edge of the river, and swings north to join the A13. This is a pleasant place as Thames-side villages go, and the harbour and quay are worth a visit if only for another look at the ever-changing pattern of life on the Thames. Off the main street is Beacon Hill, which gives commanding views over the surrounding area and also of the very old chalk quarry that stands due east of the hill. The walls of the quarry rise in great steps above the dark green water that covers the bottom. To the west of the village is the military site, with rifle ranges and what was once called the largest powder-house in England. This was back in the eighteenth century and the building is now used for more peaceful purposes that offer less danger to the future of the neighbourhood.

On the A13 again, head east towards Southend for just over a mile and then turn left along Ship Lane and across the Mar Dyke for the village of Aveley. The lane travels through agricultural land until it meets the B1335. To the left is the village, a place that has grown much since the war and is now only just separated from the large London overspill town of Belhus by the Belhus Park. St. Michael's church is the only interesting old building in the village, much of it dating from the twelfth century. In its old walls many Roman tiles can be seen, while the round Norman arches stand in contrast with the later pointed English arches. Memorials to the Barretts and the Dacres—the great local landowners—can be seen inside this church. Their mansion of Belhus is now no longer standing, but the great fireplace can still be seen in Tilbury museum. North of Aveley is Bretts, a timber-framed fourteenth-century hall house, which still has part of its moat intact.

To the right of Ship Lane the B1335 rises and falls through the wooded countryside on its way to the southernmost point of the new township of Belhus. This is a completely new town, with the large Belhus Park making a natural contrast with the concrete roads and houses.

At the end of the B1335, where it meets the B186, stands Ford Place, a house dating from 1655, with Dutch gables and a Dutch-style plaster ceiling. The yellow brick west front was added later in the seventeenth century.

North of Ford Place is the delightful village of South Ockendon. Most of the cottages stand round the village green, while to the east can be seen the moated Hall and a working windmill that was originally driven by water. The whole of this part of the village stands in open farmland with trees breaking up the skyline. Also by the green are the village church of St. Nicholas, with its late Norman doorway, and the seventeenth-century Royal Oak inn, with its gables, adding to the old-world atmosphere.

Back along the B186, past Ford Place again, and up the hill is Stifford, with its thatched cottages and wooded glades. The church of St. Mary is interesting for its two heads, in colour, that stand at the top of the half-piers marking the entrance to the south arcade. There is also an hour-glass stand on the pulpit, once used to measure the length of the sermon.

Continuing east along the B186 through the rich meadow of this northern part of the urban district we come to Orsett. The village is an attractive place, with timber-framed houses and some gabled ones, notably Birch Terrace, which stands east of the church of St. Giles and All Saints. Also east of the church is Orsett Hall, a Georgian yellow-brick building in a beautiful park. Coming back west past the church, with its Norman south doorway, we can see Orsett House, built in 1740 of red brick. A mile or so farther west are the remains of a windmill, not in very good repair. Nearby the annual Orsett show is held, but see the local press for dates as no permanent date can be given.

An attractive route to Bulphan, missing out the new by-pass, is to follow the B188 north from Orsett, then turn sharp left and take the unclassified country lane up to the village. There are some old houses clustered about the village green, where the roads to the village meet each other. Standing next to the green is the church of St. Mary, with its wooden porch and wooden tile-hung tower. This is a peaceful place, in contrast with the busy life of the southern half of the district—to which we must now return down the A128 to the A13, then west towards Grays once again.

The last things to see on this tour lie on either side of the A13 at the entrance to Grays. This part of the town is often called Little Thurrock, or Blackshots, but both are now swallowed up by the main town. As you approach the roundabout on the A13, to the right you will see the large park with a brand-new indoor swimming pool, a golf course and a most attractive floral display on the grassy banks of the roadside. To the left is Hangman's Wood.

The mystery here is not who the hangman was, but what the holes that stand in the wood were used for. They are called dene holes and often go nearly sixty feet down before they open out into small circular caves. Thought to have been dug about the time the Romans came, guesses as to their use have ranged from chalk mines to grain storage chambers, but nobody is really sure. Have a look; your guess is as good as the experts' here.

The beautiful village green at Arkesden.

St. Andrew's, Greensted (circa A.D. 1013), the only surviving log church in England.

Hatfield Broad Oak. "... the village pump, which has all the elegance of a Georgian coffee pot."

Leigh-on-Sea. "... watching the fleet of 'bawleys' bringing their catches to the world-famous Leigh cockle sheds."

Dutch cottage museum at Canvey Island. "They have restored this ancient cottage to all its former glory."

" If you go roaring round the by-pass you will miss South Weald, and that
would be a pity, for it is such a peaceful place."

HADLEIGH

HADLEIGH castle is probably the most interesting historic ruin in the county. It stands on a grassy hillside overlooking the waters of the Thames estuary and the distant Kent coastline. Hadleigh, Thundersley and South Benfleet form the Benfleet urban district.

Work on the castle started around 1230. Hubert de Burgh was the man responsible. At this time he was, in effect, the ruler of all England during the minority of Henry III. Two years after starting the castle he fell from the king's grace and the castle and its grounds reverted to the Crown. Various governors were appointed to look after the castle, which was used by the early Edwards as a hunting lodge while they chased the deer of the local forest. Much of this forest now remains in the form of woodland glades scattered all around Hadleigh.

In the mid 1300s Edward III rebuilt the castle almost completely as a protection for the area from the many French ships that tried to sail up the river and attack local villages. This was the golden age of Hadleigh castle, for its royal chambers and towers rang to the sound of the king and his guests and knights. The remains that are visible today are of the later building.

Gradually the castle and its park fell into disuse, and in 1551 Lord Rich of Leez Priory bought it for £700 from Edward VI. He never lived there and used it only as a place from which to sell stone for building churches and other buildings.

The visitor today can see only the great south-east and north-west towers and the remains of the moat. It was these towers that inspired Constable to do his now famous painting of Hadleigh castle.

A few yards east of it is a long ridge called the saddleback. This is thought to have been used as a training ground by the knights who protected the king.

The castle is now registered as an ancient monument and many people spend an afternoon looking around and picnicking on the grass. The view from here is quite tremendous, both down river to the sea and across Canvey Island to Kent. It is a sight worth seeing on a stormy day, with great clouds racing up river to London and the river seeming to be racing in the other direction out to sea.

At the time of writing the Essex County Council has put forward proposals that would extend the present area of the park to over 1,000 acres, and this would form a new national park on the banks of the Thames.

Standing at the head of the road that leads to the castle (Castle Lane) is the church of St. James. This church is even older than the castle and was built in 1130. Built as a place of refuge as well as worship, it is one of only four churches in England to retain its semi-circular apse.

On the other side of the A13 from the church and castle, and a little inland, is a forty-acre nature reserve. Here around 200 species of plant life can be seen, together with much wild animal life. For the nature lover this is indeed a haven and a delight.

When leaving these delightful spots it is a sudden surprise to come upon the busy heart of Hadleigh again, for all these places are only a few moments' walk from the main road that cuts the shopping area of the town in half.

Thundersley is a rapidly expanding place, with parades of new shops to match the modern housing estates. This is a pleasant place, surrounded as it is by wooded glades and parks. West Wood and Thundersley Glen are two of the largest of these, the former being ninety acres of woodland.

The parish church of Thundersley, St. Peter, dates from 1200. Built from ragstone and shingle, it is typical of many Essex churches. The wooden tower is still supported by its four original huge wooden upright beams.

Nearby is Daws Heath, a small residential district whose many acres of open land are protected against development.

Few people think of South Benfleet as a naval port, but this is just what it was way back in the 890s. At this time it was a main base camp for the Danish forces and their ships lined Benfleet Creek. King Alfred ended all this by attacking the camp and destroying the ships.

For many centuries after this South Benfleet was a fishing port with a small timber-exporting trade. In more modern times the creek is used as an anchorage by the many yachtsmen who make this part of the creek their own.

Being a tidal river, the outgoing water leaves exposed a large area of mud flats. These are the hunting grounds for many hundreds of birds, some quite rare. Along the edges of the flats and the marshland many types of sea plant life can be found.

The church of St. Mary stands in large grounds, and although it is very old in parts the most interesting sight is the unique fifteenth-century oak porch. The outer arch of this porch is made from two entire sections of a tree. They have been erected so that the wide part of the tree is at the top, forming the top of the arch.

Finally, having walked round the 400 acres of Shipwrights Wood, watched the wild life and yachts and seen the church, the two very old pubs of South Benfleet, the Anchor and the Hoy and Helmet, make a welcome resting place.

North Benfleet stands some distance away from its namesake in the south. It is in fact a quiet agricultural community just off the busy A127 arterial road. Although sharing the name Benfleet it comes under Basildon for local government services. North Benfleet's little twelfth-century church has an interesting tomb at the entrance to the porch, that of John Cote, " a soldier of Waterloo." The inscription makes interesting reading.

THE HANNINGFIELDS

THE Hanningfields are best known today for the reservoir which drowned half the area and is a vital source of water supply for a large part of south-east Essex. Water is delivered to it through a nine-mile pipe from the rivers Chelmer and Blackwater at Langford.

This 874-acre reservoir, which cost over £6,000,000, has changed the face of the countryside in a most interesting way. Bird and plant life on its margins has altered to suit the new environment. From the number of cars which stop on the roads that skirt the reservoir it seems that a stretch of water has a great deal of fascination for man. The changing moods of sunlight and shadow, wind and calm are reflected by the water in endless variation. The feeling is so old, yet the reservoir has only been there since 1958.

Beneath its waters lie the remains of a once great house, Fremnells, which dated back to Tudor times. There are men about who still remember working in the big house. The gradual stocking of the waters with fish makes it of interest to fishermen for miles around, though the number of rods is restricted and the fishing is for the moment rather expensive.

There is still plenty of countryside left to explore, however, and a choice can be made of any number of little side roads down which to wander. South, east or west there is a Hanningfield to greet you.

East Hanningfield's church was completely burnt down in 1883, but within two years the present building had been erected. The parish registers were preserved, which is very fortunate, for they go back to 1540, recording the " hatching, matching and dispatching " of a little village through 400 years of British history.

In the rectory garden is an old well, the oldest artesian well in the county and, at 475 feet, the second deepest.

West Hanningfield church is worth a visit, though it has to be looked for closely on the map. It is built in the Perpendicular style. The belfry, as can be seen from within, is constructed on a timber frame, an unusual and ingenious method used in places where stone was not easily available to build a tower strong enough to take the weight.

Lack of stone in fertile Essex caused builders many a headache. You will see here that the south porch is also of early wooden construction. There is one early monument, dated 1361, recording the burial of John, son of Isobel Cloville, and it is interesting to find the name still preserved in nearby Clovile Hall.

South Hanningfield is a scattered village on the way to Downham, with quiet side roads and copses where bluebells make their contribution to the magic of late spring.

What more can one say of the Hanningfields? They are fair in the sun and the reservoir is mood-evoking at all seasons.

INGATESTONE

INGATESTONE in modern days is renowned out of all proportion to its size for the wonderful exhibitions of valuable and often unique documents and original material staged every year at Ingatestone Hall by the staff of the Essex Record Office.

These exhibitions cannot be over-praised for the originality of their conception and for the contribution they make to our greater knowledge of the ordinary men and women who peopled the past and left their mark in Essex history. They are shown annually from May to September daily except Sundays and Mondays.

A visit to such an exhibition is also an opportunity to view the outside of a great pre-Elizabethan house in all its rambling glory—Ingatestone Hall, which has remained in the Petre family since Sir William, son of a wealthy Devon tanner, had it built about 1540. Pevsner, the great authority on architecture, calls it " one of the most characteristic of its period in England."

The Hall is not open to the public, but there is a car park at the gates and people can proceed on foot up the long straight drive through the picturesque gatehouse arch, with its eighteenth-century clock turret, and on up to an entrance to a wing of the Hall on the left-hand side. This wing, rented to the county council, forms a series of exhibition rooms on two floors. It includes some permanent exhibits, with a number of interesting Petre family portraits in the long gallery, where a spinet bought by the Friends of Historic Essex is an important feature.

The village itself stands some way from the Hall. It lines the great Roman road from London to Colchester, now known more prosaically as the A12. But the village, happily, has been by-passed for through traffic, so that it is possible to drive slowly through the main street and appreciate the picture of Georgian brick harmonizing with the occasional timber-framed building of an earlier age. The Petre almshouses towards the south of the village look very old, but are in fact Victorian imitation Tudor, which, mellowed over 100 years, looks pleasant enough.

From early times the church was hidden by tall buildings lining the street, but when these were demolished recently the space was turned into a lawn which gave a view of the church and set off to perfection its interesting Tudor brickwork. Inside you will see an iron hour-glass stand on the north wall of the nave. The pulpit used to stand here and the parson was expected to time his sermon. The most interesting monuments are those to the Petre family, of whom the doyen, Sir William, kept his head, literally and metaphorically, through the reigns of Henry VIII, Edward IV, Mary and Elizabeth by suiting his religious convictions to the prevailing conditions.

Only recently the other old house of local interest, The Hyde, built in 1766, was burned to the ground by a demented servant and is no more. A left turn half-way down the main street from Chelmsford leads out into beautiful Essex countryside, to Stock and the Hanningfields.

The Ingatestone by-pass has actually made it more difficult to get at its associated village of Fryerning. Once you are there, though, you will admit that the map-reading and signpost-following were worth while. Fryerning is a pretty little place with gently rising hills to vary the landscape and trees to give it an air of seclusion. The church, with its early-sixteenth-century brick tower, stands in a churchyard and cemetery which is a model of neatness.

In the vestry can be seen an unusual curio—a palimpsest (or two-sided) brass, used once in the fifteenth century to record the burial of a now unidentified woman and then used on the other side to commemorate, 100 years later, one Mary Gedge of Tudor time.

There is Roman brick in the fabric, which shows that Fryerning already had some sort of settlement just after the birth of Christ. A thousand years later the village came into the possession of the Knights of St. John of Jerusalem, called the Knights Hospitallers, and the place got the name Ging Hospital.

Ingatestone and Fryerning are combined in one civil parish, which includes the hamlets of Green Street and Mill Green, where the windmill still stands, though its sails will never turn again. Mill Green Common is an extensive area of grass and bushy woodland. Tucked away in its greenery is the Viper, claiming to be the only pub in the country with this name. Lyndsays farm is an interesting building, dating from the 1400s.

Margaretting lies on the Chelmsford road two miles north of Ingatestone. If you do not know what a tree of Jesse looks like, go and see the stained glass in the east window of St. Margaret's. This wonderful work was done in the fifteenth century, and is probably the best example of its kind in the county. Many of the old houses have gone, but it is a pretty little place still.

Mountnessing, wound about by the River Wid, is in exactly the opposite direction on the A12. Approaching it a lovely old windmill comes into view, crowning a nearby hill. The village is bisected by the busy road, but the church stands well away, reached by a side road on the left towards London. It is an interesting place. It has a great wooden belfry of stout oak timbers in a complicated framework and a notable old oak chest made by hollowing out a solid baulk of timber. You will also see in a glass-fronted cupboard the huge fossilized rib-bone of an early elephant or mammoth. The west front is made of bricks which in 300 years have mellowed to harmony with their rural surroundings.

On the right-hand side of the main street Thoby Priory stands on the site of a previous foundation of Augustinian canons founded in the twelfth century and suppressed in 1525. An arch and part of a wall are the only reminders.

The village gets its name from the early lordship of the Mountney family.

LANGDON HILLS

THE Langdon Hills, while being the highest point in south Essex, are also said to be the first range of hills in a straight line all the way from Russia. While not taking sides in this dispute we have yet to hear of anyone, even on a clear day, seeing the launching of a sputnik! What you *do* see from here is the finest view of the Thames and the surrounding countryside that has ever inspired a poet to verse. The peal of bells from the church on top of the hills echoes down the wooded slopes and sets to flight the many birds that make their home there. This area is to be preserved for future generations, as it is now part of the green belt.

Nearby is the village of Laindon, with its twelfth-century hill-top church. The church has long been a landmark for travellers to Southend, but is well worth leaving the road to visit. The tower is supported by massive wooden posts and the nail-studded door has been hanging for nearly 500 years. All of the original wood that went into the construction of this church came from surrounding trees. Attached to the church is a most interesting priest's house made of lath and plaster.

PITSEA

PITSEA is the focal point for a group of three villages that stand astride the busy A13 road. They are Pitsea, Vange and Bowers Gifford. The two limiting boundaries of this group of attractive rural villages are the " foothills " of the Langdon Hills and the mighty Thames. In days gone by the Thames came right up to the edge of the habitations, but over several centuries it receded, leaving behind evil-smelling marshland.

There are many local legends of the fishermen who lived on these marshes and eked out a poor living from the then very broad river. One of the most interesting of these stories concerns the habits of the fishermen in getting wives. It would seem that the gas that came up from the marsh soon killed off the womenfolk of the fishermen. To obtain new wives they raided the villages nearby and carried off any woman they fancied!

These days are long since gone, and now the marsh forms part of the agricultural land which takes up much of the area. The A13 runs along the edge of this land, and on a clear day you can get a panoramic view over the low land and the river.

It was from Vange in 1620 that the Dutchman Cornelius Vandenanker set about draining the marsh, and so successful was he that he became a rich man by selling off the land he drained.

Pitsea and Bowers Gifford are gradually growing together to form a garden town, and much evidence of modern planning can be seen from the road. Most striking, after the statue of the nymph, is the new shopping area that stands next to the statue. This new shopping zone has a service road, a post office and a wide range of shops. The main bus service stops nearby and the railway station is only a few minutes' walk away. There are also several new housing developments that seem to be blending in well with the new outlook of the area, the tone of which was set in 1964 with a new twelve-sided church. Pitsea is the keystone to this development, since London is only a short train journey away by the fast electric service. It is equally possible to reach the coast in a short time by bus or train.

While these villages are primarily looking to the future they do contain many things of historic interest. All three have small hillside churches several centuries old. The church at Bowers Gifford contains a brass memorial to Sir John Gifford which is the third oldest military brass in Essex. It was Sir John's family that gave the village its name. Also in the village Bowers Hall and the rectory both have homestead moats. These were used for exactly the same purpose as the moats round castles.

At Pitsea the 350-year-old Pitsea Hall is still standing near to the more modern railway station. Another hall house in Pitsea is Great Chalvedon Hall. This is a two-storied house with timber framing and was built in the 1600s.

In Vange another timber-framed house can be seen. This is called Hill Farm House. Nearby is Merricks House, which has been reconstructed but is still in part sixteenth-century timber-and-brick construction.

So as you travel through these places look out at the new and spare a thought for the men of old who spent their lives driving back the waters of the Thames.

RAYLEIGH

SITUATED near to the coast with fast road (A127, A13 and A130) and rail links to London and the northern part of the county, Rayleigh is an ideal place for the commuter. So it has proved since the war, with an ever-expanding population that has now passed the 20,000 mark.

The town centre stands on a hilltop giving views of the surrounding fields. No better view can be obtained than from the church that crowns the top of the main street. This is Holy Trinity church and it looks most attractive, as it stands surrounded by trees and grass and yet is right in the heart of the town. The inside is very light and the timbered roof can be clearly seen. While in the church the medieval alms box, carved from solid oak, should be looked for. Near the church stand several picturesque buildings, including one 400-year-old house with an overhanging upper story.

Just off the town centre is Rayleigh Mount, a National Trust property. This is the site of a Norman castle that was the only Essex stronghold recorded in the Domesday survey of 1086. Nothing now remains above ground, but excavations have revealed much of interest. The site is in a small park.

Although covering the largest area of land in the Rayleigh urban district, Rawreth has a very small population. Unspoiled by development, the village retains its original rural beauty. The landmark of the village is the church spire, which stands pointing to the sky and acts like a welcoming beacon. The view from the church porch gives a good picture of the area with its undulating pasture land cut by the farm hedges.

Nearby is Hockley, a favourite summer spot for many local people. Here are the famous Hockley Woods, the remains of a royal hunting forest. Present-day visitors will find a place to park their cars, a playground for their children and a cafe with which to replace the burnt energy. The woods themselves consist of 213 acres of trees and tracks. An hour or two spent wandering down the narrow tracks with the sunlight sending its golden shafts down beneath the tall trees is time well spent in this age of rush.

The village itself is fairly small and stands on the Rochford to Rayleigh road. Having good electric train services and frequent bus services, it is a slowly growing community in a pleasant corner of Essex.

RETTENDON AND RUNWELL

RETTENDON and Runwell lie in a convenient position to be taken together. Rettendon is divided by the A130, a busy road these days with Chelmsford—Southend traffic. The village spreads down the road from the Bell at the Hanningfield crossroads to Rettendon Place a couple of miles away.

Chancellor, the Chelmsford antiquarian, said in 1894: " The site of the church is very elevated, and its lofty tower is a conspicuous object for many miles round." For hundreds of years it has withstood the boisterous winds that always seem to blow around the hilltop. There is little left of the original building, probably because it was not well constructed in the first place and endless repair and restoration has been necessary.

From the church the view is extensive, taking in a panorama of the course of the River Crouch. From here 1,000 years ago one could have had a grandstand view of the battle of Assandun (Ashingdon), when the Danes under Canute beat the Saxons under Edmund Ironside, " and thus for a time became masters of the kingdom."

Earlier history, almost another 1,000 years back, is evinced from a fourth-century rubbish pit excavated recently near Rettendon Hall Farm. A roman kiln is indicated, to support the evidence of Roman occupation first shown by the finding of a Roman stone coffin by the river in the nineteenth century.

Down the hill past Rettendon Place one approaches a roundabout where the A130 and A132 meet. Straight over, the road runs on through Battlesbridge, still in the parish of Rettendon. Though some people like to tie the name up with the battle fought in the vicinity, it is more or less accepted that the bridge was named after the Batailes, a local family of note in medieval times. However, Canute is said to have brought his boats up to this very spot to prepare for evacuation if the battle went against him, and today you can still see the occasional large coaster which has come up the Crouch to discharge by the mill at the bridge.

Runwell is on the A132, spreading towards, and almost merging with, Wickford. It takes its name from the Running Well, said to be the site of an ancient shrine, which rises on Poplars Farm. It has a pretty little church in among the trees. Runwell mental hospital is set in 500 acres of pleasant country and comprises small units on a villa system with a central administrative block.

ROCHFORD

REPUTED birthplace of Anne Boleyn and certain home of many smugglers, Rochford is today a little stripped of its former glory. Much of its administrative area has been taken over by its giant neighbour Southend, but the small town has a character that Southend has yet to match.

The narrow streets of the town centre were built in those far-off days when the motor-car was unheard of and so are ill suited to handle the traffic of these hurried times. A by-pass is now open for through traffic and a one-way system has been introduced on the old roads. One advantage of this, apart from the speeding up of traffic, is that the visitor who returns through the town will see a different part from that which he saw on the outward journey.

Among the things to be seen are many old buildings standing along the roadside, but they grow fewer each year as redevelopment takes place; recent victims are a row of weatherboarded shops. Like most old market towns, Rochford has many pubs, and although they account for the smuggling in this area the parish church of St. Andrew was the storage centre—gin and tea were hidden in the tower! The church stands surrounded by the golf course, the green of which sets off the red brick of the church. The golf course has another link with the town's history: Rochford Hall, one-time home of the Boleyn family, is now the clubhouse.

Rochford no longer holds its market—the last one was held in the late 1950s—but it does have an airport. The airport is called Southend's, but the land is part of Rochford.

Leaving Rochford for Hawkwell, the road is guarded by rows of tall trees that gradually give way to open farmland. Along this road is the Cock inn, a pleasant pub with a playground for children and a reputation for good beer and snacks.

Hawkwell is a small place with a large playing field and a church with a wooden bell turret. The church is famous for its silver chalice dating from 1662, which is still in use today.

South-east from Rochford is Sutton, a village with a population of under 300. Sutton is approached by a tree-lined road that leads to the most interesting thing in the village—the church of All Saints. The wooden spire of this church is supported by massive timber framing, while the timber porch, dated 1633, is protected by a thirteenth-century doorway. Behind the church is Sutton Hall, dating from the sixteenth century.

The other small village in this group is Eastwood. Although it is rapidly being swallowed by Southend it retains much of its country charm. As at Sutton, the church is the focal point for the visitor. Notice the door to the church, for it is nearly 700 years old and the ironwork that holds it together comes from an even older door. Inside the church the Norman font is an unusually fine example of the stonework of the period. Near the church are several thatched cottages to give an old-world feeling to the scene.

SOUTHEND-ON-SEA

THE most accessible place on earth! This might well be the claim of this popular seaside town, situated at the junction of the Thames and the Channel. People arrive here by land, sea, river, road and air, all looking for that special something that makes the difference between a town and a seaside resort.

Southend has as many faces as it has means of entry. For the day-tripper who wants noise, bingo and hot-dog stalls the answer is turn left at the longest pier in the world (1⅓ miles) and you will find fun in plenty. If you are for the quiet life and want scenic beauty, turn right at the pier and walk along the sea front towards Westcliff and Leigh. Here you will see gardens tastefully laid out, the cliffs, and an exciting view over an estuary dotted with the colourful sails of many sailing ships.

Sports enthusiasts are well catered for with six yacht clubs, angling from the pier, golf at the wooded Belfairs Park, bowls, tennis, rugby and association football at Priory Park, and a host of other sports, including flying, swimming, county cricket and hockey.

For the more adventurous there are many flights from the airport to the popular holiday centres of Europe—you can even take your car!

While there is little of great historic interest in the town, several things worthy of note do remain, including the parish church of St. Mary, with its remains of an old Saxon doorway.

Nearby, at Priory Park, there is a museum housed in part of the ruins of the priory of Cluniac monks, and in the cellars there are the remains of the old crypt. The park itself is some forty-five acres in extent and is the centre of sports of all kinds as well as being a beautiful place to walk through.

Southchurch Hall, a thirteenth/fourteenth-century timber-framed manor house, is enhanced by its moat, now turned into a series of ponds. The Hall is used as a library and so remains open to the public.

Southend caters for many tastes, and throughout the season runs a series of festivals. In late April there is the spring flower festival, when every corner of the borough that will grow anything is a mass of colour and the Cliffs Pavilion houses a really outstanding display.

In August it is carnival time, and for a whole week anything goes, culminating on the final day—a Saturday—in a procession in which the newly crowned carnival queen takes part.

September is the month of the Whitebait Festival, an ancient festival now centred on Southend. On the morning of the festival there is the blessing of the fishes, which takes place at the pier head (an electric train service is available if you do not want to walk the mile and a bit out to sea).

As autumn arrives it has long been a tradition for Southend to turn on its illuminations. From late August to October thousands of colourful lights and displays attempt to turn night into day. Of special interest are the displays along the pier and the " Never Never Land " for children.

Part of Southend, but retaining its own character, is Leigh-on-Sea. Here the " old town " is a haunt of locals and tourists alike. One can never tire of sitting in the surroundings of an old pub or on the sea wall watching the fleet of " bawleys " or cockle boats bringing their catches to the world-famous Leigh cockle sheds. For lovers of sea food this place is a Mecca.

Another part of the borough, Westcliff-on-Sea, is well known for the views from the cliffs that give it its name, but also of interest is the " Crow Stone " that stands a little way out from the beach and marks the limit of the Port of London's authority over the River Thames. The original stone is now on show in Priory Park.

Other places to visit nearby are Rochford, an old market village with narrow streets and the reputed birthplace of Anne Boleyn; Hadleigh castle, the most important late-medieval castle in the county, rebuilt by Edward III but now in ruins; and Shoebury east beach, where you can park your car on the grass next to the sea.

STANFORD-LE-HOPE

R EVOLUTION is in the very air of this corner of Essex; the names of the villages have stamped their mark on the history of our country. Stanford, Corringham, Fobbing, Mucking and Horndon, their names roll forth like battle honours, and well they might, for it was the people of these villages who started the Peasants' Revolt of 1381.

Thinking themselves already overtaxed (and things have not changed much, have they?) the villagers faced the call to Brentwood for further taxation with little joy. One or two rash acts by the king's tax collectors sparked off a revolution that led to many innocent people being killed. The revolution was aimed at getting freedom of land tenure for the villagers and culminated in a march to London and a meeting with the king. Promised pardons and the freedom they wanted, the villagers dispersed—only to be routed out by the king's army and tried for treason.

This then is the inheritance of this corner of the county, described by Kipling as being " . . . down by the Lower Hope, dear lass, with the Gunfleet Sound in view." They have still not lost their flavour for revolution, only using revolution in its literal sense of being change. As you travel through this part of the world you cannot fail to see the evidence of modern housing and planning that is slowly changing these rural villages into growing towns.

The largest of these villages, and gateway to them all, is Stanford-le-Hope. It stands just off the A13 road at its junction with the old London road. The entrance to the village is barred by the railway level crossing. When the gates are closed—and this always seems to happen whenever you arrive—the traffic piles up the steep Church Hill, which leads to the town centre. Just the other side of the railway station used to be Stanford Creek, where boats could come inland from the Thames and unload at the wharves. The creek is now filled in and a new housing estate covers the area.

Pride of place in the town centre goes to the parish church of St. Margaret, which is guarded by its massive 400-year-old nail-studded door. The church, with its backcloth of trees, looks out over the whole town, past the war memorial that stands on the road island, and away towards Corringham.

Most of the historic buildings of Stanford stood in the vicinity of the church, but nearly all have now gone. Still remaining is the King's Head public-house, reputed to be the old haunt of smugglers when the ships could navigate the creek. This pub was also a coaching station on the London to Southend route. Another place of interest lies on the way to Corringham—Hassenbrook Farm. Alone in the town this building still retains its wooden beams and odd corners. Nearby is the new Hassenbrook School, with its unusual brick mosaic entrance hall.

Following the road, we arrive at Corringham, a once truly rural

village; but now the old village green looks out on to large new
housing estates that are gradually joining up with those from Stanford. There is still a pleasant blend of the old and the new, however,
and to sit outside the Bull inn with the sun shining through the
trees that surround the church is a pleasure not to be missed. Both
the pub and the church are quite old, the tower of the church being
Norman. For many years the church had a 600-year-old brass of
Isabel Baud, but in recent times the location of this has been lost.
However, the chancel still has its civilian brass dating from 1460.

In many old deeds the village green is spoken of, but recent
inhabitants looked in vain for its third of an acre of open space. The
latest thought is that the small triangle of grass that stands in front
of the church is all that remains of it, the roads that run either side
of the church having gradually eaten the green away.

A short drive from Corringham along narrow country lanes
brings us to Fobbing. This is a small village sitting at the edge of
the marshes—and on a damp day the mists still roll in, giving the
place a ghost-like quality. Like many villages on the banks of the
Thames, it was left high and dry as the land drainage schemes
forced the river back into a deeper but less wide channel. One can
gauge how close the river used to be from the fact that a cannonball
from a Dutch man-of-war was found in the churchyard. The river
is now a mile or more away and the range of the cannon was not
more than 500 yards.

The tower of the church (St. Michael's) dates from the fifteenth
century, but much of the rest of the church is of eleventh-century
construction. Inside the church the font and the remains of an altar
tomb are of special interest. For the more adventurous it is possible
to climb the tower and get a wide view of the surrounding countryside and river.

While in the village Wheelers House should not be missed. This
is now converted, but still retains its outward appearance of a
fifteenth-century country house. Most striking are the 300-year-old
chimneys.

The heavyweight boxer Billy Walker now lives and trains in
Fobbing, and can often be seen around the village.

Stretching away from Fobbing and down river towards London
are the small " oil towns " of Thames Haven, Shell Haven and
Coryton. These were built to handle the vast quantities of oil that
are landed at their jetties. With their miles of pipe lines and huge

storage tanks they look like a scene from some science-fiction film.

Part of this region, but lying north and south of the main connecting road, are Horndon-on-the-Hill and Mucking. Horndon lies north of the A13 and is an agricultural village with an interesting history of royal visits (Elizabeth I) and burning at the stake (a local landowner in 1555). Much of this history can be brought to life by the thatched houses and the timbered inn that crowd together in the village centre. Older than all the houses is the church. The Norman doorway leads to a 600-year-old font of unusual and simple design.

The ill-named Mucking lies south of Stanford, and its quaint old farms and cottages give a " rural England " feeling as you travel through.

STOCK

THE approach to Stock is still pleasantly rural. Though the parish extends as far as the Ship, " a well-known old roadside hostelry " on the Chelmsford road, the village itself still has a solid nucleus in its lovely church, its old inns—the Cock, the Bear and the Baker's Arms—and the windmill which gleams white against skies blue or grey.

Its full name is Stock Harvard, or Stock Hereward, harking back to stirring times in Saxon history. The church is on the Billericay side of the village, standing across a wide green which preserves the full view so often lost of town churches. This pretty church was itself nearly lost when a land-mine dropped nearby in World War II; the church was damaged, and nearly every tombstone in the churchyard was shattered by the blast.

The tombs could not possibly be restored just as they were. Instead a lovely garden of remembrance was created, using the broken monuments as flagstones on paths and terrace, where seats are provided for those who wish to sit in peace.

The wooden tower and spire date from the fifteenth century, like those at Margaretting and Blackmore. The massive oak beams needed to support the belfry can be seen from within, where, on the south wall of the nave, there is a brass to "Richard Twedye Esquir" dated 1574, which has a curious long inscription showing, *inter alia*, that he founded almshouses for the benefit of four "poore knightes," which can still be seen across the green.

Newport. ". . . noted by experts for its two typical old Essex cottages."

Harlow. ". . . the new town has . . . water gardens, and the two parks."

Finchingfield. " But what is time when you can see the cottages of all periods, and all beautifully kept ? "

Steeple Bumpstead. " The village spreads round a rectangle of roads."

The windmill stands half a mile east of the church, where once four mills stood in close proximity. Village lore has it that the other three were taken down because there was not enough wind for them all!

Buttsbury, in the valley of the River Wid, is more or less a lost village. Its church shows evidence of ancient foundation and greater glory when the village was a large and thriving place of which Stock was but a hamlet. Those days are gone and attention is drawn to Ingatestone Hall, a field or two away from the church, which is of more interest to modern travellers and can be referred to under Ingatestone.

TILBURY

LOCALS have been heard to call Tilbury " the world's end," and there is even a pub by that name to prove it. For many centuries it must have seemed like the end of the world, with its bogs and marshes flooded time and again by the mighty Thames. As in so many parts of the county, land drainage has worked wonders at Tilbury and now the place is thriving—so much so in fact that there are now three Tilburys: East and West Tilbury as well as the main town.

The growth has been brought about by a string of circumstances going back several centuries. Perhaps the first major event was the building of Tilbury Fort in the days of Henry VIII. This fort has since been modified regularly at every sign of trouble until today it stands much changed but still unbowed. The fort is one of the finest remaining examples in this country of the bastioned or defence-in-depth system. It is odd to think that although manned until the end of World War I it has seen little or no action. The fighting there has consisted of shooting down a Zeppelin in World War I and a strange " battle " in 1776. Quoting from the *Ipswich Journal* of that year, we read: " The match [cricket] was a county match between Kent and Essex; feeling ran high and a fight broke out. Thereupon the Kentish men ran to the guard room and, seizing a gun, killed one of the Essex men." That then is the fighting history of this large fort. There are two other things worthy of note while talking about it. The first you can still see in all its impressive majesty—the main gateway built by Inigo Jones. The other is the visit of Elizabeth I. This visit was to review her troops when the nation was threatened by the Spanish Armada, and her fighting speech is reported to have been cheered to the echo. For full details about this fascinating building there is an excellent booklet, full of plans and pictures, produced by the Ministry of Works.

The next landmark in the development of the area was the arrival of the railway in 1852, and finally the seal was set by the building of the docks in 1884. While ensuring the future of Tilbury, the docks have also left a housing problem. The large influx of " navvies " to carve out these huge docks led to quick housing being provided, some of which has lasted to the present time, much to the embarrassment of the local authority. The future of the docks, although in doubt a few years ago, is now secure, and a process of modernization is being undertaken by the Port of London Authority. In line with this progressive policy, there is now a car ferry service to France from Tilbury. The service operates most days and offers a quick and pleasant journey across the Channel for both the car and its owner.

Next door to the Port of London docks is the British Rail dock of Tilbury Riverside. Once the home of car and passenger ferries to Gravesend, it now operates only its passenger service. The vehicle traffic now crosses the Thames via the new Dartford—Purfleet tunnel.

On a sunny day it is a pleasing sight to be around these docks and watch the host of ships from all corners of the world waiting their turn to enter the port and unload their cargoes. What adventures they must have had crossing the oceans to reach our shores!

Before leaving the town look in at the museum. This is part of the Tilbury branch library, which stands in the centre of the town. The museum there contains a collection of historic remains from every part of Thurrock, covering every period of history.

North-east of Tilbury town is Chadwell St. Mary, a rapidly growing place standing at the crest of a hill that runs down to the rest of the Tilburys. Chadwell is interesting mainly for its church, which proudly stands at the top of the hill, looking down over the river. Much of the church dates from the thirteenth and fourteenth centuries and it has Norman doorways in perfect condition. You can also see the change in the flintwork of the church between the Norman and later builders. Within the church, note the several fine paintings and a brass dated 1603. Recent house building has unearthed many remains of the Roman occupation and it seems possible that they used this high point of the region for a settlement.

A couple of miles away is West Tilbury, a small hamlet so far unspoilt by the development taking place nearby. It is still possible to drive down Guns Hill and meet horse-drawn haycarts during the autumn months. At the bottom of the hill is the church, which stands in a circle of trees, looking out across the river, with its shipping, to the far hills of Kent. Built in the thirteenth century, but with a modern tower, the church of St. James has an early Norman window. This is not, however, visible to the visitor.

A little north of the church there can still be seen the Turnpike Cottages, a reminder of those days when transport was more leisurely and the traveller had to pay to use some sections of the highway.

The third Tilbury is East Tilbury, which is rich in history but rather dull in appearance. Hidden beneath the water of the Thames, except at low water, is the site of a Romano-British settlement and ferry. Some years ago the remains of the huts could be picked out, but, alas, this is no longer possible. However, one can still visit the site and find the depressions that marked the position from which the ferry started. It is a great pity that part of this area is being used as a rubbish dump, for much of interest may be lost. From here a walk down the sea wall will bring the visitor to the other fort at Tilbury—Coalhouse Fort. This low, rectangular blockhouse was built by Henry VIII, but the remaining building is the much-changed version of General Gordon.

One way back to the village is across the marshes. This is the way for anyone wanting to " get away from it all," for here the only noise will be the song of the birds and the wind rustling the grass. The marsh is drained by deep ditches, and these are the home of rushes and waterfowl.

We must blame the Dutch for the missing tower of St. Katherine's church. Morant records that in 1667 they shelled the tower because of " its height having given them offence "! Coming back to the twentieth century, the present prosperity of East Tilbury is bound up with the vast Bata shoe factory. This is a modern place with its own housing estate for the people employed there.

Finally, let us leave you with a mystery that hangs over this region. In A.D. 630 St. Cedd, who later built St. Peter-on-the-Wall at Bradwell, founded a monastery here but nobody really knows where it was, so as you travel round keep your eyes open and you may discover a unique piece of history.

WICKFORD

WICKFORD is situated in a fold of the River Crouch and owes its name to this location. The name means village by a ford. It was probably founded by the Saxon invaders who sailed up the Crouch to its highest navigable point—Wickford. This is yet another of the Essex towns that have given their names to places in America. In this case Elizabeth Reid, whose baptism on November 27, 1614, is recorded in the parish registers, was the instrument. She married John Winthrop, a future governor of Connecticut, and when asked to think of a name for "New Town," Rhode Island, offered Wickford. This suggestion was adopted and there is now a Wickford, Rhode Island.

Half a century ago Wickford was a quaint country village, with the locals speaking with an accent so broad that it could be " cut with a knife." Now it is a booming town and much of this quaintness has had to make way for the new buildings that are springing up everywhere. Commuter country has indeed reached deep into Essex.

A little to the west are the twin villages of Ramsden Bellhouse and Ramsden Crays. The timberwork of the church at Bellhouse is magnificent, as is the view from " God's acre " just outside the church. The name Ramsden means " raven's valley," perhaps an indication of the bird life of the area years ago.

Standing on a hill to the north of this corner of Essex is the rather scattered village of Downham. The beauty spot of the village is centred on the church, which is surrounded by elm trees reaching up for the sky. The visitor standing here at the right time of year will soon see where the bluebells can be gathered.

WOODHAM FERRERS

FROM the Blackwater to the Crouch runs a string of villages that stand as guardians to the neck of land that pushes out into the North Sea. To reach Bradwell or Burnham visitors must pass through some part of this wooded belt of Essex regardless of the direction from which they come.

Guarding the southern approach roads are Woodham Ferrers and South Woodham Ferrers. It is here that the River Crouch breaks up into the several small streams that wander around the town of South Woodham. The flat agricultural land near the river gives way to hilly fields along the B1012 towards Cold Norton. On this road look out for the large radar station that sits on a hilltop; the road seems to run round and round the station before it gets away. Watch the bends on this road, for many of them are deceptively sharp.

Woodham Ferrers is just north of its southern namesake and is on the B1018. The way through the village is a twisting, hilly road along which stand houses, cottages and the church. This latter is interesting for the medieval " doom " painting of the last judgment above the chancel arch; although much faded, the picture of Christ on a rainbow can just be seen. Also inside the church is a coloured effigy of Cecilie Sandys, the wife of the Archbishop of York who built the nearby Edwins Hall. Much of the Hall is still standing today and around it the moat can be seen.

Stow Maries, north-east of Woodham Ferrers on the B1012, is a small village standing 100 feet above the Crouch. Its old cottages, many of them thatched and in fine condition, stand on the rising village street. In this region keep an eye open for any odd-shaped mounds—they are probably the remains of medieval salt works.

Surrounded by trees, the road leaves Stow Maries and twists its way up to Cold Norton, a larger place than the previous hamlet and standing 100 feet higher. Beacon Hill is the highest point in Cold Norton and a mixture of weatherboarded and modern houses stands on the slopes of the hill and along the main street. From the hill there is a long view down towards North Fambridge and the River Crouch. The church of St. Stephen was built in 1855 in the style of the fourteenth-century stone churches. The pulpit was carved out of oak saved from a Norman church that stood on the site of the present building.

In the centre of this region is the large parish of Purleigh. The village is clustered on the top of a hill and there are fine views over the neighbouring farms. The hedges and trees that outline the limits of each field give a mosaic effect in the wide vista that spills down the hillside from the church. This is the church of All Saints, and it attracts visitors from America as much as those from England. The reason for this is that the great-great-grandfather of George Washington, the first American president, was vicar of the church from 1633 to 1643. In honour of Lawrence Washington the flint tower of the church was repaired at the expense of citizens of the U.S.A. The fabric of the church lives up to all this attention;

built of knapped flintstone with glazed brickwork, it has a Tudor brick porch with a 600-year-old strap-hung door. When passing through the doorway look for the beautiful modern glass interspersed with fragments of the original fourteenth-century glass. The altar and altar screen are both modern in design.

Just outside the village at the hamlet of Howe Green there is an entrenched mound about 150 feet across. It is thought to be the site of an early castle and is listed as an ancient monument.

Mundon stands in splendid isolation in the north-east corner of this group. It covers a large area considering that the population is under 300, but these lucky few are close enough to the Blackwater for the air to be quite bracing. The most historic part of the place is a short distance from the main street with its small wood. The entrance to this historic world is through the rustic gate of the now disused church. Within the circle of the great moat, which must once have been filled with water and aquatic plants, stand the church, Mundon Hall and a Stuart barn. Within the church notice the Tudor timberwork of the belfry (one of whose bells is contemporary with the woodwork), the squared-off Norman font and the porch. Finally in this group is the tiny parish of Hazeleigh, remarkable for the nearby woods, an iron church erected in 1893, and Hazeleigh Hall, the sixteenth-century home of the Alleynes. Once in Hazeleigh it is only a short journey to the beautiful and historic town of Maldon, a full description of which is given in a separate chapter.

SECTION THREE

AWAY TO THE WEST

AWAY TO THE WEST

ARKESDEN and the beautiful villages south of it

THERE can be few areas, even in so rich a county as Essex, where man and nature have combined as perfectly in village after village as they have in the region we are now about to visit: five villages within six miles of each other and each a beauty in its own right (well, that is the claim), so let us begin our exploration of these borderlands with the prettiest of them all—Arkesden. The best approach to this village is from the north of the A11 and then the B1039. We leave the B road soon after Wendens Ambo and turn left down the lane that first climbs the hill and finally twists its way through the trees to the outskirts of the village. Towards the bottom of the hill, encircled by trees, are the village church and a group of perfect thatched cottages. The great square tower of the church stands on the foundations of an early Norman round tower, and in the grounds of the church notice the " remembrance " plaque set in the giant stone. Passing the church, we cross the small brook called Wickham Water by a narrow bridge and turn left, past a green with a water pump on it, to follow the course of the stream through the rest of the village. Along this lane stand many cottages, all neat and tidy, with their thatch or tiles in good repair—one is reminded of the musical " Brigadoon " and could almost expect the place to disappear when the sun goes down. At the end of the village are crossroads where a wooden bench looks out from under cool trees that are watered by the stream; then on to the road we must take on the next part of our journey—on towards Clavering.

The road to Clavering winds its way between banks of tall trees that offer welcome shade from the hot summer sun. At the crossroads bear right to join the B1038 and soon after this watch for the pleasant village green at Hill Green. Clavering itself is a rather scattered place and takes in all the various " Greens " round about, such as Roast Green, where two windmills can be seen, these having now been put to a new use. The main village, which stands on either side of the main street, is a pleasant mixture of old and new. Particularly nice is the kerbside facing the local inn, the Fox and Hounds; it looks as if care has been taken to cultivate a special roadside border. The village church is situated along a lane at the west end of the main street and is worth a visit for three reasons: (1) the church itself (St. Mary and St. Clement), which was built in the mid-fourteenth century (the chancel screen and the roof are things to note); (2) the moat of the now vanished Clavering castle, which is very near the church and is seventy-five feet wide and eighteen feet deep; (3) the many attractive houses that line the way to the church. At the end of this part of the village notice the Grange, an early-sixteenth-century house with close-set timber-framing.

Our next village is Berden, and to get there we leave Clavering by the road to the left at the top of the hill in the village centre (left as you enter from the north).

Here the road runs through open countryside which has pockets of woods dotted about the landscape. Just after passing under the giant electricity-carrying pylons turn right for Berden. The centre of the village is marked by a signpost; the road posted Little London is the one to take when you leave. Facing you as you enter the village is the lane to Berden Priory; the house is about half a mile along on the right and stands on the old priory site. It is a pretty place with plenty of exposed timberwork, but the real joy is the covered well-house with an open tread-wheel for raising the water buckets, which is of the seventeenth century. Following our road out of the village we pass a timber-framed house, the church of St. Nicholas (which has parts dating from the eleventh century and brasses dating from 1473 and 1607) and Berden Hall, a red-brick Elizabethan residence (1580) with three gables on each side which can be seen from the road behind the trees.

Keep bearing left as you now travel on to the attractive village of Manuden. The lanes are high banked and run past the occasional farmhouse and cottage. At the T junction turn right and follow the road towards the village. A row of white houses shimmering in the sunlight is the first sight of Manuden, and the village lives up to its promise. The main street is spacious for a village, and the well-kept houses and cottages with their colourful walls, thatched roofs and overhanging stories are worth seeing. To the right as you enter the place is Manuden Hall. This was rebuilt in 1889, but two of the gables on the west front are original sixteenth century. At a bend in the road you will find the church of St. Mary; between it and the roadside is the churchyard, probably laid out in Saxon times. The chestnut trees flanking it are, in their own way, equally old. Inside, the wonderful chancel screen is almost as it was left by the old craftsmen who carved it with loving hands. There is also a marble statue to Sir William Waad, who was captor of Sir Walter Raleigh and was also connected with the tracing of the Gunpowder Plot conspirators. Next to the church is a row of brick cottages of the nineteenth century. We could run on for another 100 words praising the beauty of this place; but they would be no substitute for a visit, so we will leave what has already been said to tempt you and pass on to our last village, Farnham.

As you follow the lane through the pleasant country look out for the cluster of thatched cottages that stands just before the Three Horse Shoes pub, for here is an interesting road sign pointing the way right to Farnham. It warns that the road is closed at times of flood, so if it has been raining a lot keep well clear! Most of the time all will be well and you can safely follow the lane, keeping left at the bends, into Farnham. As you travel this road look out on the left for Hassobury Park and the large Tudor house, built in 1868, that stands in the centre of it. The village church of St. Mary is along a lane east of the habitations and is cradled in a corner of the park. Rebuilt in 1859, the church is noted for the Flemish glass kept from the old building and now sited near the organ chamber.

So we end a brief tour of this part of Essex, but in Farnham you are only a few hundred yards away from another county—Hertfordshire—and a short run along the B1004 (the road from Farnham joins it) will take you into the large town of Bishop's Stortford. Here you can sample the pleasures of this pride of another county before returning to Essex along the A120.

BLACKMORE, DODDINGHURST AND STONDON

BLACKMORE is popular as the object of an evening drive. In summer the verdant pastures and shady trees are so refreshing. Whichever way you come it must be by country lanes, for the village lies in the centre of the triangle made by the A roads 12, 122 and 128, which connect Chelmsford, Brentwood and Ongar.

Most people end up at the Bull, a sixteenth-century inn, or its companion on the other side of the road, but a quiet stroll round the village is more rewarding. The narrow road to the church has an eighteenth-century atmosphere about it, with houses huddled together for comfort and doors opening on to the street. The church is quite a treasure for its big tower constructed entirely of timber in three definite stages. Stand inside and look up—you will marvel at the massive baulks so cunningly assembled. An expert has dated it 1480, so the craft of some long-dead carpenter lives on.

The fabric of the church is fundamentally Norman. It was founded as the church to the Augustinian priory of the twelfth century, but was turned into a parish church on the dissolution of the priory in 1527. It stands within the old moated site, with the adjoining Jericho House, which, though much altered, was one of the favourite hideaways of Henry VIII when affairs of state lay heavy on him, so the saying among his courtiers that he had " gone to Jericho " became part of our language. The brook by the house was consequently called the Jordan!

South-west out of Blackmore to Tip's Cross a right-hand lane leads to Stondon Massey, almost an urban area in the countryside, with its own light industrial estate to the north-west past the church. The first settlers chose the higher, gravelly ground, and that is exactly what Stondon meant in their language. Massey, or Marcy, was the name of the ruling family in Norman days when the church was built, with a wooden belfry added a bit later.

Inside you can see a very nicely executed Jacobean pulpit with a reader's desk beside it, all carved in oak, and a couple of ancient brasses. The Hall stands behind the church; the oldest part, the north wing, was put up 500 years ago.

Stondon House, between church and village, has been rebuilt twice. William Byrd the musician lived here for thirty years up to 1623, and conducted one lawsuit after another about his ownership. South again, and still in the web of country lanes, you can find Doddinghurst and its hamlets. It has been favoured in recent times for secluded residential development, but the old houses were very much scattered, and some, like the Hall, the Place and Park Farm, have vestiges of moats to prove their lineage.

The church of All Saints has a stout thirteenth-century belfry of timber with a shingled spire above it, and inside it is unusual to find the rood beam, which carried the cross, with its figures, of sixteenth-century German work, still in position. Nearby the old priest's house still stands after 400 years.

From Doddinghurst it is but a stone's throw to Kelvedon Hatch and the A12.

CANFIELD, GREAT AND LITTLE

IF you want somewhere to spend a quiet afternoon Great Canfield is the place.

This is a parish large in extent, hemmed in by the B184 to the

east, the B183 to the west and the old Stane Street (A120) to the
north, with little side roads trailing round to hamlets like Bacon
End, Hope End Green, Puttocks End, Taverners Green and Hell-
man's Cross, but it is the bit of village by the church that is most
interesting. Cottages of all periods line the approach and with their
pretty gardens make a lovely introduction to the church of St. Mary.

It stands very much as it was built for the new Norman overlords,
though the wood-shingled spire and the fine south porch with its
battlements are of the fifteenth century. In the church, whether you
believe or not, pay your respects to the thirteenth-century artist who
painted the mural at the east end of the chancel between the two
windows. This painting is expertly assessed as one of the finest of
the Madonna and Child in the whole country. Though the colours
have faded the beauty of line still astonishes. There are other features
to be quietly enjoyed, including monuments to a branch of the
great Wiseman family.

Behind the church rises the forty-five-foot mound raised by those
same Normans under the first de Vere, Earl of Oxford, for their
castle. It was probably a pallisaded dwelling on a motte and bailey
(a mound with a ditch around) rather than the great stone castle of
the story books. A moat around it was filled by the River Roding.
There is nothing here but peace.

Little Canfield is not so quiet. The A120 hurries folk through
it from Dunmow to Bishop's Stortford, but the church, way down
its own little track to the south, looks on with serene indifference.
It was largely restored by a vicar who was an amateur architect; the
result is a richness in detail, as in the chancel, and an unexpected
juxtaposition of embellishments from all periods. There are an old
chest and some brasses of the late sixteenth century to be examined.

CHIGWELL and either side of it

THE hungry jaws of London bite ever deeper into our county,
and the last gulp took the boundary up to Chigwell and its
neighbours. In spite of being part of the conurbation of the
capital, Chigwell retains much of its country freshness. Pevsner
calls it in his *Buildings of England* " the first real village as one leaves
London in a north-east direction." Perhaps this description is a
little misleading, for Chigwell is certainly of town size these days,
as the traveller will discover.

Typical of the town is the High Road, which runs through the heart of the place. Opposite each other at the London end of the town are the fine golf course and a new technical college, a contrast between the beauty of nature and the undoubted attraction of some modern design. Passing the railway station and hosts of modern shops we reach the Essex end of the town, and here several things claim our attention. Let us commence with St. Mary's church, a Norman building that has doubled in size over the years. Entering by the original south doorway, look for the most interesting brass to Samuel Harsnett, a real case of local boy makes good. Harsnett was once vicar of Chigwell and rose to be Archbishop of York, but asked to be buried in his old church. The brass is life size and his vestments are completely represented. While in the town he founded the grammar school, which is situated next to the church. The school was built in 1629 and the large schoolroom remains to this day, with its queen-posts and even some of its original windows.

Across the road stands one of the most interesting of the many old inns of the town. This is the King's Head, a timber-framed building that has seen much addition without losing its seventeenth-century charm. We single this one out because of its connection with one of our greatest writers, Charles Dickens. Readers of his *Barnaby Rudge* will recognize the King's Head as the Maypole of this novel. Perhaps many of the people he saw there found their way into the finished book.

From this end of the town Vicarage Lane runs down to meet the B173, which carries us along to Chigwell Row, Hainault Forest and Lambourne. The road climbs the slope towards Chigwell Row, and at the crossroads stands the church of All Saints, facing out on to a green on which stands the five-bay Hainault Hall. The yellow and white stone church was built in 1867 but is in the thirteenth-century style. From the church you can look across to Hainault Forest, once the haunt of kings but now a recreation ground for everyone.

On the way to Lambourne the unclassified road runs along the edge of the forest and there are fine views over the Roding valley to the tree-covered horizon. The fine church lies along the lane past Bishop's Hall. The church of St. Mary and All Saints has great charm and the various alterations made over the years have all blended well with the original twelfth-century design. Inside the church there is a good wall-painting of St. Christopher and the

small stained-glass windows are of seventeenth-century Swiss glass.
Nearby is Lambourne Place, a residence built in 1740 as the rectory.
It is two stories high and has seven bays. West of the church along
a narrow lane stands Lambourne Hall, which was built in 1571.

To the west of Chigwell is its sister town of Buckhurst Hill,
approached along the B170 (Chigwell Rise/Roding Lane). Before
entering Buckhurst the road crosses the River Roding and the
railway line. Just south of this road is Queen's Road, the main
shopping street of the town, while even farther south lies a small
part of Epping Forest that is now completely surrounded by housing
but lives on under the protection of London's green belt.

ELMDON and its satellites

THREE churches in three miles—hard to believe, but it is a fact.
Go west to Elmdon and from the fifteenth-century tower of St.
Nicholas you can look south to the decaying church of Wenden
Lofts and south-west to the church of the Holy Trinity at Chrishall,
and there is not a mile between each of them.

But for the tower, Elmdon's church is Victorian, though inside
evidence, like the large brass of about 1530 to a man, his two wives
and nineteen children, points to the continuity of worship on this
site. The village really needs looking for down country lanes miles
from the main-road melee. It stands high on the chalk, the dying
fling of the Chilterns, and has its fair share of interesting old houses
in thatch and tile with trees all about.

Elmdonbury, just to the north, preserves in its last two syllables
the old name for a manor house, for one stood here of old and the
little pools to be seen about are the remains of the moat. There is a
moated mound nearby which marks the site of the Norman
fortification.

To the south, Wenden Lofts is a village which seems to have
exploded into smaller hamlets scattered all about—like Lower Pond
Street, Duddenhoe End, Bridge Green and Coopers End, which is
right on the track of the old Roman road. Lofts Hall, which marked
the centre of the old village, was burnt down years ago and only an
Elizabethan dovecote, hemmed in by farm buildings but most
splendid of its kind, remains to mark the vanished glory. The new
Hall is in the same park but much nearer the road.

Chrishall is west of Elmdon, hardly a mile as the crow flies but a good deal more by the " rolling English road." You can get to it from the south past Lofts Hall and then via the B1039, when you come first upon the church, standing up all alone on its own little hill. Among several interesting brasses there is one particularly beautiful and famous example, worth going miles to see, in memory of Sir John de la Pole and his wife, tenderly depicted holding hands. Set in the floor under its own arch, and almost life size, it is very hard to believe from its fine condition that it has weathered 600 years of history. Behind the church, in Park Wood, there is what we might call in Essex the inevitable Norman castle mound, nucleus of the old settlement.

The road runs on up to the crossroads, centre of the newer village, with some very satisfying scenery, any number of old cottages built of the local material, timber and plaster and clapboard, and behind them big open fields looking " fat and fruitful." Chrishall Grange is two and a half miles away to the north, with the Cambridgeshire border squeezing it on three sides. It is a pleasant brick structure which has stood now for over 250 years.

From the little lane between Elmdon and Chrishall on the north side there are superb views over into Cambridgeshire and Hertfordshire. In a straight line to the east lies Strethall, though again the road is entertainingly circuitous. Here an interesting pre-Conquest church stands by the track of the old Roman road which passes unknown under today's fields and houses.

If you enjoy wandering at will down country lanes, just taking in the sights and sounds, this is an area for you. Try finding your way from here down to Langley, a border village equidistant between the B1038 and the B1039. Right-angle and dog-leg turns bring down your speed and show up the scenery.

It is in this village just near the church that you can stand on the highest point in the county—484.7 feet above sea level. This is at Upper Green; the other half of the village is down at Lower Green. Look in the church for a number of interesting reasons, including the double-hammerbeam roof to the nave. Its timbers, some nicely carved, are of the fifteenth century.

EPPING, its forest, town and nearby villages

EPPING FOREST—the very name conjures up a picture of a land of space and air, of trees and shrubs, of grass and water, sunlight and shade, and in fact it lives up to all of these.

It stretches for six glorious miles from the town of Epping in the north to the edge of London in the south, and is bisected into two equal parts by the A11. Even a drive along this trunk road will show some of the beauty of the forest, for the road is lined by tall, cool trees. To the right, just outside the town of Epping and quite close to the road, lies Ambresbury Banks, a fortified earthwork thought to be the stronghold of Queen Boadicea.

To enjoy this quiet land to the full, however, you should either walk along the many tracks that wend their way through the 6,000 acres or use the car to drive along the two roads that cross east to west. The first of these is at the Wake Arms inn, where six roads meet. From here roads run east to Theydon Bois and Loughton, and to the west a loop goes via High Beech to join the A11 again at our second intersection by the Robin Hood inn. Near the Robin Hood there is usually a quiet spot to park or picnic or take a short stroll into the forest.

A little north of this road, hidden in the semi-darkness of the forest, you will find the ancient British camp called Loughton Camp. This was almost certainly a fortress, since it stands on high ground. Monk Wood, one of the most attractive parts of Epping, is close by and is a good place to watch for the deer that still inhabit the forest. At night time beware of them on the roads, for they are inclined to rush across the path of oncoming vehicles.

Let us now look at the towns and villages that have the pleasure of being close to this finger of green that points its way from the drabness of London to the richness of the Essex countryside.

The town of Epping is an ideal place to start, for its roads leave in every direction to link together all the places about to be mentioned. For the visitor Epping consists of only one main street, but how fine it is, with trees and grass verges giving a feeling of space and freedom. Shops and houses in a variety of styles blend attractively together, although few are of any historic importance. This is a little strange when we realize that the town goes back to Saxon times, but it is probable that the change in the location of the main road has much to do with this. The Roman road, part of which runs near Coopersale even today, fell into disrepair and a new road, which the present A11 follows, was built to replace it. While being a present blessing to Epping, the forest has in the past been the source of no little trouble. For instance, to be caught chasing the king's deer meant losing a hand, while all dogs in the town had to

Hatfield Broad Oak. "... the parish church, where the wooden effigy of the founder is still preserved."

The church of St. Thomas the Apostle at Bradwell-juxta-Mare, on the estuary of the Blackwater seven miles from Southminster.

A cottage near Moyns Park on the road from Finchingfield to Steeple Bumpstead.

Burnham-on-Crouch. "Covering three miles of country lanes, we arrive at Burnham. This is the yachting centre of Essex."

have three claws cut off each of their front paws to ensure that they could not chase deer.

Travellers to the town were always in danger from the highwaymen, as Samuel Pepys recorded after his visit in 1660. In the colourful days of coaching Epping was a stopping place for many routes; Epping Place, just off the High Street, is one of these rest places, and one can well imagine the horse-drawn coaches speeding down the High Street to escape the clutches of pursuing highwaymen. It is to these coaches that the town owes its many inns.

The church of St. John is fairly new—only 1899—and perhaps the most striking feature is the tower constructed in 1908. It has three big battlements and two bell openings on each side. The explanation for this lack of an old church in so old a town is that in medieval times the village of Epping Upland was the home of the parish church.

Epping Upland lies north-west of Epping on the B181. This is mainly a farming village, and the farmhouses are mostly of interest, some being moated and nearly all dating from the sixteenth and seventeenth centuries. Two of the better known ones are Parvills and Takeleys; the former stands about a mile west of the village and the latter a quarter of a mile east of the village. Standing on the crossroads that lead to these houses is the much restored church of All Saints. Built in the thirteenth century as the parish church of all Epping, it now remains, much changed, as a village church.

To the south-east of Epping in the charming Roding valley lie the three Theydons—Mount, Garnon and Bois. Theydon Mount is approached from Epping via Coopersale Street and Fiddlers Hamlet.

Our lane to the first of the Theydons runs through countryside that is typical of the Roding valley. Broad fields are marked with clumps of trees that were once part of the forest but have long since been isolated by the agricultural needs of the country. An old farmhouse standing surrounded by its lands and the odd roadside cottage are the sights that will greet the traveller hereabouts. The approach to Theydon Mount will give a clue to the second part of its name, for the road has to climb a quite steep hill to reach the small village centre. Apart from the church and the " big house " there are only a few cottages to mark the centre of the parish; everyone else is scattered in the surrounding farms. Hill Hall was built in the 1550s by Sir Thomas Smith, and his first-hand knowledge of French styles of the period (he was Elizabeth I's ambassador to France) led him to design in the Renaissance style. Although part of the Hall was later altered the south front and courtyard remain in his original style. The Hall is now used as an " open " prison for women. Standing in a corner of the grounds of the Hall is the church of St. Michael, which was built in 1613 in the Gothic style. Inside the church are tombs of the Smith family.

The way south to Theydon Garnon is along the narrow lanes that make travel in Essex so interesting; some new joy is waiting round each bend in the road. Like its sister to the north, this Theydon is also a quiet, isolated place. Even the church is wrapped round with a curtain of trees. This is the church of All Saints, whose brick tower was built in 1520, though the rest of the building is later. There are several brasses in the church, one of the priest William Kirkeby being three feet long and dating from 1458. While inside note the two dormers in the nave. Although they look Victorian they are in fact much older.

Heading west, we join the B172 and go right to reach the last of the Theydons—Theydon Bois. This is the largest of the three and has an attractive village centre. As we enter the village from the east the first sign we see is of the Central Line that serves as a fast link with London. It is good to realize that in spite of this attraction to the commuter the village has not been spoiled, as you will see when the really splendid green comes into full view on the left. Cut into two parts by an avenue of tall trees, with the traditional pond with its swans, this green really is the heart of things in Theydon Bois. Around the circumference stand the cottages, and radiating beyond them are the streets that make up the rest of the place. To the right, at the end of the green, stands the church of St. Mary, built in 1844 to replace an earlier building. This church is guarded by two oaks, and has a memorial to Frances Buss, one of the pioneers of education for women. Beyond the church the land runs back towards the forest and makes an attractive setting for the local golf course.

South of Theydon Bois, and marking the border with London, is the town of Loughton. Apart from its close proximity to Epping Forest there is little here for the seeker after open spaces or quaint buildings. Here the traveller is indeed back in the second part of the twentieth century, with a large new shopping centre and ever-expanding housing estates making this a busy town centre. Looking around, the visitor will find much that is modern and at the same time pleasing to the eye: the new railway station, some rows of houses and many of the local schools, of which some are newly built and some housed in older buildings refurbished for this purpose.

Anyone enjoying Epping Forest should spare a thought for Loughton, for it was from here that Thomas Willingdale fought his battle to have the forest open again for public use after much of it had been closed by private persons. Although a poor man, his courage led to the Corporation of London supporting him, and after a long legal fight Queen Victoria officially reopened the forest to the public in 1882.

Before leaving the forest area let us mention again High Beech, a village to the west of the forest. Its name comes from the multitude of beech trees that surround the ridge on which it stands. From here the visitor can view London, Epping and Hertfordshire, as well as the famous Dick Turpin's cave. Whether Turpin really used the cave is not certain, but many locals believe he did, and there is a pub standing over the cave as a useful memorial to him. High Beech church has one of the best settings of any church in the country, for it is surrounded by trees and the beautiful lanes lead up to it from all directions.

HARLOW

" FORMERLY of greater importance than now, once having a market and being a seat of the woollen manufacture, it consists chiefly of one long street with many ancient houses." How surprised the writer of the old guide would be to see it today; and Harlow is a place worth seeing as it comes to completion as a new town after twenty years of planning and building under Frederick Gibberd.

It actually takes in Great Parndon, Little Parndon, Netteswell and Latton and the hamlets in between. The best way to see this area is to take the town for what it now is and then to discover how the best of each of the old communities has been kept to give character to the new.

If you approach from the east down the B183 from Hatfield Heath you pass through old Harlow first, with the most pleasant view around the bend in the road at Mulberry Green. The parish church is not 100 years old, though the many ancient brasses displayed demonstrate the true age of the site. Harlowbury, site of the ancient manor house, with its chapel of simple Norman construction, lies more to the north.

A right turn at the first set of traffic lights takes you down to a roundabout, where the second exit will take you with a bang into new Harlow and the sight of the Temple Fields industrial area, an eye-opener in factory site planning. If you go on down Edinburgh Way, cross the roundabout and continue down Elizabeth Way you will be at the other end of the town, where the Pinnacles industrial area has been developed. Go east on Fourth Avenue and you will have driven right round Little Parndon, once one of the smallest parishes in Essex. On your right hand is the town centre, for pedestrians only, with car parks all around and easy access planned.

Straight on past the roundabout the Town Park borders the road on the left and Netteswell, the old village, lies over on the right, its thirteenth-century church dwarfed by the recent development, like Hugh's Tower, incorporating flats, known aptly by the local wags as the huge tower! On the far side of the next roundabout you will see Stow neighbourhood centre, an example of good residential planning, of which a number are scattered about.

There is another to the south, for instance, which extends the old village centre of Great Parndon with its fifteenth-century church; and yet another to the east at Latton, where part of the old Augustinian priory remains and the church of St. Mary has some interesting features, including brasses and fragments of early wall painting.

Over at Potter Street, where only the name remains to remind one of its ancient trade, a big new shopping centre is the prominent feature.

Just about 2,000 years ago the Romans built a temple here. Its site is 250 yards west of the railway station, and the hollow in the hill on which it stood is associated with the theatre with which it was the accustomed concomitant.

Today people come into Harlow from a wide area to worship at the modern temple of sport; for the new town has a fully equipped sports centre, a heated indoor swimming pool, ten-pin bowling, golf, even water gardens and the two parks for less dedicated recreation. There are no fewer than twenty publications available from the public information office about the life and landscape of this brave new town, including a very useful suggestion for a tour by car of the main features.

HATFIELD FOREST

" LET'S drive into the forest!" In these days of fumes and frustration on the road the suggestion sounds so refreshing but is hardly practicable. Yet our county can offer more than one spot where it is possible literally to drive in among the trees, and Hatfield Forest is a shining example.

It has the extra advantage of being administered by the National Trust, which means it is open to the general public. There are 1,049 acres of it, grassy glades in which to walk or picnic; trees, great oaks and hornbeams and graceful silver birch; and plenty of space in which the family can lose itself for an afternoon.

You will find it on the Ordnance Survey map at TL5320, three miles east of Bishop's Stortford. Access is from Bush End and Woodside Green. The charge for parking at the moment is three shillings, half-price for motor-cycles.

After you have left the car it is a good walk to the far end of the forest, where there is a small lake with a few boats and fishing by permission from Shell House, an eighteenth-century pavilion. It is a matter of personal opinion, but on our last visit the lake and the pavilion, where tea and snacks were available, seemed over-patronized and we were glad to retreat to the cool depths of the forest.

Driving there and back is a reward in itself. You can pass through Hatfield Broad Oak—a name to conjure up a rural scene in anybody's imagination. It is a pleasant parish, with houses of all periods in a harmonious gathering about the village pump, which has all the elegance of a Georgian coffee pot. The place grew from the nucleus of the Benedictine priory in order to serve the needs of the kings of England when they came to hunt in the royal forest of Hatfield.

The priory, founded in 1135 by the progenitor of the de Veres, Earls of Oxford, has long since vanished, but part of its chapel remains as the parish church, where the wooden effigy of the founder is still preserved in all his knightly splendour—a bit thin in the legs, weathered by time and defaced by souvenir hunters, but still with his little dog at his feet.

Hatfield Heath is a great place for cricket on a summer Sunday. The green is broad and the houses round about, with trees behind them, form a backdrop to the true drama of village cricket. Note the warning of the 1885 guide book: " The hill on the Chelmsford road, one and a quarter miles from Hatfield Heath, is *dangerous for bicyclists* and should be ridden with great care."

On the other side of the forest is Great Hallingbury, once a part of the same royal forest and still attractively wooded. Both here and at Little Hallingbury Roman bricks have been used in the fabric of the church.

Prehistoric camps existed at Portingbury Hills and at Wallbury Camp. The latter, in Great Hallingbury, covers thirty acres and has a double rampart.

In its history and in its facilities Hatfield Forest has a lot to offer.

KELVEDON HATCH and a rural ride

MIDWAY between Ongar and Brentwood on the A128 is the starting point for a visit to a series of tiny places whose real interest lies not so much in their history as in the countryside that surrounds them.

The word " Hatch " as part of the name of the village of Kelvedon gives the first clue to the locality, for it means " forest gate." While houses, churches and the like now occupy much of what was the forest of Essex, broad belts of it still remain to entice the eye. Kelvedon Hall is the first place of note, and it stands some way north of the village along a lane to the west. The Hall, which was built in the mid-eighteenth century by the Wright family, is of red brick, with Tuscan columns supporting the pediment over the main doorway. As you enter the main part of the village you cannot help but notice the rocketship-like shape of the radio booster station. Across the road from this is the church of St. Nicholas, built in 1895 to replace an earlier church that stood by the Hall. A little farther along, on the same side of the road, you will see through the trees the early Georgian house called Brizes. From here onwards the whole of this side of the road is taken up by farmland. A nasty S bend marks the end of the village, but our route takes a side road just before this. It is Crown Road, and the signpost says Dudbrook and Navestock. Immediately into this lane is a gravel area where it is possible to park and walk back the few yards into the S bend and look at Farrington House. This was built in 1855, but has recently been restored and decorated to make a pleasing sight along a busy main road.

Navestock is the next landmark—or, to be accurate, the next three landmarks! A word of explanation: first we pass through Navestock Side, where most of the population live, then go north to see the church and Hall, and finally come south again to the hamlet of Navestock.

Our lane soon comes to a junction, but we keep sharp left and follow the road signposted Navestock and Havering. At the top of the slight hill we find Navestock Side, with its attractive old green where cricket has been played since the eighteenth century. Opposite is the Green Man pub, where thirsts can be quenched after a hard game. One or two of the houses nearby are partly weatherboarded. At the black-boarded farm building with a hoist that hangs over the road turn right down Princess Road (signposted Ongar and Epping) and head towards Navestock church and Hall along a road that winds its way downhill between rolling acres of wooded farmland. You must go up the narrow track that leads to the church of St. Thomas, for here is one of the finest rural churches in Essex. It stands just beyond the metal farm gate, its elegant timber spire a thing of beauty pointing up from the well-tended churchyard. Pass through the timber gatehouse and inside the whole church seems to be created out of wood, although some is so covered with whitewash that its natural beauty is lost. Here also are monuments to the Waldegrave family, who held the manor for four centuries up until the nineteenth. Next to the church is Navestock Hall, built in the sixteenth century as a manor house, which now has a most attractive look about it with its timber framing set off by the tall trees and gardens that surround it.

We now retrace our steps a little by turning left at the end of the church lane, but only for a few yards; then the road we follow goes right (signposted Navestock Heath). At the junction with the road to Sabines Green we follow the Havering road for some really wonderful views. Soon after passing under the power cables slow down, or even stop, and look to the right for a breathtaking view down the valley and across the distant hills. These lanes are narrow, and even though they are little used beware of driving and watching the scenery.

At the B175 turn right and head for Stapleford Abbots and Passingford Bridge. Stapleford Abbots is a scattered place and there is little of historical interest to be seen from the roadside, although several of the local farmhouses, such as Blackbush and

Bons Farm, are quite old. By the Rabbits public-house a narrow no-through lane leads back to the church of St. Mary; the road surface is not good, but it is passable. The church stands at the top of the lane on the left, but much of the building is too modern to be of great attraction. Go round the back, however, and it is a different story, for on the side of the church is the tiny brick Abdy chapel, which was built in 1638. From the chapel one can look out over the churchyard and its extension next door and down the valley beyond.

Onwards towards the A113 and the narrow bridge across the Roding at Passingford. The bridge itself is quite old and parts may even be medieval, but of more scenic beauty is the three-story weatherboarded mill to the left. Once driven by a water-wheel on the Roding, it now has an ultra-modern turbine hidden away inside to provide the power. To the right as we cross the bridge is the wooded park of Sutton, while on the left a little farther on, near the telephone kiosk, we turn left to follow the lane signposted Coopersale and Epping as we make our way to Stapleford Tawney. It is only a few yards to the next turning, a sharp right-hander, and then a pleasant run into the tiny village, with its interesting old farmhouses and its thirteenth-century church. St. Mary's has an avenue of tall trees leading to it, but high above them stretches the wooden bell turret with its shingle spire. Hidden by the trees is Great Tawney Hall, an eighteenth-century farmhouse probably built to replace Stapleford Tawney Hall, which stood next door and of which only a garden wall and a dry moat now remain. The road now seems to run in a straight line, but beware—it really goes at right-angles and ahead lies the private drive to Little Tawney Hall.

All around us now are miles of open farmland, and we are looping through them on our way to Toot Hill and Stanford Rivers. At the crossroads go down by the old Mole Trap public-house with its attendant boarded cottages. A right turn at the T junction and you will soon start to see where the " Hill " comes into Toot Hill, for the road rises and falls like the big dipper at the fairground. As a point of interest, a left turn at the junction will soon bring you on to a three-quarter-mile section of an old Roman road which runs through some quite wooded places.

Stanford Rivers owes the second part of its name not to the fact that the Roding forms part of its boundaries but to the family who held the manor in the thirteenth century. The church you see among the trees to the left is St. Margaret's, and it dates from the twelfth century. The wooden belfry is supported by four posts and has a leaded broach spire which has hanging in it the only Joseph Carter bell in Essex. The west window of the church has been blocked by a slab which has a primitive figure carved on it. An interesting brass in the church is to a " chrisom child " who died in 1492 within a month of being baptized.

We end our tour of these rural parts at Little End on the A113. The impressive but drab building you see before you was the Ongar workhouse—now a tent factory. A short distance north is Chipping Ongar, but this must wait for another chapter.

THE LAVERS—and south to North Weald Bassett

THREE sister villages make up the Lavers, more or less in line across the rural hinterland to the north of the A122. They need signpost reading of a high order to ferret them out. It is hard to believe that two or three miles east of the bustling new town of Harlow there are Essex villages so unaltered by the passage of time and the hand of the " planner."

Magdalen Laver can be approached from the Harlow side off the A11 or by going north from the A122. It offers quite a collection of old houses, and a church which though much restored has many interesting features, including the fourteenth-century screen. Over to the west Wynters Armourie has a name as intriguing as its history. From an original building surrounded by a moat in Saxon days there developed a fourteenth-century aisled hall to which alterations and extensions have been made down the years. The church is tucked away down its own access through Hall Farm, but the road itself runs on north then east past Great Wilmores to High Laver and the crossroads where the church of All Saints shows in its corners Roman tiles re-used by its Norman builders. The item of greatest interest in this village and the object of no little pilgrimage over the years is the tomb of John Locke the philosopher, author of the famous *Essay on the Human Understanding*. He lived at Otes (the manor house, demolished in 1822) as the guest of Sir Francis Masham from 1691 till his death in 1704. He is buried in the church-yard and a tablet on the south wall in the church is inscribed with an epitaph written by the philosopher himself. Go east by the church, then north and east again past the oddly named America Farm and

Church Farm with its remnants of a moat and you will arrive at Little Laver, a diminutive village which has lost its old mill and can only boast of a much-repaired church, though the font evokes its former thirteenth-century glory.

From Little Laver the road running south past the Red House and New House (with a very old moat!) takes you to Moreton, three miles north of Chipping Ongar, and to welcome refreshment at the 400-year-old White Hart inn. The traveller of the 1880s found it " a village pleasantly situated beside a stream with well-wooded banks," and so you will find it today. St. Mary's church has an eighteenth-century brick tower. Well-meaning Victorians " restored " the interior, but the massive Norman font of Purbeck marble withstood the enthusiastic onslaught.

At Moreton End, roughly south-west of the church, stands a cottage with a past. It was once the guildhall of the religious guild of All Saints, founded in the 1470s, and its timber framing is original —something to be enjoyed. The old mill which looked so attractive became an economic embarrassment in recent years and was demolished completely.

Out of Moreton to the south you cross the Cripsey Brook, and by taking either of the roads you will arrive in the parish of Bobbingworth, where the village borders a spacious green. By the church, virtually rebuilt in 1840, stands Bobbingworth Hall, one of the three manor houses. Another one was Blake Hall, on the left-hand side of the road running south to the A122. The present Hall is a rather fine Queen Anne house in a spacious park which has been in the Capel Cure family for years.

Take the A122 to the west and you will cross the track of the old Roman road; soon the massive network of aerials announces the imminence of the wireless transmitting station at North Weald Bassett. Let us break down the name—North is to distinguish it from South Weald, near Brentwood; Weald is the old word for the forest which once was all-embracing here; and Bassett refers to the great local family of early days.

London's tentacles have reached out here in the shape of the railway station which connects with the Central Line; consequently the place has grown rapidly in recent years.

During World War II the Royal Air Force had a fighter base here from which the " few " flew to the defence of London in the Battle of Britain. The barracks erected in those days are just now being refurbished to help accommodate large numbers of servicemen returning from abroad as military commitments are reduced. The old airfield is a favourite stopping place for families who want to watch members of the gliding club based here getting airborne and coming in to land. But be careful; parking on the side of the road here is definitely a hazard to fast-moving traffic.

Weald Hall, now a farmhouse, lies on the opposite side of the airfield. There is a way round to it through Woodside and Ducklane which offers a very peaceful vantage point from which to watch the gliders.

The church was badly damaged by fire in 1964, so that, despite the lovely scenery, it does not justify the detour to the north to see it. Perhaps the best remaining symbol of North Weald's past is the King's Head inn, a pleasing seventeenth-century contrast of black timbers and white plaster.

MATCHING AND SHEERING

AT Hatfield Heath there is a maze of roads meeting. Look out for the one to Matching and give yourself a treat. As you go down it look for the signpost which says " Matching Hall and church only." Up this tiny lane—a no-through road—you will come to a gate which bars the way, though pedestrians can pass. Here you are in another world.

Matching Hall is of Elizabethan construction at least, but it is on a moated site which goes back beyond the Conquest. Water still flows in the moat, mirroring the flowers and providing a haven for a host of wild and farm fowl. There is an ancient dovecote still standing by the water's edge which once provided birds by the hundred for the tables of the Hall. An old thatched and weather-boarded barn by the gate has another dovecote high on its gable.

Opposite stands the church of St. Mary the Virgin, amid oaks and chestnuts, while the rectory is almost hidden in a wooded fold behind it. In the church, behind the pulpit, put up in 1624, is a niche where people did penance in full view of the congregation for acts of wrongdoing. The fifteenth-century tower has outlived the rest of the fabric, which was almost completely restored in 1875. It looks across the tombstones to a couple of cottages. The end one, with a Victorian letter-box built into its wall, has an interesting history. Though largely restored it was first built by one Chimney, further identity unknown, who planned it with small rooms downstairs and one large room above, dedicated to the use of poor people as a place to hold their wedding celebrations after the ceremony, and it is still called the Wedding Feast House. It is a rather homely example of the fifteenth-century builder's craft.

There are some pleasing short walks to be had over the little hills and dales through which a stream meanders, deep in its bed, to feed the pond which you have to skirt on your way from the main road. Here it is bliss indeed to lean on the fence and just look at trees and sky and water, and listen to the tumult and the shouting of the birds that busy themselves in, over and around the little lake.

The beautifully harmonious group of church, Hall, cottages and rectory makes up Matching. The people come to church from nearby Matching Green and Matching Tye. A right turn at the junction, where we leave the no-through road, and we go on to Matching Green, a place that lives up to its name, with houses scattered all round the green, on which weekend cricket is a popular spectacle. Do tour round it until you spot the garden with the heads —yes, heads in concrete, on grotesque bodies, caricatures of well-known figures, all done by an old gentleman who actually wears false teeth he made himself of the same material! There are any number of well-kept old houses here to please the eye.

On towards Harlow and we come to Matching Tye, another attractive little village in the same tradition. Here the road has a branch through Collins Cross and Newmans End, passing the edge of the Down Hall estate and running into Sheering, an unremarkable village straddling the Hatfield—Harlow road (B183). The church has some interesting stained glass, but the houses to note, Sheering Hall, Durrington Hall and Aylmers, are all off the main road almost into Harlow. By continuing from Sheering to Hatfield Heath we shall have completed a circular tour

NEWPORT and both sides of the road

THE A11 running north through Essex is a useful springboard for exploration of the countryside around Newport, which is the next considerable centre between Saffron Walden and Stansted Mountfitchet, with side roads to a number of interesting little places.

Newport's mile-long main street is its chief delight, and is noted by the experts for its two typical old Essex cottages. One is Monks Barn, of the fifteenth century, and the other is Crown House, built in the early seventeenth century and richly decorated with the plaster work called pargeting in 1692. It has been called Nell Gwynne's House—the crown by which it is now known representing the interests of a certain king! The market here was transferred to a growing Saffron Walden in 1144, but its inns, like the Coach and Horses, built in Elizabethan days, kept busy on the great thorough-fare. South of the railway bridge look out for the eighteenth-century prison, with its big gable, now converted to houses.

The church is a fine building. The chancel and the transept (the arms of the cross-shaped building) date from the 1200s, the nave is a century later and the south porch was completed in the fifteenth century. The tower is just about 100 years old. A very interesting treasure within is the travelling altar-piece. It is made in the form of a chest which when opened shows a beautiful late-thirteenth-century painting of the crucifixion.

Just to the north Shortgrove Park stands on the right-hand side at the end of the village. It contains a mansion of the middle 1600s altered to its present appearance in 1712. The A11 to the north of this is covered in our Saffron Walden section, so let us retrace our steps and branch out from Newport on the western side, via the B1038 through Cuckingstool End.

This little part of Newport holds a whole history in its very name, for a cucking stool is recorded as far back as the thirteenth century, and the *Oxford English Dictionary* says it was " an instrument of punishment formerly in use for the punishment of scolds, disorderly women, fraudulent tradespeople, etc., consisting of a chair . . . in which the offender was fastened and exposed to the jeers of the bystanders, or conveyed to a pond or river and ducked." There was in fact a large pond here, since drained, from which the old village name of Newport Pond derived.

It is no great distance along the same road to Wicken Bonhunt. On the way you will pass Bonhunt Farm on the left, where there stands a Norman chapel in its original form which has been used since as a stable and a barn. In the small, tree-shaded village, hall and church stand side by side, both rebuilt but worthy still of notice. The barn by the hall is Jacobean, and on the other side of the road the o d Brick House shows the Bradbury coat of arms above the door—a local family of note.

Through the village a left-hand turn takes you south down a narrow lane past Coldhams with its moat to Rickling, a village which has moved. The old village round the church has practically vanished and the new settlement over the years has gathered round Rickling Green a mile to the south; but the old church stands at the bend in the road, its chancel, after 600 years, leaning visibly to the north. On the stonework round the priest's door you will see the sundials scratched to mark the time for mass. If you keep heading south you will pass Rickling Hall, an early sixteenth-century manor house on the courtyard plan, which has lost the great hall which was its main feature but has retained its interesting gateway. Behind the house a castle mound denotes Norman occupation.

Rickling Green is so near the A11 and Quendon that it is joined with that village in parish matters, but it keeps its own centre in the green, around which the houses make a pleasing picture. Quendon lines the main road, its features clear to any through traveller. The church is much restored, with little " local " interest. The most eye-catching erection is the fountain by the road, under a tile canopy on wooden pillars. This is a modern outlet for the ancient well which flows here, marked in an earlier age by the nearby horse-trough. A noticeable house, nicely Georgian, is Quendon Court.

The " big house " is Quendon Hall, standing in its park to the north of the village. In its grounds there is a beautifully constructed octagonal dovecote, almost as big as a small house, dating back to the days of our first Queen Elizabeth.

Off to the west, lost down the lanes, is Widdington. Its very isolation has lately been its attraction to those in search of the quiet life, and consequently it is a popular residential area. The little green has a nucleus of cottages, but houses line the lanes as well. To the east the smallest of roads leads out to Swaynes Hall, Mole Hall on its moated site and Thistley Hall, to peter out at Amberden Hall, built in 1560, the manor house of a lost village.

Back in Widdington the Hall is tucked away behind the church. It was built 500 years ago on an earlier moated site of which a vestige remains. The church of St. Mary has been largely rebuilt, though once inside the architectural detective can find clues to a much earlier building. On the other side of the road stands Priors Hall, which incorporates in its own old walls an even older (thir-teenth-century) building of stone, part of the very first homestead on this site.

From here the road runs north then east to Debden. This pretty village is the centre of a large parish. The church, rather isolated down a tiny lane, was connected with Debden Hall, in whose park it stands. The Hall was demolished in 1936, but the park is still a remarkable feature, containing an extensive lake fed from the Debden Water, and forming beautifully landscaped surroundings for the church, which dates from the thirteenth century, with later additions. Look at the font—would you guess it was made in 1786 of an early kind of concrete called Coade stone? On the north side of the village the old windmill, once so dilapidated, is now an unusual house.

Way over the other side of the parish on the A130 from Saffron Walden a De Havilland Venom plane announces the entrance to Debden airfield, now the home of the R.A.F. police training depôt.

THE ONGARS and others

CHIPPING ONGAR is the last place you can reach from London on the underground via the Central Line and Epping. The station car park is always full, for commuters have found that this little Essex town offers an increasing number of " desirable residences." Its one main street makes a pleasing afternoon stroll, and the shops are interesting, for the town serves a considerable rural area and has done so from the Middle Ages. Its very name, Chipping, is the Saxon word for a market.

After the Saxons the Normans. They built a timber castle on a forty-eight-foot mound overlooking the church. Though the castle has gone, some of the brickwork (filched from a local Roman ruin) remains in the gateway to the inner courtyard. The outer yard had an earthwork which embraced all the medieval town and can still, in part, be traced. The ruins on the mound today are only the remains of a brick summer-house built in 1744.

The church, says Pevsner, is an " uncommonly complete Norman village church," and therefore is worth looking at outside and in. Where the road to the church branches off from the main street there is an interesting house, dated to 1642, timber-framed, with prettily finished brackets to support the overhanging upper story. The King's Head, almost opposite, completes a trio of historical buildings. It has been there since 1700 and offers today a variety of meals and sandwiches at the bar.

The Congregational church gains glory from connection with two famous people. One was the pastor Isaac Taylor and his literary family, of whom a daughter, Jane, wrote " Twinkle, twinkle, little star." The other was David Livingstone, who stayed here for a year from 1839 in a room over the archway to the church while training to be a missionary.

Other places of historical or scenic interest are grouped north of the town, or south round the junction of the A128 and A113 at Marden Ash, where the Hall dates from about 1700. But for real history take the lane west to Greensted, or walk there across the Cripsey Brook and through the meadows. This diminutive and isolated hamlet is well known throughout the kingdom for its un- usual church, which was built in Saxon times, probably as a resting place for the body of St. Edmund as it progressed from London to interment at Bury St. Edmunds. The construction is amazing; the nave walls are solid trunks of oak trees split down the middle, standing on a wooden sill with a brick plinth (both of which are Victorian replacements). The nave roof, too, is a later restoration, but some of the charming dormer windows are Tudor and the tower, white and weatherboarded, is graceful in its Saxon simplicity. The house beside the church is Greensted Hall, a Victorian reconstruc- tion of an Elizabethan home.

East of Chipping Ongar, on the tightest of right-angle bends in the A122, stands High Ongar. Its wide street gives a good view of the varied collection of houses and inns, with pink-washed plaster and old timbers showing the age of some places. St. Mary's church, like the hymns, is ancient and modern. The nave is Norman, with a very ornamental doorway, and the tower is Victorian. Sit in the family pew inside and imagine you are the squire of the eighteenth century who occupied it with his wife and children every Sunday. Between the Ongars the River Roding runs, offering pastoral views and riverside walks.

Between them too are the " Four Wantz " crossroads, now turned into a roundabout. The B184 north from here soon runs into open country, where the side road runs off left to Shelley. The church and Hall are relatively modern, though the Hall can boast of rem- nants of sixteenth-century stencilled wall decorations. On the other side of the main road Boarded Barns Farm reminds us that medieval Essex had no stone to quarry, but the forest provided baulks and boards in abundance. Farther north you will pass Fyfield school,

Thaxted. " Let your eyes wander down the main street and up the hill to
the church."

" Harlow is a place worth seeing as it comes to completion as a New Town."

Southchurch Hall, "a thirteenth-century timber-framed manor house, is enhanced by its moat."

" Modern Billericay has taken pains to preserve as much of its past as possible."
Chantry House in the High Street.

one of three Essex County Council secondary modern boarding schools. Farther on is Fyfield itself, though the Hall and church are to the east, with footpaths to and from them along the river bank. The Hall, like Lampetts to the north-west, derives from the aisled hall with central fire and no chimney which was all the rage among the rich men of the fourteenth century. Many of those old timbers are in position today, though the buildings are much altered and extended.

The church of St. Nicholas has also altered over the years as the population grew, but its older parts, like the nave, date from the twelfth century. The village is close-knit in an area usually dotted with out-of-the-way farms and cottages, because it was a place of much greater importance in the past, as indicated by several old houses standing on even older sites. The next stop up the road is the Rodings, which have their own place in our book.

South of Fyfield the one-inch map shows a disused airfield, the only acknowledgment of the part the Norton Mandeville aerodrome played in World War II. The old runways are fast disappearing; their concrete has found a new value as hardcore for building sites. The church and Hall, which virtually constitute Norton Mandeville, are way down an ancient lane from Norton Heath, the hamlet on the A122 which is remarkable for the fact that the heath or green round which the houses gather was never seized and enclosed by the local lord, as happened so often to village common land. On the other side of the A122 the side road goes down to Blackmore and yet another chapter in this book.

THE RODINGS

EIGHT little places all called Roding—what a headache for the Post Office ! They all take the second half of their name from the little river which divides them four and four and runs down to Barking Creek.

Travelling out of Chelmsford on the A414, the first of these villages, Berners Roding, is signposted at the Four Wantz, an old local name for crossroads, on the Chelmsford side of Margaret Roding. The tiny side road wanders round to an even narrower lane which ends—and you are there. The little church has just one bell, made in 1594, in a wooden belfry which rises above old cottages, some with thatched roofs, which have sheltered families for 300 to 400 years.

I.S.E. 8

Farther along on the main road we arrive at Margaret Roding with its church of St. Margaret, which has " some of the best Norman work in Essex," to quote the rural district guide. It also has another of those old oak chests which are the pride of our village churches. Then comes Leaden Roding, standing on a very sharp corner where the A414, bending to the right, is joined by the B184 from Dunmow. Its name comes from the church, the only one in early days to have a leaded roof, which is the oldest in the group. Its shingled spire over a pretty weatherboarded bell turret points up out of the trees, contrasting with the new rectory built alongside in 1967. Within, look for the very graceful Jacobean pulpit of wood, beautifully proportioned, rising from a central stem.

By proceeding on the A414 we can turn left and get via a side road to Abbess Roding, which in early days belonged to the abbess of Barking. The church has some interesting incidentals in it, like the eighteenth-century hour-glass stand. Rookwood Hall has barns which were built when Henry VIII was on the throne. From Abbess to Beauchamp Roding, where church and cottages reflect the peaceful progress of life in a typical Essex village.

Back on the A414 our way lies to White Roding. On the left we pass the drive to Colville Hall, where Roman remains in the brook testify to the pleasantness of the situation as found by these and later settlers. The Hall is a beautiful old place in itself, but it also has a classic Tudor stable, unrestored and unspoilt, with original door and framing with herring-bone infilling. Cammas Hall, Merks Hall and Mascallsbury are other old houses of note in the White Roding area.

It is called white, no doubt, from the appearance of its newly built church back in the days of the Normans. It is the biggest church of the group, standing in harmony with the windmill, which has been rebuilt, and the old rectory, which was originally a moated homestead—fortified against the Viking marauders. From White Roding a turning by the Black Horse takes us on to Cammas Hall and deep countryside with hardly a habitation until we reach the outskirts of Hatfield Broad Oak.

To see the rest of the Rodings we must go back to Leaden Roding and take the B184 towards Dunmow. Now on our left and right as we pass Roundbush Green lies Aythorpe Roding, reached from the crossroads at the Axe and Compasses. The windmill adds a touch on the skyline. The church and Hall are miles from the village out in the rich farm land on the banks of the Roding itself. The moat which once ran round the hall is now a pond on which the ducks bob in tranquillity.

The village is a place of ponds and streams. Both the Roding and the Can flow through it and there are old farmhouses and rustic views enough to please the most ardent camera addict.

It is a lovely long straight road through Aythorpe Roding to High Roding. At 292 feet above sea level it is hard to see how the place got its name, but at least it is fifty feet higher than Leaden Roding!

The village lines the old Roman road, a pleasing view of varied architecture, with lath and plaster predominating. The youth hostel down the road to the Easters is converted out of an old tithe barn which still displays " a wealth of old timber." The church, as so often in Essex, was built next to the Hall by the squire for his own convenience, so it stands today next to High Rodingbury, now a farmhouse, and it can only be approached down a long narrow lane which ends in a field of corn. If you want quiet in the country you will find it here.

Let us leave the Rodings on the note set by the British Motor Corporation: "Pretty local scenes, with green meadows and fragrant hedgerows, typifying the quiet, inherent beauty of English country-side."

SAFFRON WALDEN and a circle round it

IF you want to go to Saffron Walden you can hardly do better than arm yourself with a half-crown copy of the official hand-book, which in its comprehensiveness and its contributions by experts is a model of its kind. It is available at the municipal offices in Hill Street.

The town owes its significance to the Normans. They built its castle and established its market. Slowly the houses spread down and around the castle hill. In medieval times the place grew wealthy from the culture of the saffron crocus, used as a dye, a medicine and a condiment, and even as a perfume. So important was it that Walden became known as Saffron Walden.

By the end of the eighteenth century the industry had died, but the name persisted. Other industries waxed and waned, and today a variety of light industries provide employment without obtruding on the charm of this old Essex market town. Put your car in the spacious park on the common and you will be in a good position to start your tour. Before you do you can have fun on the big earth maze at the eastern end of the common. Its origin is totally lost in the mists of time, though some ancient fertility rite is probably indicated. It was being recut even as far back as 1699, when it cost the corporation fifteen shillings.

Up the hill across the road from the car park are the remains of a castle, close by the museum. Only a piece of rubble stands to remind one of the Norman fortification of about 1100. The museum is a must—it was built in 1834 by the local natural history society, and is now subsidized by several local bodies. As well as good displays of general subjects there is much to be gleaned about the neighbourhood.

Across Museum Street, on the same spur of higher land which commended itself to early settlers, stands the parish church of St. Mary, the largest church in the county, 184 feet long and eighty feet wide. It dates largely from a big reconstruction early in the sixteenth century, though the spire was not added until 1832, replacing a wooden structure, like a lantern, which is said to have been put up as an experiment by Winstanley, the lighthouse builder, who lived at nearby Littlebury.

In the church are some interesting monuments, including one to Thomas, Lord Audley, builder of the first Audley End house, and no fewer than four old chests to interest the antiquary and the woodworker.

The Roman Catholic church is of interest in that it was converted in 1906 from a timbered barn of the fifteenth century. The Society of Friends' ancient meeting house had to be dispensed with in 1879 when a bigger building was needed to cope with the increase in numbers after the opening of the Friends' school here. The Congregationalists have also progressed—from a barn in Abbey Lane in 1656 to the elegant chapel built in 1811 and subsequently restored.

The charm of the town lies in the way houses and shops have been altered down the years to make them liveable in according to the taste of the time, like those fifteenth-century buildings in Bridge Street and High Street. Nearby, in Church Street, you can see a good example of an old Essex art—decorative plaster work called pargeting—on the gables of the house next to the Sun inn, which itself has plaster designs of the last century.

Many a Georgian front conceals a roof of mellow tiles which gives a clue to the real date of the building. Bridge House in Bridge Street has been so disguised, but its splendid chimneys show its true age.

We can go on about Saffron Walden and its charm for pages, and still not do it justice; but you do not have to know all the whys and wherefores, all the dates and facts, to enjoy a town like this. Just wander through it, do a bit of shop-gazing, take in all the atmosphere of a sleepy market town, have lunch in one of the old inns, and you will go home refreshed.

You cannot, however, go home without saying that you have been to Audley End, a mile or so to the west with access from the A11. It is not the hamlet but the great house of the same name which commands the attention. Today it is in the care of the Ministry of Public Building and Works, and is open to the public from April to October, Tuesday to Sunday and bank holidays, 11.30 a.m. to 5.30 p.m., for a small fee. There are coach and car parks and refreshments are available.

Sir Thomas Audley, later made Lord Audley of Walden, was Speaker in the Parliament of 1529-35, when the dissolution of the monasteries enriched the king's servants. Audley received the abbey of Walden, which he altered to suit his needs before it passed to Thomas Howard, made Baron Howard de Walden in 1597. This man, once England's Lord High Treasurer, built a great house here by 1616 which vied in size with Hampton Court—so big, in fact, that it was never fully furnished or completely occupied. Charles II bought it in 1669, and called it his new palace, in place of his houses damaged under Cromwell; but it cost £50,000 and he was not able to pay it all, so it reverted to the Howards in 1701. Its present-day condition is due to a £100,000 overhaul by the first Lord Braybrooke in 1788. A full guide at the house will give you details. Let us just add that the gardens, with the river running through and the fountains behind the house, have much to commend them, while the miniature railway is helpful when the children get bored.

From here the busy A11 heads north. Immediately on the western side rises Ring Hill Camp—a sixteen-acre Iron Age earth fortress marked today by the " temple to peace " erected by Lord Braybrooke. Up the road we run into Littlebury, a village on the River

Cam with hills on its western edge, and home of Henry Winstanley (died 1703), the celebrated builder of the Eddystone lighthouse.

The wool trade brought development here, and it gained importance too as the summer residence of the Bishops of Ely, of which Gatehouse Farm is said to be a part. In the church admire the ancient linenfold carving of the wooden font case, the largest and most ornate in the county, and see at least one of the brasses—to James Edwards, who died of the plague in 1522.

From Littlebury, road and rail hug the river on to the Chesterfords. Little Chesterford comes first, a small place with one great feature—the thirteenth-century manor house adjoining the church, which is said to be the oldest inhabited house in Essex. The east wing is the original house, built of flint and stone about 1190, when the living quarters were on the upper floor only, with access by an outside stair. A dovecote, a practical medieval way of assuring a supply of food, stands nearby. The church itself is of the thirteenth century, though the pretty bellcote is Victorian.

Great Chesterford spins a web of lanes between A130 and A11 south of their junction. This is a case of departed glory if ever there was. The village is large still, a reminder of the business its market once attracted. Its great glory was in Roman days, for then it ranked as a town and the old straight roads can still be detected here and there. The walls were still being knocked down in the eighteenth century—to provide rubble for the roads. Today a couple of really old inns and many an old house give pleasure to the sightseer. The church has shrunk over the years, and the tower has twice fallen. A sad note is sounded by the brass of 1600 to John, seventh son of Lord Howard, who lived only twelve days.

The busy A roads cross the border into Cambridgeshire, while we turn leisurely eastwards from Great Chesterford to Hadstock, which stands high on the B1052. Its ancient church, built in flint by the Normans, still has shutters on some windows which predate the use of glass. Those who believe that the battle of Assandun took place at nearby Ashdon (but see also under Ashingdon) say that this church was built by the victorious Canute in thanksgiving, on a much larger scale than it appears today. The porch is 500 years old, but it protects a door nearly as old again, iron bound and inches thick, on which could be seen for hundreds of years the skin of a Dane, nailed there after he had been flayed for robbing the church.

The well in the churchyard was probably sacred in pagan times, the dwelling of a water god, which was why the Christians put their own church there.

The manor house is Elizabethan, as its massive six-shaft brick chimney implies. With the old thatched cottages grouped round the ancient green this is a calendar-picture place without a doubt. To the north and east a Roman built his home, and one of the lovely mosaic floors was discovered in the last century and relaid at Audley End.

Ashdon is the next village in our circle round. Early settlement here is evidenced by the four great barrows directly to the north on the parish boundary, called the Bartlow Hills. They are the largest burial mounds in Europe, where Romano-British V.I.P.s found their rest. Most of the excavated treasures were lost in a fire.

On the way south to the village proper we pass half a mile east of the site of a Roman villa on Great Copt Hill, now just a scatter of stones. The church, standing on a hill above the valley of the little River Bourne, makes a charming view, with its embattled tower standing out against the sky. It was probably built in Saxon days; look at the pillars in the nave and you will see that their bottommost parts are curiously different from the upper parts, and may be elements of the original structure. If you want to know what a king-post roof is have a look at that over the south chapel, which dates from the fourteenth century.

In those days the church was the social centre of the village. Even trade and craft associations were connected with religion, so it is not surprising to find the ancient hall of the Guild of St. Mary next door to the church. It was built of strong timber framing about 1480 and suffered many indignities before it was carefully restored as a pleasant residence in 1960. Hillocks in the field to the south are the only memorial to the cottages that once clustered about in the old village here on the hill.

Down in the newer village there is many a picturesque scene where the little river runs. The Rose and Crown is worth a visit because it still shows some of the painted decoration of the seventeenth-century walls, including some texts in old Gothic letters.

To the east Waltons is an old house with a fine Georgian front but with a much older history behind it. It was badly burned in 1954 but has been restored with alterations. Its owner, Mr. E. Vestey, was responsible for the restoration of the post mill in the fields across the road.

The road opposite the inn runs down to Radwinter past Water End and Bendysh Hall, another place altered by a recent fire. Radwinter is a large village with hamlets like Maypole End and Stocking Green along the road to Saffron Walden, and no fewer than eight manor houses, shown in names such as Broadysh Farm, Bulls Farm and Brockholds, almost into Wimbish, which dates from the middle of the sixteenth century. The church and the houses and shops about it make an unusual nucleus, because they were designed by the same architect in a rebuilding of the church in 1870. His name? Eden Nesfield. But the wooden south porch is a fourteenth-century survival, and is interesting because it has a projecting upper story, rarely seen in Essex.

Wimbish is plainly written on the map, but it is hard to pinpoint as a village. Instead odd hamlets cluster about junctions between the B1053 west of Radwinter and the A130 to the south, with names like Wimbish Green, Upper Green, Tye Green, Howlett End and, way over to the west, Cole End and Thunderley.

A drive around the area will show more manor houses and other ancient and beautiful places than can be catalogued here. Judge for yourself by counting the number of old moated houses shown on the map—you will find many more than a dozen!

The church and the Hall have to be looked for on the right down the road from Maypole End, prettily situated near a pond fed by the River Pant. In the church you must look for the " unusual and delightful " brass to Sir John de Wantone and his wife, more than 600 years old. The bell on a stout wooden framework in the churchyard is the only reminder of a tower twice built and destroyed.

As Newport has its own chapter we shall complete our circle by crossing the A11 and taking the B1039 to look in on Wendens Ambo, where the railway station, oddly enough, is called Audley End (to please the people in the " big house "). Ambo is Latin for both, the point being that Great and Little Wenden were made one as far back as 1662. The tower of the remaining church is very old, it may even date before the Conquest, while the rest of the building incorporates a variety of styles and there is some good wood-carving. The little road to the church, overlooked by a jumble of cottages, is a wonderful scene for the camera.

We can end our tour by musing on the timelessness of our Essex countryside and the passing effect of man on its beauty while trying to find, in a field now reached from a side road south of the church, the remains of a Roman villa—once the splendid home of a proud man, now just a few bricks and rubble beneath six feet of earth.

STANSTED MOUNTFITCHET and the villages round its airport

LET us call it plain Stansted; everyone else does in these days of controversy about the position of the third London airport. The town stands in an angle caused by the junction of the A11 and A120 roads, and as we write it is still a fairly quiet and attractive old town. Stansted was originally a Saxon township and was one of the many places to be plundered by the invading Normans. It is to these Norman rulers that the present town owes the second part of its full name, for it was the Mountfitchets who were granted the lordship of the manor.

Just north of the present railway station the remains of their castle can still be seen. Gravel digging has spoiled parts of the building and the visitor must expect to see only the occasional foundation showing above ground. To the east of the castle are extensive areas of ornamental gardens which contain Stansted Hall and St. Mary's church. The Hall was built in 1871 and replaces an earlier building. It is in the Jacobean style, with stone dressing on the brick. This is an attractive house with gables, mullioned windows and clustered chimneys that are quite typical of the period copied.

Although the church of St. Mary the Virgin has been very much rebuilt over the years it is still possible to wander through the Norman chancel and the three archways that the ancient rulers of our land must have used. This church holds much of interest, and the effigy of a knight—thought to be Richard Mountfitchet, who died in 1300—in the north chapel should not be missed.

The main street of interest to the visitor is Lower Street, which runs down the slope of the hill away from the castle remains. Along this street stand several old houses with exposed timberwork, all of varying height according to how much the original owner wanted to pay for his home. On the corner of one street a great cluster of trees indicates the present rural nature of the township. In keeping with this is the windmill that stands on the southern side of the town and which is preserved in good order.

Radiating to the north-east from Stansted are several small

villages, all threatened in some degree by the proposed enlargement of the airport. We are assured that no immediate catastrophe will befall these pleasant places, but the long-term future would seem less secure, at least as far as their retaining their unspoiled rural look is concerned; so if you wish to see these places as they are at the time of writing you are advised to put off your visit no longer and come with us now on a visit to the " airport villages " around Stansted.

Following the B1051 away from Stansted towards Elsenham, we pass the edge of the ornamental gardens and a couple of small woods, one on either side of the roadway, before entering the village proper. This is a sleepy place, with thatched cottages gleaming as the sunlight reflects off their whitewashed walls. The octagonal building you see is the old well-house, and it was erected over the well in memory of Lady Gilbey, wife of Sir George Gilbey, who resided at Elsenham Hall. The Hall, a red-brick Georgian mansion, lies a little south of the village in pleasing grounds. Nearby is the parish church of St. Mary, which is of Norman origin, built in stone with an embattled western tower. There is elaborate carving around the south doorway and in the chancel. About a quarter of a mile north of the village is one of the " reclaimed " houses of Essex. This is Elsenham Place, a timber-framed building with two symmetrical wings. Some of the woodwork was brought here in 1937 from The Close in Saffron Walden when this was demolished.

Continuing along the B1051, the traveller has the choice of going on to the small parish of Chickney or turning left and going up into Henham. Since both are most attractive places, it is worth having to double back to see them.

Chickney stands on quite high ground and is a rather scattered place, but the scenery is good wherever you are. The main village is only a little distance from the B1051 and is the home of a church that has stood for more than ten centuries. Near to it is the Hall, which for all its Tudor look was built no earlier than 1935. A mile and a half north of the village is a charming fifteenth-century residence called Sibley's. This is a timber-framed house with period fireplaces and a sixteenth-century partition in the hall.

While you will find Chickney attractive, Henham has won a prize as a best-kept village. It is situated on what in earlier times would have been described as " healthy ground," that is on a hilltop, and the chief sources of the River Cam flow to the north and east, making the surrounding country lush and verdant. The village green is the centre for the visitor, for all about it are the attractions of the place. Not least of these is the large green itself. Standing round the green are thatched cottages whose long gardens make a colourful scene during the summer months. The church of St. Mary stands here in the heart of things as it has done since the thirteenth century. In the churchyard is a relic from the early days of medicine, when the dead were needed for anatomical research. The body-snatchers would stop at nothing to get their hands on a new corpse, and to prevent desecration an iron cage was sometimes placed over the grave. In this churchyard one of those iron " hearses " can still be seen.

Leaving Henham, we follow the lane north-west, past the moat that once protected Henham Hall (now demolished), under the railway and on to the ill-named hamlet of Ugley. It is really a pretty little place, with cottages, old farmhouses and a glorious setting for its church. From a distance only the sixteenth-century brick tower can be seen above the tall chestnut trees that surround it. Closer inspection is not recommended, for the main part of the church is fairly modern, as is the Hall that is close by; but once again there is a redeeming feature for the searcher after historic Essex. In this case it is the large barn that was built in 1680 and which has three entrances. Leading off the end of the main street is a bridleway that cuts across the fields, making a most pleasant walk to the sister hamlet of Ugley Green. Before leaving these two places we must record an interesting outcome of their name. Everywhere else in the country the local Women's Institute takes the village name as the first part of its title—here they call it the Women's Institute of Ugley!

The next part of the tour will not be as pleasant, as we must now leave the quiet green lanes to join the busy A11. Proceeding towards Stansted, look out for Orford House about a mile after joining the trunk road. This was built by the Duke of Orford about 1700 and is a red-brick two-story house in seven bays. Passing through the outskirts of Stansted and over the railway, it is soon time to leave the fumes of the A11 and pass once again into the solitude of the exciting Essex countryside.

Birchanger is the name to look for, and it awaits you just left of the trunk road. The narrow lane you are travelling along twists and turns its way through the fields, and the village is spread thinly on either side of it. Although many of the trees that once gave the village its name have long since gone, clumps of them still remain to break up the skyline and add a background to the Hall and church. This church is yet another St. Mary's and is interesting for its two Norman doorways—the south door only being rediscovered in 1930. The houses end at Duckend and a few hundred yards farther on the lane comes out on to the A120.

From the way this road is driven straight across the county it takes little guessing to arrive at the conclusion that it was built by the Romans. To the south of the road lies Hatfield Forest (which has its own chapter in this section of the book), while a mile or so farther east is the last village we are able to visit on this tour—Takeley. The first place to see is the church of the Holy Trinity, which stands alone up a side road to the left, just before you enter the village proper. While the structure of the church, Norman and Early English, with re-used Roman bricks, is of interest, the thing of glory lies inside. This is the impressive font cover, which is six feet high and is built tier upon tier like the pinnacled spire of a cathedral, and dates from the fifteenth century. The village can be said to live up to this preview, for it contains several half-timbered cottages, farmhouses that are 300 years old, and barns to match. North of the village are the cool woods, a proper place to end this circumnavigation of the Stansted hinterland.

THAXTED

FROM a height of 181 feet the spire of the magnificent church of St. John looks down on a town that typifies this county of ours. It can see the many historic buildings that nestle at its feet, the streets where Dick Turpin is reputed to have delivered meat, and in the distance the fertile land cut by the many narrow twisting lanes that spread like tentacles to join together the surrounding villages.

Thaxted gets its name from two Old English words: *thaec* and *sted*. The first was the name of the material used in thatching and the other means " place " (one might say " the place where reeds grow "), and to the west of the town the River Chelmer still flows— the source of the reeds.

The town was a thriving place when the Normans arrived, and under them it continued to expand. They enlarged the Saxon church and organized the clearing of wooded areas and their conversion into farm land. The farmers paid their rents by working for the lord of the manor; in fact most transactions were of a " payment in kind " sort until the end of the thirteenth century. At this time the cutlery trade arrived in the town and payment in money became more common. The mystery of why the cutlers came to Thaxted remains to this day; the local water supply may be the reason, but nobody is really sure. By the end of the sixteenth century cutlery had disappeared and weaving took its place, only to share the same fate.

It is to the cutlers and weavers that the present visitor owes so much, for they provided the money for the building of the houses and the guildhall and for a further expansion of the church. Let your eyes wander down the undulating but rather straight main street, past the wonderful sight of the fifteenth-century guildhall and up the hill to the church. This is a town steeped in history, and the visitor can be excused for thinking he is seeing a film set of the fifteenth century, for all along the main street everything gives the impression of being of the same age; indeed, this is the beauty of this town—everything is so perfectly matched. Future generations are being assured of their chance to see this beauty, for in 1967 the Essex County Council adopted the " Thaxted plan " to preserve much of this town. To mention all the buildings of interest would take a volume much larger than the present one, but we hope the few we can bring to your attention will give a " flavour " of the town.

Dominating all other structures in Thaxted is the church of St. John the Baptist. Surely this is one of the jewels in the Essex crown, for its beauty is deserving of cathedral stature. Its outside is graced by ornate carving, great lengths of windows and leering gargoyles. We leave the description of the inside of this church to the "Two-penny Guide," copies of which can be bought at the church: " The wide open spaces, the simple altars, the colour in hangings, carpets and banners, enriched at the festivals by bowls of flowers standing on the paving, all combine to show the world of today the great beauty of this triumph of medieval craftsmen."

Before leaving the church let us remember Conrad Noel, vicar here until 1942, who brought colour and excitement to the place and is the inspiration of the novel *The Flag*, by Robert Shaw. The present vicar, the Rev. J. Putterill, might well become the subject of a novel, for he is fighting the good fight to save his church from the vibration that could topple it if the new Stansted airport gets off the ground. All lovers of Essex must wish him well in his battle to preserve this magnificent church.

Behind the church stand the whitewashed almshouses. These are two blocks of cottages parallel to each other, one with thatch and the other with a tiled roof. Looking between them and out into the countryside Thaxted's last windmill can be seen; it was built in 1804 out of local bricks.

Opposite the church, at the bend of Watling Street, is Clarence House, a lovely example of red-brick Queen Anne building that was once the home of the Clarence and Heckford families.

At the bottom of the hill is the fifteenth-century guildhall, which, although restored, is a grand sight as it stands on its " island " between the roads. This is a three-storied building, the front ground floor being an open, paved market house. Here vast wooden pillars support the upper levels, and an interesting relic of the past can be seen. This is the pole with an iron hook on it used to remove burning thatch from nearby dwellings in the days before fire extinguishers were invented.

At the top of Town Street is the Priory, where in 1938 repairs revealed a wall painting and a unique—to Essex—wagon-roof supported by a fifteenth-century king-post. A little lower down the street and on the opposite side is the Recorder's House—now a restaurant. In 1550 this was the home of Serjeant Bendlowes, the first recorder of Thaxted. Much of the woodcarving that decorates the outside of the house is original.

At the bottom of Town Street the B1051, Park Street, runs off to the right, and along here is Park Farm. This is an interesting building with a projecting upper story and plenty of interior timber work. Even the barn was built in 1550. Two miles farther along this street is the historic Horham Hall, where the first Elizabeth lived for a time. Originally built in 1470, it has passed through many changes, but the present building is attractive in its own right. Much of this dates from the early 1500s and was built by Sir John Cutte, treasurer of the household to Henry VIII. It consists of mellowed Tudor brick and stonework. Part of the moat is still in existence, but on the eastern side it has been filled in and a most picturesque gatehouse occupies the site.

South of Thaxted lies a crescent of five small villages, each with its own attraction for the visitor. To the west of the A130 lie Broxted,

Tilty and Little Easton; just off the A130 is Great Easton and east of this road is Lindsell. Apart from Broxted, which is on the B1051 a few miles south of Horham Hall, none of these villages is approached by a numbered road, but all are reached from attractive country lanes that are well signposted. This is farming country and the lanes twist round the corners of fields, plunge down short slopes and offer really poetical views of the countryside. Here and there the aspect is blocked by one of the many small woods that dot the region, only to reveal a few yards farther along a new scene and a new farm crop.

Let us start what must be a brief tour of these villages in the west with Broxted. This is one of the " hill " villages of the county, as it stands some 370 feet above sea level and offers a panoramic view of the neighbourhood, including the nearby windmill. In the village are plenty of shady trees and an interesting group of buildings. The church, with its weatherboarded belfry, dates from the thirteenth and fifteenth centuries and has Roman tiles in its walls. Nearby are the gabled church hall, a seventeenth-century brewhouse and a couple of old barns; all in all a very pleasing sight.

Gracing the valley of the River Chelmer and a short distance east of Broxted is the village of Tilty. In the twelfth century the village was chosen by the Cistercian monks as a site for an abbey; little still stands of this building, although recent excavations have revealed many foundations. St. Mary's, the present parish church, was probably a chapel to the abbey and has three lancet windows of the period, but much of the outside decoration is more modern and almost certainly reflects a partial rebuilding programme. Inside the church are several fifteenth-century brasses. Watered by the Chelmer, this is indeed a " green and pleasant land," as the local woods will testify.

Due south lies Little Easton, one-time home of Frances, Countess of Warwick. She lived during the reign of Queen Victoria at Easton Lodge, which was just outside the village. She was renowned for her generosity and her gardening. Sad to record, the Lodge has now gone and we have lost another of our stately homes. The village, however, remains, and its many thatched cottages with their well-kept gardens are perhaps a fitting memorial to Lady Warwick. The more usual memorials are in the ancient church of St. Mary, which stands on the edge of some beautiful parkland; these record the Bourchiers, the Maynards and Lady Warwick, as well as the

famous Dame Ellen Terry, who worshipped here when visiting
Lady Warwick. While in the church look for the paintings of the
seated prophet and scenes from the passion.

Great Easton is situated just off the A130, about one and a half
miles north of Little Easton. The village street runs west from the
main road and passes many attractive cottages and farmhouses
before it arrives at the war memorial, behind which stands the very
early Norman flintstone church of St. John. The houses round this
area often display ornamental plasterwork, bargeboarding, half-
timbering or Tudor chimneys. On the outskirts of the village the
road crosses the River Chelmer and there is a shallow ford to
navigate.

Half-way between Dunmow and Thaxted, and two miles east of
the A130, lies Lindsell. The road to this village is worth the journey
for its own sake as it gently rises from the busy main road to reach
a height of 300 feet in the quiet of the village. The compact village
centre is typical of many others in this part of the world, but the
approach to the village church of St. Mary is unusual. To find it
the visitor must pass through the courtyard of Lindsell House (a
gabled building with projecting upper stories) and there it stands,
unusual in its finish of pebble and red-brick dressing, and in the
position of its tower, which is at the south-western end of the aisle.
The church contains a dug-out chest and a brass of Thomas Fytch
dating from 1514.

WALTHAM ABBEY

AN ancient town set in the corner of an historic county—this
is Waltham Abbey, or, as many know it, Waltham Holy
Cross. The Holy Cross part of the name commemorates the Dane
Tofig, who nine centuries ago brought his wondrous cross to the
settlement at the edge of the Essex forest and built a church to
house it. The present church takes its name from this, being called
the church of the Holy Cross and St. Lawrence.

King Harold was responsible for the establishment of the abbey,
and it was built on the site Tofig had used some twenty years earlier.
After his death in 1066 the body of King Harold is reputed to have
been carried from Hastings and buried in the abbey church. There
is a story connected with King Harold and his fight against the
Danes that explains the presence of the two River Leas. At the time

Great Warley " has a surprising number of historical associations."

The Hanningfield reservoir " has changed the face of the countryside in a most interesting way."

Tower mill, Stansted Mountfitchet.

MYDDYLTON PLACE.

"We can go on about Saffron Walden and its charm for pages, and still not do it justice."

in question the River Lea was of fair size and subject to flooding. The Danes used it as a means of communication and moored their ships near Waltham, a fact that Harold noted with regret. He is said to have hit upon the plan to divert the river and leave the ships high and dry; certainly the river is now flowing down two beds, so there may be truth in the story.

The town grew in size and various rulers used it as a base for hunting in the nearby forest, and they usually stayed at the abbey. In 1540, with the dissolution of the abbeys, the future for Waltham changed from the possibility of becoming a cathedral city to that of a market town. This is ironic when we remember that Thomas Cranmer, architect of the Reformation, was living in Waltham when plans for the break with Rome were being made.

Over the years the demand for wood for the construction of homes and ships increased, so the forest was gradually cut back until the town was no longer at the edge of it, but only close to it. These spaces have not been wasted, for the visitor will see the great areas of glasshouses that now surround the town and provide much of its wealth and employment.

Let us take a brief look at this pleasant town as it stands today. The approach roads are the A121 (east and west), the B194 (from the north) and the A112 (from the south). They join each other near Sun Street in the heart of the town. On this corner are the abbey gardens, and west down into Church Street is the abbey itself.

After the Reformation much of the original church was lost and the present building is only about a third of the size of the older church. Parts of the original have been excavated and Harold's grave is marked by a stone. Parts of the foundations can be seen by appointment. Once inside the church the eye is drawn upwards by the stout Norman pillars with their carving and decoration. In the Lady chapel you can see parts of the old walls and at the back is a small museum. Behind the church runs the Cornmill Stream, which is crossed by an old Saxon bridge known locally as Harold's Bridge. Nearby are the shallow depressions thought to have been the abbey fishponds.

In the market square stands the oldest inn of Waltham, the Welsh Harp, a timber-framed building that was used by pilgrims to the shrine of King Harold.

As a market town since the twelfth century Waltham maintains the tradition, and markets are held every Tuesday and Saturday in the market square. Twice a year, in May and September, fairs are held under a charter that dates back to Henry III.

The visitor to Waltham cannot help but be aware of the many streams that flow about the town, and mention has already been made of some of these. They are an attraction in their own right, as they are the home of many wild birds. The River Lea flows between verdant banks and joins together large areas of water north of the town, with the great King George's reservoir to the south.

North of Waltham, along the B194, are the two small hamlets of Nazeing and Roydon. The road to them is pleasant as it skirts round the hills to the east and looks out on to the river to the west. Nazeing is one of those places that seem to be in every direction you go, but most people live in the part called Nazeingbury or Lower Nazeing. Like Waltham, this is a market-garden region and the traveller is likely to come across yards of glasshouses round any bend in the road. To the west, on the River Lea, is Keysers, where it is possible to rent a boat and go messing about on the river. From the river the land rises until it reaches Nazeing proper. The thirteenth-century flint and stone church of All Saints stands north of the village, and from it one can look down on to the valley of the river and into Hertfordshire. South from the church past the old cottages, which are as attractive as ever they were, we come to Nazeing Park, which was built in 1814. The wooded parklands fill the diamond-shaped roads that run along its four sides. So we run on into the famous Nazeing Common, a wild and windy place on the hilltop that dominates the area.

Roydon is due north of Nazeing and is almost on the banks of the River Stort, while the Lea is only a short distance away. This is a pleasing old village, and in fine weather it is good to get out on to the river near the mill for boating, swimming or fishing. The local church is dedicated to St. Peter and is nearly 700 years old. Notice its octagonal font with the superb carvings of human heads on it. Near the church stands the village green. Fine old houses, many of them weatherboarded, run south from the church along the main street. The village is proud of its connection with the famous Sir Thomas More, who married Jane Colte, a local girl. She was a daughter of the Colte family who owned Nether Hall. This lies south-west of the village and is now in ruins, but even they serve to show the glory that once belonged to the moated house.

THE WILLINGALES

IT is such a pleasant little tour from the county town through Writtle and along the Ongar road to the signpost which points to Willingale. From there on the narrow country roads are little-frequented and driving is a pleasure through good Essex farm-land, past the famous war-time aerodrome at Norton Mandeville to one of the strangest sights, church-wise, in the whole county; for here you can see two well-built, well-cared-for churches standing in the same churchyard.

Older villagers recall loitering there on a Sunday evening, listening to evensong on both sides, for one church belongs to Willingale Doe and the other to Willingale Spain. The names of these adjacent villages derive from their post-Conquest owners, William D'Ou and Hervey de Spain. The legend that they were built by two sisters in rivalry is disproved by the difference in their ages, which is very visible in their architecture.

St. Andrew's is probably Saxon, with a pretty little spire, but St. Christopher's, dating from the fourteenth century, is more interesting in the way of brasses and monuments. Now the parishes are united and services are held in St. Christopher's only. From the churchyard, which is on an eminence, there is a pleasing view of Essex countryside.

You will find a genial landlord at the Bell, opposite the churches. He pointed out the local joke that there is one Bell between the two churches! The journey towards Chelmsford can be made in another direction through the village and out into open country past Shellow Bowells, a tiny parish abutting on to the old Skreens estate, where a large mansion dating back to the Skreene family of the fifteenth century once stood. It was demolished early in this century, though the foundations can still be traced. Skreens itself lay in the parish of Roxwell, which comes into view very prettily over a rise in the road. The large farmhouse on the left, called Dukes, was built in the sixteenth century and is kept in very good repair.

The village street still bends alarmingly, hugged closely by an interesting variety of houses and shops. The vicar at the time of writing, the Rev. Philip A. Wright, M.B.E., has what is probably the best collection in the county of old Essex farm and household implements and " bygones," many of which have been illustrated in *Essex Countryside*.

Following the road on to Chelmsford, look out for a sharp bend just before it meets the A414 by the Hare and Hounds. Across the road there, over by the river between Boyton Hall and Chignal Hall, there is evidence of considerable Roman occupation.

SECTION FOUR

LOOK NORTH

LOOK NORTH

ALPHAMSTONE, PEBMARSH, LAMARSH and the BURES

L YING along the winding valley of the River Stour, these villages are contained by a triangle formed of the A133, A131 and A604. A good place to commence any exploration of these villages is Alphamstone, whose central position along a country lane allows ease of travel to the other villages in the vicinity. The village stands on the high ground overlooking the river, and one of the best views can be obtained from the churchyard. The present burial ground covers a site used in the Bronze Age for the same purpose, and urns from here can be seen in the museum at Colchester. The much-restored thirteenth-century church stands near the fork in the road at the eastern end of the main street and has several things of historical interest. The wooden doors, built when our armies fought with bows and arrows, are the portals to the rest. Sunlight entering the church passes through stained glass that was created in medieval times, to fall on the 800-year-old Purbeck-type font. As previously mentioned, the houses and cottages of the village spread themselves along the lane, which is bounded by the undulating farmland that is so much a feature of this corner of the county. Many of the houses and farmhouses are old, but none has anything as old as the 120-foot-long weatherboarded barn that can be seen at Clees Hall. This barn was built in the sixteenth century and has a queen-post roof. To find it, take the left-hand fork at the western end of the village and after three-quarters of a mile turn left down the narrow lane; the Hall lies at the end of it.

By taking the right-hand fork the road leads us on over fairly level ground to the village of Pebmarsh. Here the village has grown up round a T junction in the lanes and around the fine old fourteenth-century church that was built just west of the junction. Many of the buildings, including the post office, date from Tudor times, and scattered around the outskirts are many other fine examples of Tudor building. Perhaps the best example is Stanley Hall, which lies nearly two miles west of the church. While in the village look for the attractive timber-framed and plastered house called Mill House, for it connects this rural place with a modern industrial giant. From 1798 to 1900 the house was attached to a silk mill which formed a starting point for the now famous Courtaulds firm. The mill is no longer standing.

The visitor cannot miss the church of St. John, for its many battlements attract the eye, but its chief interest lies in the age of a brass of Sir William Fitzralph. This dates from 1323 and is almost certainly the oldest in Essex.

East from Alphamstone, and reached via the right-hand fork near the church, is the small village of Lamarsh. Here the visitor will see many attractive cottages lining the lane that runs north towards the church of the Holy Innocents. The lane runs parallel to the railway and the river, while to the left the fields climb the gentle hillside. It is worth the journey to see the very pleasant church just for its round Norman tower, although much of the rest of the building has been restored. North again lies the sixteenth-century Daws Hall; this old house stands protected by a belt of tall trees.

South from Lamarsh the roads follow the winding course of the river to arrive at Bures hamlet. This is an interesting place, for most of the village is across the county border in Suffolk and is called Bures St. Mary. It is sad to report that most things of interest, including the church and a fine building called Bevills, are in Suffolk and therefore outside this present volume, but on our side of the border you can rest at the sixteenth-century Eight Bells inn. The village has a most attractive river aspect; even on the busy A133 one can look across the fields and the river and see the mill and its attendant house standing by the gently moving waters.

The other Bures is called Mount Bures and is only a short journey along the A133, turning right at the signpost and crossing the railway line to reach the village centre. It was near this railway line in the nineteenth century that an interesting Belgic tomb was found, dating from A.D. 43. Behind the church is the reason for the Mount part in the name of the village. Here the Normans built a castle and the remaining mound is thirty-eight feet high. The mound is now a wooded and secluded place and offers very pleasant views over the village. The church of St. John was also built by the Normans, and they used many Roman bricks in the construction. These can still be seen, particularly round the windows in the west wall.

THE BELCHAMPS

ST. Pauls, Otten and Walter; these are the three little Belchamp villages that lie against the county border with Suffolk. They are tiny places set in the midst of rolling farmland, with that almost professional quiet that our Essex agricultural villages offer to the traveller tired by his journey along busy main roads. To reach this corner of solitude, leave the A604 at Great Yeldham and head north-east to Belchamp St. Pauls.

The houses and cottages of St. Pauls, the largest of the three villages, stand round the pleasant village green. Yes, the first impression is of a neat, attractive place, and closer inspection will not shatter this picture, for the village was voted the best-kept place in Essex in 1966 and 1967. A plaque to commemorate this can be seen in the community centre, a well-designed building with light rooms and a well-kept thatched roof. You will look in vain for the usual church at the edge of the village green, for the local place of worship is about a mile north of the village, near the sixteenth-century Paul's Hall. It is worth the trouble to visit the church, St. Andrew's, for its chancel seats have misericords decorated with flower and leaf motifs. The church is one of only two churches in Essex to have these. There are also brasses to the Golding family, of whom Arthur Golding (1536-1605?) is the most interesting. He lived across the road from the church at Paul's Hall and is famous for his translations of the classics. Not only have students over the years thanked him, but Shakespeare is also reputed to have used the Golding translations in his own works. The Hall is still standing, one wing being timber framed, and in the other wing some of the original windows remain.

Belchamp Otten lies south-east, and on the way there look out to the left for the remains of an old windmill. Otten is the smallest of these villages and is really little more than a cluster of houses and a church along the road. The church of St. Ethelbert is small but shows traces of many periods; the nave, for instance, is Norman, but the belfry is nineteenth century, built on much older wooden cross-beams. Scattered round about are many old farmhouses and cottages, some of them timber-framed.

The lane to Belchamp Walter is a twisting, turning route that heads south to Puttock End before going east to the village. The houses of this village stand along the crossroads that mark its position on the map. From the village the land runs gently down towards the Belchamp Brook. This is another place where the church stands away from the main habitation but near the Hall. To reach them, continue over the crossroads as you enter the village and make for the woods ahead of you. Round them to the right you will find Belchamp Hall and St. Mary's church opposite it. This is a fine little church, worthy of its setting. Its massive round font and the north side of the chancel are Norman. Notice also the recess in the north wall of the nave; the rich carving might indicate that it was the entrance to a now lost chapel. The Hall was built in 1720 of white and red brick, and it has some fine wood panelling inside. An older house lies due south of Puttock End at St. Mary Hall, on the way back to join the A604. The house is a timber-framed building built in the late sixteenth century and stands at the end of the hamlet on the left.

BORLEY and the northern corner of Essex

HIDDEN in this eastern corner of north Essex are the fields that produce much of our staple diet. It is lovely countryside, with lanes winding their leisurely way between fields rich with crops, and saved from becoming too open by the many small woods that serve as wind-breaks. To the east runs the River Stour with its slow-flowing waters cutting their way between Essex and Suffolk; what more charming boundary could any county ask for?

Scattered among this feast of nature are the four villages that make up this chapter, and we start with the most famous of them, Borley. The village is at the south end of the B1064, and it is this road that we shall use to link the villages together, although it is necessary to branch off it to left and right to enter some places of interest. The main village of Borley lies along a lane running west about half a mile south of the B1064 and is famous for once housing the most haunted house in England. This was Borley rectory, which was the scene of many strange happenings, but the house was burned down and later demolished. However, they say that on really dark nights . . . but enough of that and back to the sunlight and the small group of cottages that makes up the present centre. In the heart of things is the small stone church with its interesting, well-cut yews that line the approach to the building. Within the church there is a large memorial to Sir Edward Waldegrave, who spent his life in and out of the Tower for his religious beliefs during the reigns of three monarchs.

Rejoining the B1064 we head north for half a mile, then bear right to visit the hamlet of Liston. The seventy people who make up the population of the place live along the lane near to the large grounds that once housed the local Hall. Standing on the right is the mainly Norman church, although the tower is much later. As you look out across the valley of the Stour into Suffolk the pinnacled tower you see in the distance belongs to the church at Long Melford.

Back on to our classified road again, we follow it into the largest village of the group, and one of the most interesting—Foxearth. This is typical of the best in Essex villages, for it seems little spoiled by the passing of time and there is much to look at, including the old post office building and the moated house that stands on the right at the end of the main street. This is a timber-framed house that was originally built in Elizabethan times but has been restored. Since the restoration in 1885 the church of St. Peter and St. Paul looks rather Victorian, but inside the painted rood-screen and the stained glass give away its real age.

Heading north again past Pentlow Street we reach the most northern hamlet in this part of Essex. This is Pentlow. The River Stour flows along the end of the village street, and in the rectory garden is a fine tower that offers broad views across the county border and over countryside that Gainsborough made famous in his paintings. This was built by the Rev. E. Bull as a memorial to his father. One of the few round towers in Essex is a feature of St. George's church, while inside is a fine monument to the Kempe family.

The parish is rich in historic houses, but they are rather spread out. Particularly noteworthy are Pentlow Hall, a manor house built in 1500 which has exposed timber work, and Bower Hall, which lies well west of the village and was built in 1600. The latter also has a barn that is 100 years older than the house.

Just across the river the A1092 runs east and west and offers a fast link with most parts of our county.

BRAINTREE AND BOCKING

IN ancient days our forefathers hacked their trails through the dark forests of Essex, and the Romans came and built their long, straight roads over the same tracks. Where two tracks crossed a settlement sprang up, perhaps just a rest house for travellers and stables for a change of horses, and soon the nucleus of a community was established.

Braintree developed in just this way along the Roman Stane Street where it is crossed by the Chelmsford—Halstead road. There is evidence of a prehistoric lake-village. Considerable Roman occupation is shown by the large number of their coins found hereabouts.

In medieval times, and even into the eighteenth century, Braintree people made a living from the many pilgrims who sojourned here on their way north to the shrine of Our Lady of Walsingham in Norfolk or west to that of St. Edmund at Bury St. Edmunds in Suffolk. The Reformation reduced this trade for many a long year, but inns which might have decayed were taken over by the Flemings who flocked here to escape religious persecution. Early history of the town is not easy to come by. One reason may be the Great Plague of 1665, brought here perhaps by some scared refugee from London. A third of the population died and the life of the town was disorganized. One continuing aspect of its life, however, has been the cloth trade. From the fourteenth century Essex sheep kept Braintree and Bocking looms well supplied through to the eighteenth century, when crepe and silk ousted wool as the main manufacture. This town is also proud to have woven materials for royal robes, including the wonderful purple velvet of George VI's coronation ensemble.

A saunter from Braintree through the main street to Bocking combines old and new in pleasing comparison. On the right-hand side of the High Street as one approaches Braintree is a splendid fountain which fronts St. Michael's church. This fountain, of a bronze boy holding a fish, is just one of the many evidences in Braintree and Bocking of the benevolence of the Courtauld family since the original company of the Courtauld group first began production of silk in 1816 in Bocking. They turned to man-made fibres in the 1890s and expanded rapidly, so that the group now employs over 100,000 people.

Other examples of the Courtaulds' interest include the electric clock in the tower of St. Michael's church and the old drinking fountain in the market place. The town hall was built in 1928 on a corner of the old Fair Field overlooking the market place, entirely at the Courtaulds' cost. It is a little history in itself, for it contains murals by Maurice Grieffenhagen which show scenes in the history of the town and its neighbourhood.

Courtauld beneficence includes the William Julien Courtauld Hospital in Braintree and the buildings of the Bocking United Services Club, incorporating the village hall. Similarly, the institute at Bocking End which now houses the Braintree museum was presented to the council in 1960, though it is a building of the Victorian period.

The public gardens (entrance from the Causeway) and the recreation ground (entrance from Coggeshall Road via John Ray Street) are further Courtauld bequests.

The recently introduced one-way system has made it easier for the motorist to thread his way through the town centre, where several old inns show the town's ancient role as a travellers' rest. The Horn, the Boar's Head, the Horse and Groom, the Swan, the Bull, the Wheatsheaf and the Six Bells, together with the White Hart, now a Trust House hotel, all have an outward picturesque antiquity which cloaks an interior that is comfortable by any modern standard.

While Braintree's buildings, ancient and modern, side by side, give an air of vigour and prosperity the atmosphere of Bradford Street is that of an old print. The pity is that the old buildings there, which form such a charming picture together, are in some cases being allowed to fall down so that their sites may be exploited commercially. In the same street old gateways to coaching inns long since demolished can still be discerned.

There is a commercial building of earlier days which has become an object of beauty and interest in Bocking. It is the fine windmill which has been restored and can be seen in Church Street. While commenting on industry it is only fair to include the name of Crittall, for it was in Bank Street that metal windows were first produced by F. H. Crittall when he was running an ironmongery business which dates back to 1635 and is said to be the oldest continuing business in this trade in the country.

To get to Dunmow you take the road from Braintree through Rayne village, which has been more or less disjointed by the speed of modern traffic past its picturesque old houses. On the way to Rayne you pass a holiday caravan site catering for thirty-six caravans, complete with restaurant and swimming pool. In the same direction a stop at the Barn restaurant will bring before your very eyes, as they say, the most overwhelming collection of " bygones " and old country implements and objects. There are even cartwheels on the ceiling! It is a most intriguing place.

The B1053 from Bocking to Wethersfield offers a diversion on the left to Panfield, a village adjoining the urban district of Braintree and Bocking. The Hall, now a farmhouse, is a noteworthy building which dates from 1546 and still shows Tudor features.

Priory Farm marks the site of a small " alien " priory, part of St. Stephen's abbey at Caen, which was suppressed long before the Reformation, because it was in fact a French enclave on English soil when war with that country broke out. Edward Bangs, one of the Pilgrim Fathers, was christened here in 1591. A plaque in the church recording this fact has been presented by an American descendant.

THE COLNES and CHAPPEL

FROM Chappel going westwards you will take the A604, and you will need to cross the River Colne three times to see five villages in as many miles. The river and its crossing points were the reason for the making of these villages, which today offer a scene that is peaceful to the eye and the soul, with slow waters, low meadows and gently rising farmland.

At Chappel, road, rail and river run. The village was allowed a chapel of its own in 1355 because winter conditions prevented attendance at the nearest church, and so the place got its name; but it was not until 1533 that the village was granted full church status. That old chapel still stands on its riverside site as the village church, stoutly made of stone, and looking down all of 200 feet to the ever-rolling Colne. With the houses clustering about it and the more recently built spire pointing from their midst it makes a very pleasant view.

The railway crosses the river on a 1,000-foot-long viaduct, brick-built and time-mellowed, a good example of Victorian engineering skill enhanced by the simple proportions of its thirty or so graceful arches built around the middle of the last century. The station is on the other side of the river, to the north near Wakes Colne.

This, the first of our Colne villages, is named after a branch of the Wake family who married into the lordship of the village in the thirteenth century. Wakes Hall is a mid-nineteenth-century re-building of the old family residence.

The church of All Saints gives evidence in doors and windows as well as in walls of its Norman foundation; and houses like Little Loveney Hall up the lanes to the north past Wakes Colne Green and Crepping Hall to the east through Rose Green give evidence of fifteenth- and sixteenth-century building, though their sites date back very much farther. Old House Farm is appropriately named—it has housed hopeful humanity for 300 years.

From the hamlet of Wakes Colne Green, which has its own attractive share of old houses, it is a roundabout but refreshing route west then south through good-hearted farmland to White Colne church. Or you can go west along the A604 and turn off by White Colne station, where the village has developed more in recent years, and go on north to the church, which has been " drastically restored " though the seventeenth-century pulpit remains. The big houses of former times when the village hung more round the church are farmhouses today, known as Bart Hall and Berewyk Hall. This, the smallest of the Colnes, is farthest from the river, yet in days long gone by it was swamp-land, acres of it.

Cross the river for the second time and you are in Earls Colne, named after the de Veres, Earls of Oxford, who lived in the Hall next the church. Coller, the popular county historian, said in 1861: " May be called a town, standing on the southern bank, and several good mansions with their belting woodlands scattered over the undulating landscape; the fair scene presents a very favourable sample of the rural districts of the county "—and we can echo that description today, for the village is almost a town, so favoured is it as a residential area, yet its old charm is still retained by its village nucleus.

The road climbs up from the river past interesting old places like Colne Ford House, which stands astride the boundary between White Colne and Earls Colne. There is a leaden plaque dated 1724 denoting the line inside the house. Outside it is richly plastered or " pargeted," with " 1685 " picked out within the pattern. The Priory, too, has a history. Though now an eighteenth-century mansion in red brick imitating the Gothic style it stands on the site of a Benedictine priory founded about 1100 by Aubrey de Vere, who later became a monk in his own foundation. He and his wife, Beatrice, sister of William the Conqueror, are buried here.

Other old houses of lath and plaster with timber framework carry on their façades the crest of the de Veres. Tucked away down its long drive off the junction of the Halstead and station roads is Colne House, the home of Mr. Arthur Evans, head of the internationally known Halstead firm of Evans Electroselenium, which has been described by us in a separate pamphlet. The grammar school is large for the size of the place, but its importance goes back to its foundation in 1520.

As to the church, let us refer to the rural district guide, which says that it " dates from the fourteenth century and has a large number of features of interest, ranging from its splendid sixteenth-century tower and its timbered roofs to its pre-Reformation church silver."

In a typically serene Essex village the locals will tell you that the real beauty spot is Chalkney Wood, east of the village, where the trees creep down to admire their reflections in the River Colne.

The last crossing of the Colne is made down the road past the station. Over the bridge the road rises up to Colne Engaine, so called after the lords of the manor of 600 or more years ago. The church gathers the houses round its homely skirts. Its tower is of brick, a Tudor rebuilding on a fourteenth-century base in which you can detect much Roman material, indicative of the great age of the settlement here. Charming lanes lead from the village centre to all points of the compass, passing hamlets with intriguing names.

In the parish, but way over on the lane to White Colne, lies Colne Park, the big house, much enlarged about 1900 in its own beautiful grounds. And so we complete five miles of Essex homes and churches, history and beauty.

DUNMOW

HAVE you repented your marriage, waking or sleeping, during the last year and a day? If not, Dunmow is the place for you, for here in this pleasant town, situated on high ground overlooking the River Chelmer, the Dunmow flitch trial takes place each year.

Originated in the reign of Henry III by Robert Fitzwalter, who offered a flitch of bacon to the first couple to convince an all-bachelor jury of their married happiness, the trial fell into disuse, but was revived in 1855 by Harrison Ainsworth and is now a great attraction at holiday time.

Dunmow consists of twin villages, Great and Little Dunmow, which stand astride the old Roman road of Stane Street. Here many old remains have been found, suggesting that Dunmow was a Roman station on the road from Colchester to St. Albans.

Great Dunmow, as well as being the home of the flitch trial, houses several interesting buildings. The old Town Hall, built in 1578 and enlarged in the nineteenth century, is interesting for its steep roof. The fourteenth-century parish church contains a priest's room over the ornamented south porch. Also worth seeing are the decorated font, the fourteenth-century chest and the sixteenth-century sealed charters of the town.

Little Dunmow has the original Dunmow flitch church within its bounds. The church is the only remaining part of a priory established in 1104. Buried here is Robert Fitzwalter, who, as well as being the founder of the flitch trial, was one of the leading barons who opposed King John and was appointed to ensure the working of the Magna Charta. The church also contains a thirteenth-century chair, said to be the chair in which successful claimants for the flitch were carried.

West of Dunmow lies Hatfield Forest—1,000 acres under the control of the National Trust. Picturesque old cottages and farmhouses dot the area, blending with the modern developments.

Across Stane Street and to the south-east is Barnston, a rural place with a poplar-lined street that rises until it reaches the Norman church. This church is interesting for many reasons, and the tourist should not miss the double Norman piscina (it is the earliest known example), the 300-year-old altar table and poor box, and the 500-year-old timber that supports the tower. The condition of these things today bears testimony to the loving care that the craftsmen of old put into them.

Near to the church is an Elizabethan hall house that is quite typical of its period, with attractive windows and a large central chimney.

FELSTED

"GEORGE BOOT made this house 1596" is the interesting message inscribed across the front of an old place in Felsted. Now it is a bank for half a day a week and a restaurant all the time. A good meal can be enjoyed here, but prior booking is essential.

The village owes much of its character to Lord Rich, who got rich as solicitor-general in Tudor times. In 1564 he founded the school, which is now in the top rank of public schools and can boast the education of three of Cromwell's sons. The original schoolroom, typically Tudor with overhanging upper story, still stands facing down the B1417, with the headmaster's house by its side. It has an archway to allow access to the church of the Holy Cross, where members of the Rich family are buried in the Rich chapel under some very fine monuments thought to be designed by Epiphanius Evesham.

The charming old buildings and the interesting scenery make it worth while stopping to stroll about. To the north-west, over Priory Bridge, there is a landmark visible for miles around—the great chimney of the sugar factory, here in the depths of Essex countryside. The sugar you take in hotel or restaurant in Essex, or out, for that matter, may well have originated from the roots of sugar-beet sown and grown in Essex clay and rendered down at Felsted. Down the B1417 at Hartford End there is an old watermill which shows additions through 200 years to Victorian times.

Stebbing stands on the other side of the A120 to the north of Felsted on what is, for Essex, fairly high ground, with the church of St. Mary the Virgin as its crowning glory.

Two points about this church are of interest. One is that it is all of stone in a stoneless county and the other is that it was built and remains entirely in the style of the fourteenth century.

The one feature above all to notice is the carved stone rood-screen. This is like the one at Great Bardfield, and there is only one other example of its type—in far-away Trondheim. Sit in the church, and for a few minutes be with those patient builders of the fourteenth century.

In the village the Friends meeting house has 1674 inscribed on its wall, but it seems that the building was almost completely re-built in the eighteenth century.

The group of interesting old buildings near the church includes Parsonage Farm house, showing its old beams. The road running north-west just past the church takes you on into the village and then past Stebbing Park, where a fifty-foot mound rises out of a moat, the mystery site of a castle which legend has it existed before the great invasion. The road runs on to Bran End and the B1057, which leads to Duck End and so on to Lindsell.

In the other direction, way down towards the A120 you come to Stebbing Green. Porters Hall there can still boast a moat, though the present house is only 300 years old! Nearby is the site of a considerable Roman building from which tiles and pottery were excavated in recent times.

FINCHINGFIELD

DURRANT'S handbook of 1887 tells us that Finchingfield is "a large parish, containing a considerable village, and, in addition to many good farmhouses, not a few large old manor houses, most of them now much reduced, though once inhabited by families of good position." In eighty years the wheel has turned full circle; Finchingfield has appeared on calendars and posters all over the world as a symbol of the British village, and "families of good position" have paid well for the privilege of living in such a beautiful place. No one who has visited it will disagree, for its setting is so much in its favour.

Roads from all directions descend a hill to merge by the village pond, where any through traveller has to negotiate the hump-back bridge with room for only one vehicle at a time. But what is time when you see the cottages of all periods, and all beautifully kept, stepping away up the hill to the crowning glory of the old church of St. John the Baptist? You want to stay and discover more. Round the green, for instance, there are thatched cottages and a windmill raising its white arms heavenwards.

Make time to appreciate the ancient craftsmanship and current beauty of buildings like the guildhall (next the church), Parsonage Farm house, the butcher's shop and Sculpins, where a couple of hundred years ago Sir John Marshall kept open house to all comers every Thursday. The church, you will find, has its own guide. Its great strong tower is of Norman construction, having stood for nearly 900 years. Among the interesting and instructive things to see within is a monument to a William Kempe (1628), who undertook a vow of silence for seven years.

He lived at Spains Hall, adding an air of whimsical charm to a Tudor mansion which already had a history behind it. Muilman's *History of Essex* says: " The manor of Spains Hall, which has a mansion about a mile north of the church, was one among other estates with which the Conqueror loaded Alan Fergent (second son of Eudo, Earl of Bretagne) for assisting him in his conquest of this kingdom." The book, which was published around 1770, goes on to explain that a later tenant under the de Veres was Hervey de Ispania, and that is why the house is known as Spains Hall today.

Several generations of the Spain family were succeeded by William Kempe, then the property passed by marriage to Sir Swinnerton

Dyer, Kempe's sister's husband, in whose family it remained until it was purchased from them in 1760 by Samuel Ruggles, who, as Coller says, " belonged to a family which had ' gentlemen of note ' as early as 1298." The house has remained in the same family ever since, devolving to Sir John Ruggles-Brise, the present Lord-Lieutenant of the county.

The chance of visiting Spains Hall when the gardens are open to the public on certain days in aid of charity should not be missed. The visitor will be struck by the very rural nature of the surroundings on the side road off the B1057 even before the drive is reached. Down the drive the view of the house is very pleasing. The Dutch-looking red-brick gables date from the end of the fifteenth century. Wright summed it up in his *History of Essex* of 1832: " The fine old Gothic mansion of Spains Hall, standing in a varied and well-planted park, appears from the style of the architecture to have been built in the reign of Elizabeth; the entrance hall is spacious, being about forty feet in length, with width and height in due proportion; and it is lighted by one handsome window, divided into bays extending nearly its whole length." Nikolaus Pevsner explains the architectural features succinctly in his Essex volume of the " Buildings of England " series.

But books will not compensate for the view of the house and garden, which has as far as possible been preserved in its original form. World War II shook the old house with bomb-blast, but luckily only a chimney-stack actually collapsed. The three-story porch leads into the hall, which runs to the same height in one story, with elaborately carved beams which are said to be original, while the view through the mullioned windows has not changed greatly in 400 years.

The lake south-east of the house represents one change, for it was once two of seven fishponds said to have been excavated by William Kempe himself—one a year for seven years, for this was the period of this unusual man's self-inflicted silence. He said something in haste, apparently about his wife, for which he was so ashamed that he made a seven-year silence his penance. In the church, in Kempe's chapel (south aisle of the chancel), you will find his tomb with an inscription recording this fact and showing that he died in 1628 at the age of seventy-three.

One other feature which must have been there in Kempe's time is the cedar overspreading the lawn at the side of the house. It is much larger now, of course; its girth is twenty feet or more, and it still keeps growing, though its main branch was broken off by a recent heavy snowfall. Over the years flower beds have disappeared in its growing shade.

The garden above it, full of roses, is surrounded by the old Tudor wall, marked with the first Ruggles's intials, with the " prayer-house " embattled in the same red brick to break the line and interest the eye.

From the centre of the village the B1053 will take you on to Wethersfield. You may notice an unusual number of American cars on the road, but they are not all tourists. Many belong to American airmen and their families who live in the district, for Wethersfield, pretty village that it is, has given its name to the great airfield inconspicuously tucked away on its outskirts, on which American planes are based.

Like Finchingfield and the area around, Wethersfield is hilly—to Essex eyes that is—and here the slopes run down to the Bourne Brook, while the Pant meanders on the western boundary of the parish, which includes hamlets like Beasley End, Blackmore End, Rotten End and Brickkiln Green.

Its eastern neighbour is Gosfield, where there is a lovely big lake —but be warned; it is noisy! The water-skiers weave patterns of spray over the 100-acre expanse. A little haven is roped off for the paddlers and there is space for a few rowing boats, which can be hired by the hour. A lot of the noise comes from the miniature fairground on the bank, supported by refreshments and amusement booths.

You *can* get away from the noise, but not right round the lake. There is access from the road to each side, but after you have gone so far swamp and thicket bar the way.

Though life at the lake may seem a bit brash today it has had its glory in the past, for it is part of the estate of Gosfield Hall, a much-altered house of the sixteenth century which was visited by good Queen Bess and, in 1807, by Louis XVIII of France.

It is an impressive place, lived in, extended and modified by generations of owners, one of whom, Earl Nugent, who died in 1788, was responsible for making the lake. Nowadays it is open to the public on certain days—your public library will tell you when.

The village street shows how old can mingle with new, including some " neat half-timbered houses " and a village hall built by the

Courtaulds of Bocking fame about 100 years ago. The church dates from the fifteenth and sixteenth centuries and is a peaceful place to look around, with some splendid monuments and an unusual brass to Thomas Rolf dated 1440 which has no fewer than ten adulatory verses in Latin.

Shalford lies farther to the south-west, including Shalford Green, Jasper's Green and Church End. The church was built in the 1300s; it has some old stained glass and fine woodcarving. A good example of modern building in harmony with rural surroundings is the Congregational church here.

To the south-east of Finchingfield in the same pretty area the villages of Little Bardfield, Great Bardfield, Bardfield Saling and Great Saling lie on a north-west/south-east axis running to the A120 near Rayne.

The whole area is a place to tour on a sunny day, with ears to appreciate country sounds and eyes to see the story of Essex in homes and farms which hide among trees or gather by the streams.

Little Bardfield's special interest is in its small church, which has a Saxon tower dated from 1042. Great Bardfield dreams of past glory. It was once a town with its own charter for a market and a fair, but today its character is reflected in its antique shops, which may offer the discerning collector a bargain or two. Queen Elizabeth is said to have stayed here for a time to avoid the vengeance of her half-sister, Mary Tudor. Its church has an unusual and beautiful rood-screen of carved stone. Believe it or not, there are only two other examples in Europe: one at Trondheim cathedral and the other almost next door in Stebbing!

Do not miss the small museum here, which has relics of rural life of an age gone by, banished by the present machine age; but individual initiative and creativeness exist in the colony of artists, including men of note like Edward Bawden.

If you are taking the road to Finchingfield watch out for the very narrow bridge over the Pant. You need to look a long way ahead to see that the road is clear.

Bardfield Saling is also known as Little Saling. Its fourteenth-century church was erected as a chapel of ease to Great Bardfield, with a circular western tower and other unusual features.

Great Saling is nearest to the Rayne road. Like so many of the villages we visit, it has a history even from before Domesday, too long to recount in our pages. Blake House Farm is a living reminder

—it goes back more than 400 years. Great Saling Hall is a manor house of similar age, carried out in brick. Near it you will see a great elm tree, said to be the largest in the kingdom and all that is left of an imposing avenue which led across the once broad village green to the church. Great Saling made recent history by being the site of the first aerodrome built by our American allies in this country during World War II.

HALSTEAD, STISTED, PATTISWICK

HALSTEAD'S High Street, broad and clean, drops down from the church at the top of the hill to the valley of the Colne, where a bridge and a bend moderate the speed of through traffic.

At the top, St. Andrew's church dominates the skyline with its bold tower, a 100-year-old reconstruction of a building which goes back to the fourteenth century. The great Bourchier family were gathered here one by one to rest for ever in the Bourchier chapel or south aisle. Their canopied tombs with recumbent effigies have recently been restored. There is a peal of eight bells, which needs a lot of ringing; small wonder therefore that a big ringers' jar dated 1658 can be seen in the belfry, with the amusing admonition " If you be wise, fill me not twice at one sitting "—that is with ale, of course!

The old market was held on the side of the High Street, a broad space which makes a very useful car park, and there is another free park just off the middle of the High Street, so the visitor is really welcomed. You will find it a rewarding experience to stroll down the street and " take in the sights." From the top of the hill the trees and parkland in the valley beyond the town make a pleasing view. While you are here you might like to know that the cottage hospital nearby in Hedingham road was given to the town by George Courtauld in 1884. Down the High Street, Chantry House (No. 26), in its name and with bits of original hammerbeam roof, reminds us of the original function of this place, which was built in 1412 by order of the will of Lord Bourchier as a house for a priest who was to say prayers for the souls of his lordship and his family in the parish church for ever.

On the other side of the street there are many old buildings to be enjoyed; they reflect the growth of this old market town in their building, extension, reconstruction and refashioning to suit the latest style, from the fifteenth century onwards.

Over the bridge on the left a little lane, the Causeway, runs by the river to the gates of the premises of Courtaulds, the great silk and artificial fibre manufacturers. You can lean on the railing and watch the river run beneath the eighteenth-century timbered mill which spans the stream. Its bands of windows across its white clapboard front make it look as though it was put up to please the eye rather than to house workers and machinery for making silk in an age when a day's work meant literally working from dawn to dusk. From this mill, where George Courtauld set up as a silk throwster in 1782, the name of Courtauld has gone round the world.

New industry is also making its mark. At the top of the town in the Colchester road, Evans Electroselenium, producers of fine instruments based on the photo-electric cell, are housed in a very modern building with a fountain playing in a flagged courtyard and a symbolic mural in the modern style in the reception hall.

Over the river again, in Bridge Street the old Corn Exchange, built 100 years ago, still stands, though its use has changed, and the house of correction (an early kind of reformatory), twice as old, is now a flour mill. Farther on, past the site of the old level crossing, you will come upon the public gardens in Trinity Street. They cover four acres and were laid out in 1901 to celebrate Victoria's diamond jubilee. Trinity House is a seventeenth-century timber-framed house with a white-brick front added in Georgian times.

That is Halstead, but what can we say of the area around? The Colnes and the Hedinghams are covered in separate sections (see the index), so it is the area to the south centred on Stisted that awaits exploration.

Just past the bridge on the A604 east of Halstead stands Bluebridge House—still showing its early-eighteenth-century front in a pattern of blue and red bricks. Opposite it a lane runs down to Greenstead Green and on over the Bourne Brook through Tumblers Green to Stisted. Though much of the church and the Hall in its beautiful grounds date largely from the nineteenth century, the village has many buildings which in their variety indicate its early history and make picturesque subjects for the camera.

If you care to diverge at Tumblers Green you can make your way to the A120 via the tiny village of Pattiswick, which takes its name from the wick or farm of the Pate family, ancient owners of the land around. The small church of St. Mary is of thirteenth- and fourteenth-century construction.

THE HEDINGHAMS, THE MAPLESTEADS AND GESTINGTHORPE

THE A1017 is the continuation of the A131, dead straight almost from Little Waltham through Braintree and on to Gosfield, where the line falters and bends about north to Sible Hedingham. Here we shall stop to look round.

The church of St. Peter is down a side road to the left, a fourteenth-century building with a sixteenth-century tower. Inside, look for the richly decorated tomb-chest in the south aisle, said to immortalize Sir John Hawkwood, who died in 1394, a local tanner's son who rose to high rank in the army of Florence and married the daughter of the Duke of Milan.

In the village look around for the White Horse inn, with 500-year-old timbers on view; Greys Hall, in the eighteenth-century style; and the Hostage, anciently a resting-place for pilgrims to the shrine of St. Edmund (at Bury St. Edmunds). The village street is a testimony to its history; old timbers, plastered fronts, jutting upper stories, Georgian façades and tiny cottage windows all harmonize. The Swan and the Sugar Loaves stand at either end of the village, two old hostelries hospitable yet.

The Colne runs parallel to the road through the village. It must be crossed by the B1058 to get to the sister village of Castle Hedingham, which is deservedly popular with travellers at all seasons of the year. Its name comes from the great castle erected here in the twelfth century by the de Veres, Earls of Oxford, overlords of all the land for miles around. Judge how big it was by what remains, for just the keep is standing now, 110 feet high with walls of flint twelve feet thick. It is on private property, but it can be visited on Tuesdays, Thursdays and Saturdays from May to September from 2 to 6 p.m. on payment of a small fee.

In a humble cottage in the shadow of the castle Edward Bingham produced pottery at the turn of the century which is now sought after by collectors of " Hedingham ware."

The brick bridge across the ancient moat must have seemed a very modern structure when it was built—in Tudor times!

The village itself lies about and below a sharp zigzag in the main road. There are so many nooks and corners where history speaks out, so many vignettes of old village beauty, that adjectives are superfluous and space to describe them is inadequate; so the motto

Shalford, "a place to tour on a sunny day, with ears to appreciate country sounds and eyes to see the story of Essex in lanes and farms."

L/N

Stebbing.
"The group of
interesting old
buildings near the
church."

Stisted flour mill. " The village has many buildings which, in their variety, testify to its early history."

must be " See for yourself." The church is a centre of attraction, standing as it does among trees with interesting houses all about it. Its brick tower was restored to its present condition in 1616; there is an inscribed stone to prove it. Above the west window and the clerestory windows you can see emblems of the de Vere family. " The church, once it is entered," says Nikolaus Pevsner, " reveals itself as one of the most important and, of its period, the most ambitiously designed in Essex."

Sit in a pew for a while and appreciate the mystery, the history and the peace of this ancient place, along with the fifteenth Earl of Oxford, who since 1539 has rested here with his wife beneath a sumptuous black marble monument. Look for the little things, too, like the lovely sixteenth-century woodcarving at the east end of the south aisle representing the Magdalene washing the feet of Christ. Glance upwards and you will see the double-hammerbeam roof constructed in medieval times upon the old Norman columns.

There is a network of country lanes from the two Hedinghams which will take you east to Great Maplestead, where you are well away from civilization of the diesel-fume and dual-carriageway kind. The church stands high, with its squat tower, powerfully built, which has lasted for nearly 1,000 years and seems set to stand for ever. The Norman apse with its three windows is an unusually rare survival. Two lovely monuments are to be seen, charming in their seventeenth-century naïveté, in the stiffly formal postures of the effigies and in the inscription on that to Lady Deane. She was of the family which owned Dynes Hall, a mile to the south, a Tudor mansion in chequered red and blue brick, largely rebuilt in 1690 or thereabouts, which stands in its own beautiful grounds.

From the junction north of the church you can find your way through the hamlet of Lucking Street and east to Little Maplestead, " an ancient straggling village." It is quite famous for its little round church of St. John the Baptist, which is the most recently built (about 1335) and the smallest of only five such churches left in England. It belonged originally to the Knights Hospitallers of St. John and so was based on the design of their headquarters church of the Holy Sepulchre at Jerusalem. The building you see today is the result of a very thorough restoration 100 years ago. Within, however, the font, crudely fashioned in early Norman days, is a direct link with the past.

Edward Bingham learned his art at nearby Gestingthorpe, where his father carried on a garden pottery business, using the local clay. It is a one-street village lining the lane which runs north off the B1058 a couple of miles east of Castle Hedingham—just another Essex village, but with that picturesqueness which is almost common-place in our county.

St. Mary's church has a big brick tower built about 1500 which dwarfs the rest of a building altered and extended ever since its Norman foundation. The nave roof is contemporary with the tower, an unusually fine example of double-hammerbeam timber construc-tion. A brass on the north wall commemorates gallant Captain Oates of Scott's last Antarctic expedition, for he grew up in this village. Over to the east on the other side of Wiggery Wood Roman remains are turning up.

GREAT SAMPFORD

FROM Finchingfield, a model English village, to Saffron Walden, the acme of the sleepy English market town, the landscape along the B1053 might in comparison seem flat, in both meanings of the word, but that is not so. The route is, as the A.A. says, "undulating and winding in parts, through some pleasant rural and woodland scenery and attractive villages."

Little Sampford is the first, but today it is not a village as such, though the church stands as testimony to its existence. Of a number of interesting items to be seen the most curious is the break which can be noticed in the actual building of the church, said to have been caused by the death of all the workmen in the days of the Black Death, that terrible plague. Do-it-yourselfers will see how to make an oak chest out of a single block of wood. It may take them a year or two, but the example seen here has lasted 600 years, so the labour was justified.

The old Hall near the church was demolished, and the unusual house you see built on its site dates from 1936. A number of sites with indications of moats show that there were a good many big houses here in days gone by. One you can still visit is Tewes, one mile south of Great Sampford, a fifteenth-century manor house open to the public on Thursdays and Sundays from March to October.

Great Sampford got its name from a ford here across the River Pant. It is " a village of pretty gabled houses," especially near the church, which is dedicated to St. Michael. This is of the fourteenth century, of great interest if you are architecturally minded, with a bonus in the appealing animal carving on the transept arch. Look out, too, for the schoolmaster's desk and his book cupboard, for they were made in Elizabethan days.

The lime trees in the churchyard are said to have been planted by General Eustace, who fought in the Peninsular War (1808-14). He planned their glory for the eyes of future generations—a thoughtful gesture.

If you feel like a drink there is the Bull inn—but no need to hurry; it has been there since the seventeenth century!

South-west of the village, off the B1051 to Thaxted, lies the hamlet of Tindon End, which tells its own history in its name, altered over the years from St. John's End, denoting the grange here belonging to the Knights of St. John of Jerusalem. The manor was once lived in by Sir James McAdam, called in an old guide book " the Colossus of Roads " a terrible pun which alluded to the famous macadamized road surface.

STEEPLE BUMPSTEAD

UP near the Essex/Suffolk border just off the road from Haverhill to Baythorne Bridge ancient earthworks can be seen by the more persistent observer. They are not obvious or extensive, but at one time they were capped by a building—a kind of steeple, which gave its name to the settlement of Steeple Bumpstead.

The church, as always in our Essex villages, was the real centre of life in medieval times, and remains the centre of interest today. It is a well-proportioned building which owes its outward appearance largely to a big restoration in 1880.

Inside you will see a genuine " poor box," iron bound and on a long, panelled stem, which has been in use for at least 450 years. A leper's window still exists, where the poor outlawed victim of that dread disease might stand to look in on the services. Of the number of fine monuments the most touching is that to Sir Henry Bendyshe, last of a local line of baronets, who died in 1717, for it not only shows him life-size in elegant posture but also includes his dead son Henry as a tiny baby at his side. There is also a tablet here to brave Nurse Cavell, shot by the Germans in 1915, for she was nursery governess at the vicarage in her younger days.

The village spreads round a rectangle of roads with the church and a number of old houses on the southern side. At its eastern extremity, where the signpost shows three ways, to Hempstead, to Finchingfield and to Haverhill, there stands the pride of the place, the old moot hall, built in 1592, perhaps to replace an earlier building, for the moot brings echoes of the old Saxon gatherings to discuss matters affecting the community, and this would have been a good spot for such a gathering.

Records of the hall are lost, but it was early used as a school. The oak timbers, the overhanging upper story and the great chimney give the photographer plenty of scope; in fact it is a miniature edition of the famous guildhall at Thaxted and is sometimes called the guildhall in the village.

Bower Hall is the local " place," though all the bigger houses round about are overshadowed by Moyns Park, on the Birdbrook side, first built in the early sixteenth century with the main block in the later Elizabethan style, and lived in by the Gent family through nearly 400 years.

If Steeple Bumpstead is taken as the centre of a clock Sturmer will be found at one o'clock, right on the Suffolk border. Its name originally signified a mere on the River Stour, which runs on the eastern boundary, offering scenery—and peace. The Hall is way off the main road, a moated homestead now demoted, as it were, to farmhouse status.

Birdbrook stands at three o'clock, down a side road off the B1054, " as delightful a village as one could find in many a long day " says the rural district guide—enough said! At six o'clock the B1057 runs on down through pleasant country to Finchingfield, while farther round our imaginary clock, at about eight o'clock, lies Hempstead.

This is a place to stir the imagination and quicken the blood. Dick Turpin is said to have been born here in 1705, and his exploits as a highwayman, associated often with the Crown inn here, are largely imaginary in the form in which they are presented today. A ring of trees, said to mark an old ring for cockfights, is named after him. As for quickening the blood, William Harvey, the celebrated physician (died 1657) who discovered the circulation of the blood, lived here late in life and is buried under a handsome monument in the north or Harvey chapel of St. Andrew's. The church fell down in 1882, smashing its five bells and turning the place into a ruin, and was finally rebuilt only in very recent times.

Round again to nine o'clock we can see Helions Bumpstead, bordering Suffolk and Cambridgeshire. Take any side road south of Haverhill and you must arrive here. It ranges from Pale Green to Wiggens Green, and the three names cover a mile of English farming countryside at its best. Three big houses in the area are Bumpstead Hall, Horseham Hall, on a moated site, and Helions, named after an ancient family, which is said to be the site of the house of Tihil the Breton, first Norman lord of the lands around Haverhill. The church has old features, though the tower dates only from 1812.

FROM TOPPESFIELD to the border

USING the A604 as our springboard we can plunge down a number of those side roads so typical of Essex which wind around to Toppesfield, Great and Little Yeldham, Tilbury-juxta-Clare, Ovington, Stambourne, Ridgewell and Ashen. If we go north through the Hedinghams our first turn will be just past the White Hart at Great Yeldham, where the lane runs left over the old railway and passes Potters Hall and Toppesfield Hall, a much-altered seventeenth-century building, to arrive at a T junction. The northern branch reaches into the centre of Toppesfield.

The church, in red brick, dates from the fourteenth century, but its tower was renewed in 1699, and the builder's name, Daniel Hill, is inscribed, with other names significant at the rebuilding, on its western wall. South-east, past Cust Hall (fifteenth century, with an original chimney still standing) and Gainsford End, you can see Gainsford Hall and the old tower mill, now, sadly, falling down. To the north the road through Grass Green is a back way to Stambourne.

Back on the A604 the road gathers part of Great Yeldham to its verges, though much of the village lines the lane to Little Yeldham. Three tributaries wander under main and side roads to form the Colne just down the road. One runs at the back of Hall and church to feed an old defensive moat.

The church has an unusual feature. The tower was started on the grand scale in the fourteenth century, but for reasons now unknown was discontinued and in the next century a less ambitious erection was completed, the old tower becoming the two-story porch we see today. The old rectory, built at the same time as the tower, still shows its ancient timbers, and the White Hart Hotel, standing south of the village, dates from 1500. It now has a reputation beyond the county for the quality of its meals, for it is a very popular road-house, made all the more attractive by the preservation of old beams in its interior.

Little Yeldham lies to the north-east about the head of a T junction. The church has an interesting wooden belfry made in the 1400s. The lanes north and south take you by the narrowest ways to the Belchamps and Gestingthorpe respectively, with gentle contours and fair fields all around.

From Great Yeldham, too, a side road runs past Spencer Grange, a mid-eighteenth-century house refronted in the classical style with a columned porch of late Georgian days. Round a horseshoe bend the houses of Tilbury-juxta-Clare come into view—not to be confused with the Thames Tilbury! "The Court and the Hall are both good residences " says an eighty-year-old guide—and they still are. The church, like the Hall, is very isolated off the left-hand fork of the road out of the village. The trees stand about it like a sparse congregation. The brick tower is a century older than the nave and chancel, which were put up in the fifteenth century. Inside there are some interesting fragments of contemporary murals.

The narrow road goes north to Ovington, with its tiny thirteenth-century church, in pastoral surroundings as quiet as they are unspoilt where the Hall is its only companion.

The next side road along the A604 goes left under the railway bridge and on to Stambourne, a growing residential area on the Dyers End side but still showing a good old pub opposite a somewhat stark-looking church with a massive tower of Norman build. In the east window you will see a stained-glass memorial to the Macwilliams, who were responsible for much of the rebuilding of the rest of the church in the sixteenth century. Past the church one or two old thatched cottages enliven a scene of intensive agriculture. Turn right at the T junction and you will go back via Wesly End and Essex Hall to the main road—bang in the middle of Ridgewell.

Here the houses reflect a hundred and one styles of building through the ages as they gather informally among the chestnuts and limes around the village green and its white memorial cross, all overlooked by the battlemented tower of its fifteenth-century church down the lane by the Hall. On the one-inch map you can mark the site of a Roman villa south of the village, built in the days when the Colchester—Cambridge Roman road marched unhesitatingly across country.

From Ridgewell it is but a step to the north up a winding lane to Ashen on the sharply rising bank of the Stour, looking across to Stoke-by-Clare and Suffolk. Nothing of great import here—just a quiet village, a church with an old brick tower and a great peace which makes it hard to believe there was an airfield here in World War II.

TWINSTEAD and half a dozen villages round the A131

LET us leave the A131 some four miles north of Halstead and turn right towards the agricultural freshness of the countryside around Twinstead and its neighbour of Twinstead Green. The lane with its sharp right- and left-hand turn reaches Twinstead Green first and passes the few houses there on its way to the larger hamlet. This is a quiet lane where those with the time can stop and listen to the songs of birds and watch the ever-changing pattern of the clouds as they move over the nearby wooded hillside.

Twinstead is approached by passing several seventeenth-century timber-framed houses before the centre of the hamlet is reached. The church of St. John marks the middle of the place, and although it contains brasses of the Wyncott family dating from 1610 it was rebuilt in 1860 of red brick. Opposite the church is a belt of green and the site of the old moated Elizabethan Hall. Behind the church and the cottages stands an orchard that encircles the northern half of the hamlet.

We are now following the lane on towards the two Hennys, Great and Little—and a real English country lane it is, with sharp bends (keep left) and a rise and fall that would do justice to the Roman empire. But how good it is as you cross the small stream and look round the skyline to think that so close to London such wide-open spaces still exist. The Hennys are tiny places and stand along a hilltop, the restored thirteenth-century church of St. Mary at Great Henny being right at the summit. Nearby there are many old cottages with thatched roofs and plastered walls to delight the eye. Little Henny has long since lost its church and most of its inhabitants, but there are still the grounds of the Ryes, which was built in 1820.

Going back down the hill we turn left and pass the mill on the Stour at Henny Street before again going left and up to Middleton. The houses and cottages stand along the loop of the lane that leads to the interesting church of All Saints. Just before the church notice the thatched cottage that is 200 years old and still in good condition. All Saints' church stands in a pleasant spot, with trees in a circle at the back while the entrance is protected by an old porch which fits perfectly with the great door of the church. The wooden bell-turret is much later than the rest of the building, but blends in well. Within the church is a seven-foot Purbeck marble floor slab of James Samson, one-time rector of the church, that dates from the mid-fourteenth century. On leaving the village look out on the left for Middleton Hall and its homestead moat.

Along this lane we cross the county boundary into Suffolk, cross the A131 via the village of Ballingdon with its windmill, and turn back into Essex again to reach Bulmer. The countryside here is more open than the type we have seen previously on this tour, and to the north the fields gradually run down to meet the Belchamp Brook, which feeds the larger River Stour. The village has grown round the crossroads and is now the home of about 500 people. Ahead of us the lane follows a most attractive route to Gestingthorpe, but we turn left to follow another pleasant route past the church of St. Andrew on the right and the large estates and mansion of the Auberies on the left. St. Andrew's is of interest mainly for its octagonal font, which is 500 years old and in excellent condition. All about the church are fine old houses and cottages, some with thatch, some with timber framing, and many with their original chimney-stacks dating back several hundred years.

The lane wends its way to Bulmer Tye, which is on the edge of the A131; at the end of this hamlet we join the B1058 and run down the hill past the orchards and turn left to visit the last village in this chapter, Wickham St. Paul. The St. Paul part of its name dates from the tenth century, when it belonged to the dean of St. Paul's. We reach the church of All Saints well before the main village, and its most interesting feature is the ivy-covered red-brick tower which was built in 1505 from £20 left in a will. Even older than the tower is the iron-bound chest that was made in the thirteenth century.

Most of the houses lie round the small village green, and many of them are of historic interest They date mostly from the seventeenth century and are timber-framed, but the wood is covered by plaster. As we leave to complete our tour by joining the A131 at the point we started from, take a last look round and remember that some of these old houses were being built at the time Shakespeare was playing to his first audiences.

SECTION FIVE

KING COLE'S COUNTRY

KING COLE'S COUNTRY

BIRCH and the Layer villages

THIS, the first chapter in our eastern section, must be the place to explain the reason for our choice of " King Cole's country " as the section's heading. " Old King Cole was a merry old soul " we are told, perhaps because he found life in Essex so congenial. As far as our researches took us it appears that Coel was the governor, under Roman overlords, of all the district around Colchester. Differences between the tribes and the Roman occupying forces reached the point at which Coel sided with his people in a revolt against the Romans in A.D. 260. Colchester (named after Coel) was besieged by Roman general Constantinus at the head of a great army; but peace was concluded in the most satisfactory way because the general fell in love with Coel's daughter and married her. Their son, Constantine, born in 265 at Colchester, eventually became emperor.

Birch and the Layer villages conveniently occupy an oblong of which the top edge is the Roman River as it circles round Colchester and the longer sides are represented by the B1022 and the B1026, with the bottom edge aligning with the Layer Brook as it runs into the Abberton reservoir.

Let us move out from Colchester on the B1022. The first turning on the left after we cross the river by the hamlet of Heckfordbridge takes us straight to Birch, dipping down the hill and rising again by the church, which was built of flint in 1850 at the expense of the Round family, who then lived in the Hall. The spire is 110 feet high, with a clock that was added to celebrate Victoria's jubilee.

In the days when Birch was divided into Great and Little the church of the latter parish stood in the grounds of the Hall. Now it lies in ruins and the Hall itself has been demolished.

Demolished too is the clapboard post mill which the one-inch map shows at Birch Green to the south. But a moat can hardly be demolished, so it remains, south of the village opposite the inn, to signify Saxon settlement.

Birch Green almost merges with Layer Breton farther to the south, a village which combines old and new, with a name derived from the fourteenth-century local landowner Nicholas de Breton.

One of the oldest buildings, the church, was destroyed by the great Essex earthquake of 1884 and has since been rebuilt. From the centre of this small village there is a choice of ways. Let us take the road west, drive round the twisting, tiny lane to the crossroads and run south. Then we shall be in Layer Marney—again reflecting in its name the local family of repute. The great feature of this very scattered village is owed to a late scion of this line, Sir Henry Marney, keeper of the privy seal under Henry VIII.

Somewhere about the first decade of the sixteenth century he started the builders on a house suited to his exalted rank. The great gatehouse rose slowly to be a four-towered affair eight stories high in Tudor brick, with terra-cotta mullions and other features in the height of fashion. It dominated the countryside—and that was as far as it got. Sir Henry died in 1523 and his son, last of the line, in 1525. Judging from the size of the gatehouse, the splendour of the house-to-be is almost beyond imagination. Today the building still stands, dwarfing the Hall and the church which stand beside it among the trees.

The church (St. Mary the Virgin) is of typical build in our county in Tudor times, using red brick with the occasional blue to form a pattern. There are lots of architectural details inside to be enjoyed by the expert, but to people like us it is the monuments that are so astounding. They were in the older church on the site. Sir William Marney, who died in 1414, and later members of his family are represented by effigies, splendidly attired, lying on decorated tomb-chests under beautifully wrought canopies.

From this lovely spot there is no forward way; we must retreat to Layer Breton and take the road to the south past the Hall and on across the Abberton reservoir, which is fed by the Layer Brook. The reservoir is dealt with under our section "Fingringhoe to Wigborough"; let us just say that it is a lovely sight at all times of the year. We get the opportunity of seeing it again by turning left when we meet the B1026 and going north where the Hall and church of Layer-de-la-Haye stand on either side of the road. The church is largely of the fourteenth century, with an interesting wooden south porch and a couple of monuments which date back to 1500.

Past the Hall, as we approach the crossroad centre of the village we see on the left the very neat grounds and buildings where the reservoir water is treated. The village itself spreads quite attractively down the road east to Maltings Green—a reminder of the village breweries of earlier days—and gives a very doubtful access east of the church, as the crow flies, to Blind Knights, which is said to have come by its name from its use as a hospital for returning crusaders. From the village centre it is a straight run back to Colchester on the B1026.

CLACTON, St. Osyth and the villages round about

ANYONE can find Clacton-on-Sea, for it is signposted from every corner of the county, but how many of its visitors spare the time to wonder what pleasures lie along the route? In this chapter let us show you what to expect not only from Clacton but also from its near neighbours, starting with Weeley, some eight miles north on the A133.

Situated at the junction of the B1033 and the A133, Weeley is a village of growing population and is the administrative centre for the Tendring rural district. The old cottages and farms of this Saxon settlement are being added to almost daily as more people come to live near the coast. From the memorial cross in the main part of the village it is nearly a mile along country lanes to the local church of St. Andrew. It stands on a carpet of fields, with the ruined Weeley Hall as a companion, as it has done for the last 400 years. The red bricks of its embattled tower are unmoved by the restoration of 1881 that changed most of the body of the church. Look round by the ponds for the fine thatched and weatherboarded barn; it has lasted from the fifteenth century and has a king-post roof.

A short distance south and we arrive at Little Clacton, which lines the main road. Its village green, overlooked by the turret of the fifteenth-century church of St. James, stands near the bend in the road. While the plastered church has little to offer, a closer look at that wooden turret is called for; it is supported by four posts with tie-beams and curved braces. Nearby is the Blacksmith's Arms, which has been dispensing drinks to thirsty travellers for 150 years.

We are almost within smell of the sea, but let us linger a moment longer to savour the ancient mother village, Great Clacton. Its noisy child, Clacton-on-Sea, is only just down the road, but you will find nothing there as old as the church and cottages of this village. Saxons left their graves here, and Normans used the Romans' tiles in the construction of the church of St. John the Baptist. A restoration in 1865 rather spoilt the east front, but the tall, plentiful proportions of the chancel and the traces of vaulting in the nave tell the story of its Norman origin. A tablet in the church records that Eleazor, son of the famous John Knox, was vicar here in the late sixteenth century.

Walking away from the church down the avenue of limes we enter the village street, and it is as attractive as the church. Among the places to see are the Georgian Mansion House, the bow-windowed Queen's Head, the sixteenth-century timbered Ship inn, and the many attractive cottages in between.

At last! The road runs down towards the sea and ahead is the pier, stretching across the sand and sea for over 1,000 feet. At Clacton there is much to entertain the visitor—several live shows (including one on the pier), cinemas, bingo, the slot-machines, all can be had for the asking. For most it is the sea and sand that call strongest of all, and Clacton has an almost unlimited supply of both. From the caravan sites at Jaywick in the west to the residential Holland-on-Sea in the east stretch an unbroken five miles of sand and safe bathing. Behind the beach runs the modern coastal highway, with its borders of promenades, gardens and lawns. Trees and flowers are everywhere, and after dark they and the lamp standards twinkle with hundreds of coloured lights. If you need any further convincing of the pleasures of Clacton remember that the holiday king, Billy Butlin, has sited one of his camps here—a sure sign that a holiday resort has reached the top. In the grounds of Butlin's camp, and at other points along the coast, can be seen the only pieces of architecture to break the almost completely Victorian scene. These are the famous martello towers, which, built of brick in 1810-2 by the Royal Engineers, were designed to repel any attack by Napoleon. The unusual name comes from the island of Corsica, where at Torre della Mortella the British Army saw similar things in use in 1794.

Of course, there is a full programme of sport during the season. You can choose from county cricket, sailing regattas, golf, bowls, fishing and swimming, and if you are young and beautiful the annual beauty queen competition may tempt you.

While you are enjoying that ice-cream and sitting in the sun perhaps you can spare a moment to think of the journey home. To the east, past Holland-on-Sea and up the B1032 lies Great Holland, while in the west is the not-to-be-missed village of St. Osyth. The choice is yours, so let us first take you east through Holland-on-Sea

(Little Holland), with its hinterland of marsh where many types of wildfowl can be seen, and past the ruin of its old church on the edge of the sea.

Once this church stood a mile inland, but the cruel sea bites ever deeper into our shore, and gradually it has reached this church. Nearby you will see the sea walls and embankments that have been built to keep the sea back from the land.

Round the corner of the road we reach Great Holland, a tiny village clustered round a rise in the land and overlooking the sea that strains to eat it up. The charming cottages and inn are set between pine trees, and these in their turn provide shelter for many rooks. All Saints' church was built in the Early English style in 1866, but it has little of the promise of the huge tower that remains from a sixteenth-century construction.

To the west of Clacton, along the B1027, lies the village of St. Osyth. This is an old-world place that spills down a gentle hillside to finish on the edge of a pleasant creek. The creek is alive with boats and wild birds, and nearby in the old mill pond you can enjoy pleasure boats and even water ski-ing. For refreshment you can get a snack inside a martello tower, for here at St. Osyth one has been converted into a cafe.

Just off the road to the beach lies St. Clair's Hall, on a moated site. This is privately owned, but if it is open to the public when you are there you can see a most rare aisled hall dating from the fourteenth century.

Above all St. Osyth is renowned for its priory, but before we tell the story of this a word about the church of St. Peter and St. Paul that stands nearby. Most of the building is either Norman or Tudor, and the glory of the place lies in the brick piers and arches that line the length of the church. The unusual horseshoe communion rail is a stone copy of the original.

So to St. Osyth's priory and its story of faith and blood. There are various legends about the young daughter of Frithenwald, the first Christian king of the East Angles, and the following is the most generally accepted one. Osyth was so taken by the new Christian faith that she decided to devote her life to it. Her parents, however, arranged her marriage to Sighere, the son of the neighbouring king of Essex. Although the marriage took place, it was obvious that Osyth was an unwilling partner and so Sighere gave her the village of Chich and allowed her to found a nunnery there. The village was renamed Osyth, and everything went well until 653, when a raiding party of Danes attacked the area, burned the nunnery and captured Osyth. When she refused to bow before their gods the Danes cut off her head. She is then reputed to have carried her head to the church, where her remains rested. Later she was canonized and so the village is now called St. Osyth.

The priory today is a mixture of the original Norman—the Normans having used many Roman bricks—and the later fifteenth-century building. While the Norman part is in ruins the magnificent gatehouse and abbot's tower are to be seen in all their glory. The battlements and slender chimneys stand out against the skyline. From May to September the spacious grounds are open to the public at a small charge; this also often applies at Easter weekend.

Let us end this chapter with a word about witches. In St. Osyth for many years lay the bones of a reputed witch who put a curse on anyone who tried to move them; so they remained, with everyone afraid of the curse, until recent years, when they were removed to Cornwall to take pride of place in a museum. We have not heard if the curse was effective.

COLCHESTER

LIKE a spider, Colchester sits at the centre of a web of lines of communication. It is fifty-one miles from London, twenty-one from Harwich, eighteen from Ipswich and equally accessible from most directions of the compass. The favour of its situation was first found by the ancient British tribes, and Roman, Danish, Saxon and French invaders followed in their tracks.

The name comes from the Saxon for a fortress on the river Colne, or maybe from the " Colonia fortress," harking back to the settlement here of Roman veteran soldiers as a colony from A.D. 50 onwards. The Romans made for Colchester when they landed because it was the capital of the kingdoms of south-east Britain. It was then called Camulodunum, after the Celtic war god Camulos, and it had already been a going concern for 500 years. Cunobelin (Shakespeare's Cymbeline) was ruling at the time, and some experts think it is his burial mound in Lexden Park which has yielded up the rich and ancient relics now to be seen in the museum.

It is in the castle museum that the image of Roman Colchester can best be recreated, and as we write this the museum is visibly improving in the arrangement and display of its outstanding collection of pre-Roman and Roman antiquities. There is a useful guide which not only explains the many interesting collections but also outlines the history of the building which is the keep, the only remaining part of Colchester castle, a great Norman fortification. This keep outshines the Tower of London in its magnitude, and was probably planned by the same architect. It has had a chequered career of attack and neglect which only a building of its vast bulk could survive. Today a sturdy tree grows on its topmost wall, its branches waving like the banners of an earlier age.

While in this neighbourhood the associated museums of Holly Trees, showing a collection of later antiquities, and the natural history museum in the former All Saints' church are very much worth a visit.

The Normans built their castle on the remains of a Roman temple raised to honour the victories of Claudius, and the main streets of the town still follow the Roman plan, except in one interesting instance. The High Street once used to continue through the west wall of the town by the Balkerne gate, but the word " balkerne " means " stopped up " or " barred," and we gather that in Saxon times this gate was blanked off in a renewing of the old Roman fortifications against the fierce attacks of the Danish sailor-raiders.

The increase of traffic in this thriving town even before the motor age doomed all the other gates in the old town walls to demolition, so it was a stroke of fortune that closed the gate in Saxon times and so preserved it for twentieth-century eyes. Without exaggeration it is one of the most remarkable Roman buildings in this country. It had two towers, which guarded a two-lane road for traffic and two paths for pedestrians. Today a public-house is built on the remains of one tower and straddles the roadway, but part of the south tower and a pedestrian way still stand clear to testify to the structural skill of the Romans.

To see Colchester, to appreciate its antiquities, its architecture and its odd corners, requires a walk rather than a motor tour. One-way streets have reduced congestion, but the traffic flows too fast to loiter over the view from a car; on the other hand there are a number of car parks handy to the town centre, all well signposted.

In our limited space only a few points of interest can be named, but there are excellent fuller guides available in local bookshops and at the museum.

See Colchester at its most picturesque just off the High Street in the shadow of the Town Hall, built in the opulent style of 1902. In Stockwell Street and around St. Martin's church houses of all periods stand in interesting groups, many as the result of loving and painstaking restoration. On towards the east you can wander to the museums and the park which stretches clear across to the river. Past the museums in East Hill you will come to the Minories, a late-Georgian house with a wing 200 years older. It is a private art gallery above rooms of Georgian furniture, pictures (including some of Constable's early work), china and silver, together with a loan collection of Colchester-made clocks.

The latest information is that it is open free on Saturdays and at a shilling on other days, closing on Thursdays and Sundays.

Down East Hill can be seen some pleasantly half-timbered houses and across the river East Street still shows many of the old houses erected in medieval days when this " new suburb " was being developed. Here the Siege House stands, a late-fifteenth-century building, much restored, which still bears the bullet marks that it collected during the siege of the Royalists in 1648.

Back opposite the castle Queen Street runs in dog-leg fashion. Here for time out of mind the St. Denys fair was held, an eight-day celebration which later marked the opening of the oyster fishery, now performed on October 20 every year. This opening celebration goes back to the time of Richard I, who vested the Colne oyster fishery in the townspeople. The Oyster Feast, provided as the culmination of the oyster festival, is one of the few great eighteenth-century civic banquets still surviving. Though gormandizing is not on such a grandiose scale today it is an affair to which 300 and more top people, including royalty, are invited.

There is an official opening of the oyster season apart from these junketings. Off the coast near Brightlingsea an ancient proclamation is read by the town clerk and it is gin and gingerbread all round for the participants.

Farther down Queen Street, along roads at the end like Priory Street and Vineyard Street, considerable portions of the old Roman wall can be seen.

Magdalen Street is long and straight, probably a Roman way, along which Colchester's earliest suburb developed. It connects with Military Road and Barrack Street, reminders of the big military build-up here during the Napoleonic scare and of the garrison still maintained here today, and it runs on to the Hythe.

This, an old English word for " haven," may have been the town's port in Roman times. In sailing days it had a certain prosperity, but road and rail have caused a recess in the coastal trade. However, there is always something of interest to be seen by those who love the sight and sound and smell of ships and things. The quay harks back to its Victorian heyday, but the houses round the church are much older.

All around Colchester history speaks out to those prepared to listen. It took the Royal Commission on Historical Monuments more than fifty close-packed pages to do justice to the town, without even touching upon its modern amenities, so let us leave while we have pages left for other places, apologizing in advance to our critics for the omissions we must make.

There are two places along the A12 which are more or less associated with Colchester: Copford and Stanway.

" The most remarkable Norman parish church in the county " is Nikolaus Pevsner's comment on Copford. There are a number of architectural technicalities to support this statement, but the reason most evident to the sightseer is the medieval wall-paintings. These paintings were done when the church was built half-way through the twelfth century. The key figure is that of Christ seated in glory with angels about him and the apostles below them, between the windows. On the inner face of the chancel arch the signs of the zodiac are very vigorously represented.

The church is in the park of Copford Hall, a pleasing Georgian house, and the two buildings together with the old stables, all standing amid lawn and trees, make a picture worth lingering over. This rather isolated group is near the site of a Roman building which was robbed in the past to provide building material for the church.

Copford Green is half a mile to the west, but much of Copford today lies along the ancient Stane Street, where the traffic queue is often slow enough for the motorist to appreciate a number of attractive buildings.

Stanway is nearer Colchester and shows signs of urban sprawl. Its name comes directly from the street it straddles, the stone-way, or paved Roman road, from Colchester to Bishop's Stortford. A couple of miles to the south-east stands the old church of All Saints, a picturesque ruin, partly demolished in the days of Cromwell. It is in the grounds of Stanway Hall, a Tudor country seat now transformed, with the fields round about, into a very well-patronized zoo. From the B1022 a glimpse can be had of some of the animals, looking very much at home in their rural surroundings.

DEDHAM and district—Constable country

SO near is Dedham to the county border that almost every Essex visitor will have to go north to see it. Let us pick up the route in Colchester and follow the A137 to Ardleigh and thence the B1029 north to Dedham.

Ardleigh is the hub of four spokes formed by the crossroads; it is therefore rather split by the flow of traffic, but that is not new— even eighty years ago an old guide was saying " Johnny Boy's Hill, on the Colchester road, is very loose, and dangerous for bicyclists." The modern map name is John de Bois, after whom the bridge over the brook is named.

Farther on at the crossroads there is plenty of attractive architecture to be enjoyed, with St. Mary's the dominant feature, built of ragstone quarried locally, supplemented with brick and flint decoration typical of East Anglia and topped with a fine pinnacled, battlemented tower. This, like the south porch, is early sixteenth-century, though the rest of the building was largely restored with Victorian enthusiasm. Settlement here in Bronze Age times and subsequent Roman occupation has been revealed through aerial photography, and Belgic and Roman remains turn up frequently in an area to the south of the church.

That old guide tells us " Dedham is a small, quaint, decayed town." This is not true today; the wide street with the church on one hand and the inn on the other is cluttered with a new flow—of cars carrying sightseers bent on viewing what another expert, Pevsner, calls " easily the most attractive small town in Essex." It would be hard to differ with this opinion after a stroll down the one main street. Solid houses of timber framing, little cottages of lath and plaster, Georgian fronts and modern imitations—all give a lively and interesting variety to the street scene.

The battlemented·church tower, rising 130 feet from the trees in this pleasant valley of the Stour, inspired Constable in numerous paintings. It was built about 1500, chiefly by the Webbe family, wealthy wool merchants who left their marks and initials on the ground floor of the tower and their monument in the body of the church. The affluence of the wool industry at this time and place produced, through the piety of a number of merchants, a church in rich Perpendicular style. Of much to notice here we might mention the font. It looks very defaced, but that is not surprising, since it was recovered from beneath the floor of the nave in 1862! Its cover is made of oak from timbers of the old *Royal George*.

From the church the B1029 goes north out of a little square around the memorial cross, down to the banks of the sweet Stour. Here stand the mill and the seventeenth-century mill house by that famous Dedham lock known round the world through the beauty of the view as expressed by the brush of our best-known landscape painter, John Constable. He must have walked these lanes and fields oft-times around the 1820s to reflect so faithfully the scenes and moods of this beautiful area of Essex countryside.

Farther east along the main street, past the century-old steepled Congregational church, the road bends south and will eventually take one all the way back, over Dedham Heath, to the main road just north of Ardleigh. Go this way and you will come across Castle House, three-quarters of a mile down the road. This was the home of a famous painter of our own age, Sir Alfred Munnings, whose widow keeps his studio as it was in his lifetime. It is open on Sunday afternoons through the summer, when you can see some of his finest paintings of horses and racing topics.

If you go in the other direction from Dedham to the west it is not possible to stay on the banks of the Stour, but there is a lane which runs west by Lower Park to meet the river and the A12 where the new bypass round Stratford St. Mary (just over the border) cuts through the vale. Turn left and climb Gun Hill and you will soon see a signpost pointing you down a right turn to Langham. It is a pretty road, already fairly high above the river valley, which runs smoothly past fields and orchards to the village; but keep a watchful eye some way before that to spot the little driveway running north to church and Hall.

St. Mary's nave has indications of Norman origin; the tower is only 600 years old! Look in the porch for the very charming " Dumb animals humble petition." Done in cast-iron about 100 years ago, it exhorts drivers to think of their horses and give them a rest up the steep hill. This may well indicate the Gun Hill we have just climbed, and it could be that the notice was originally fixed to a horse-trough on the roadside. Church Farm nearby is a 300-year-old timber-framed building. It is featured in Constable's painting "The Glebe Farm and Langham church." From this spot, too, he took the view for another famous work, "The Vale of Dedham." Just a little farther off you can see the Hall, rebuilt in the middle of the eighteenth century.

Farther on round Whalebone Corner stands the village itself, with the back road running over the Black Brook past Blacksmith's Corner to Langham Moor, through farmland interspersed with little groves of trees. But let us go from the village centre up the lanes reaching step-like north-west so that we pass by Valley House, a great example of an Elizabethan timber-framed, plastered house, with decorative chimney shafts rising against the green backdrop of the woods, and come down past Rivers Hall to Boxted Cross and the residential development creeping out from Colchester.

Old Boxted lies farther to the north-west through orchard country, preserving its identity as a cluster of cottages around the T junction giving access to the church of St. Peter, from the tower of which the Stour can be seen meandering through the wooded vale, while the eye can follow the line of the road as it runs on north-east to a bridge over the river giving access to Suffolk. This tower is largely made of puddingstone, a natural mixture of pebble and rock which looks strangely like a modern concrete aggregate. The church was founded in Norman days, but has had to be much repaired. Its best-known monument is to Sir Richard Blackmore, "physician-in-ordinary" to William III and Queen Anne, who died in 1729.

From the church go down to the junction and turn right. Just up the next turning on the right is Boxted Hall, a 300-year-old dwelling on an earlier site. Keep going west along this road, which runs along above the river with many a pleasant view, and you will find it joins the A134 near the border. Turn south and you will find an interesting run through the Horkesley villages back to Colchester.

ELMSTEAD and around

OLD King Cole knew a nice place when he saw it, and still today there are endless interesting routes to take around his capital. Let us try a trip out to Elmstead and come right back to it in a wide circle through Frating, the Bentleys and the Bromleys.

The A133 is a very busy road and Elmstead is the first imposition of the thirty-mile limit, but it is worth slowing up to appreciate the old houses—clapboard and thatch, tile and plaster. There are two inns here, the one on the left with the unusual sign of the Bowling Green.

Some people say that Elmstead Market, as this part of the village is called, harks back to the days of the plague, when traders had to keep their distance from the village for fear that they carried the dreaded disease. It is a fact that old Elmstead lies a mile away down Church Lane, where the church marked its centre, now a remote and peaceful place in the heart of farmland.

From the north you can read the history of the church, from the Norman door re-using Roman bricks and the late-thirteenth-century windows on to details of the fourteenth and fifteenth centuries. Old stained glass from the east window has been refitted in the chancel and south chapel. There is a wonderful monument to be enjoyed—the wooden effigy of a knight, now more than half a century old, which still holds the onlooker with its simple reverence. There are other details of devotion, like the charming little brass of about 1500 showing two hands holding a heart. Strangest of all, though, is the iron cross, early nineteenth century, which is said to have started life as a hat-rack! The Hall has had additions over the years, but it dates its timber and plaster work from the sixteenth century.

From Elmstead Market the A133 runs south-east over the Tenpenny Brook, where a signpost invites us south down a side lane to Frating, which, like Elmstead, now consists only of the church, a nineteenth-century restoration with some old features retained, and the Hall, dating from the 1500s.

To find the present centre of population journey on down the lane past the orchard round Hockley Place to the junction with the B1029, then go north, and there is Frating Green, all around the junction with the A133. Iron Age people settled here and grew their crops on soil which is just as hospitable today to grain and fruit and market gardens. Old thatch and clapboard cottages harmonize with later building. The King's Arms is a charming little place; its dormer windows, nestling in the old tiled roof, seem hardly high enough to qualify as a second story.

The road runs on through big fields under wide skies to our next diversion, a lane on the right-hand side going south to Great Bentley. This is a scattered village for an unusual reason—it has the largest clear village green in England, covering forty-two acres. That is a lot of green, and who better to vouch for it than the vicar, who has to cross it every day from the vicarage to the church, which stands behind the village inn.

The church still has Norman work in nave and chancel; its embattled tower rises up among the trees, keeping watch over the cottages all round. It must have seen the smugglers stealthily approach by night to hide their contraband in the old hollow tree, for Great Bentley has a reputation as the inland depot for the " gentlemen " who operated up the Brightlingsea creeks. Something less pleasant and more factual is the plaque on the green near the cricket pavilion which records the burning at the stake of Rose Allin, a martyr to her faith.

From here go north past moated Parsonage Farm and turn right at the A133. Then the next turn on the left goes north to the sister village of Little Bentley, just three miles away. It is the church that first comes into view—a few trees about it, and beyond it the well-tilled fields. Stop for a moment, enjoy the welcoming peace it offers in the cheerfulness of its white paint and the simplicity of its furnishings. The domed, nail-studded chest just inside the door is 500 years old, but the big feature of the thirteenth-century building is the rood loft and the stairway leading to it. So many have been destroyed by misplaced religious zeal that it is a rare survival. Sit in one of the eighteenth-century pews with delightfully carved ends and let your eye and spirit rise to the ancient timber hammerbeam roof.

In the churchyard stands the old schoolhouse, altered now and doing duty as the village hall. Just down the road on the other side is a pretty little eight-sided lodge with a thatch hat, at the entrance to the considerable park and woodland of the Hall. Farther on up the road Little Bentley gathers its houses round the crossroads, in a pleasant setting.

The north road leads deeper into rich farmland, past the Fox and Hounds with its bay windows jutting almost into the road and on to Little Bromley, a pretty village in flat open country. Its pride is its church, almost a mile south-west; its old brick tower and its massive buttresses to the nave giving it the air of a great, proud ship of Christianity riding the flat, wide acres. It has been riding them since the Normans built the nave, but the chancel and the tower are renovations in the following 500 years.

From here it is easy to follow the signposts south to Great Bromley—and a beautiful surprise. The road bends round past a little bit of woodland and suddenly there is a whole view of St. George's church, standing on its mound, clear against the sky, grey with flint and stone, and battlemented all about. It is a wonderful example of the East Anglian Perpendicular style, kept in very good condition over 600 years. Inside there is a lovely brass of 1423 under its own pinnacled canopy, while the roof of the nave itself is of classic double-hammerbeam construction.

The village lining the junction with the B1029 lives up to the church. Look out for the blue and white paint of the old thatched-roofed post office, offset by the pink-washed walls of the Spread Eagle farther south. Go on in this direction and you come past the grounds of Hamilton Lodge to the junction with the A604. Here on the corner lingers the last remnant of the village—the Black Boy, with its jolly sign. On the A604 go west and Elmstead Market comes into view to make our circle complete.

FINGRINGHOE to WIGBOROUGH and the earthquake country

IN 1884 an earthquake fractured the sea bed just off the coast of Mersea Island. The vibrations were felt all over the county, but nowhere more than in this arc of villages covering the coastal margin round the island. Practically every parish in the present chapter has the year 1884 in its records—usually followed by a rebuilding of the church in the following years. The same fate was visited upon many private dwellings and pubs and inns, some of which were never to rise again.

This chapter falls rather neatly into two parts: one centred on Fingringhoe in the east and the B1025, and the other on Wigborough in the west with the B1026 as a focal point. Let us start, then, over in the east in the parish of East Donyland, which lies on the B1025 just outside Colchester. The village of this parish is Rowhedge, and to reach it we leave the B1025 and go left down the lane that runs across the hillside towards the River Colne. Away to the right, down the gentle slope, we can see the variegated greens of a patch of trees guarding the Roman River that flows to join the Colne just south of Rowhedge. Perhaps the best part of this village is the quay, with its boatyards, old houses, and view through the masts of many small ships to the town of Wivenhoe across the river. In the centre of the village is the white-brick octagonal church of St. Lawrence, built in 1838 in the style of the chapter house of York Minster. We retrace

Colchester. St. John's abbey gate. "... history speaks out to those prepared to listen."

St. Osyth's Priory : " The battlements and slender chimneys stand out
against the skyline."

Layer Marney Towers. "The great gatehouse rose slowly to be a four-towered affair eight stories high in Tudor brick."

Mistley Towers (National Trust), built by
Robert Adam, 1774.

our steps to leave until reaching the crossroads, where we turn left and head south to Fingringhoe. Notice on the left Donyland Hall, a fine seventeenth-century mansion.

An old tidal mill stands on the river's edge to the left as we cross the bridge to enter the village. The mill is now a store-house, but it remains as a rare memorial to other mills that used the power of the tide to drive their crushing stones. As we enter this charming old Saxon village look ahead past the huge old oak and the tiny pond and up to the old church that overlooks the whole place. Most theatre managers would give anything for a first scene like this— and there is more to come, for Fingringhoe was an old Roman port in A.D. 43. It includes the first Essex Naturalists' Trust nature reserve and has many fine old houses to delight the eye of the visitor. The church of St. Andrew has that typical English country church look about it. Its brick and stone walls, dotted with red Roman bricks, have that not-quite-cared-for appearance, and it is approached through trees. During the rebuilding following 1884 many fine wall-paintings were discovered, including one of St. Michael weighing souls, so something good did come out of this tragic event. Two oak treasures also grace this church; one is a dug-out chest which rests on a bier and the other is the delicately carved font cover which rises in three tiers to tower above our heads, as it has done for the last 500 years. From the church we can look down and over the famous Fingringhoe oak and the thatched cottages round the green. Fingringhoe Hall, now a farmhouse, was built in the seventeenth century on what was once a moated site. The Dutch-gabled front was restored in the eighteenth century.

Our next port of call is Langenhoe, and this lies west, down the lane and through the orchards. It is a scattered place and consists of small groups of houses and cottages around various crossroads. The parish occupies the countryside to the east of the B1025 and as far south as the oyster beds in Pyefleet Channel, which separates Mersea from the mainland. The flat and magnificent marshes cover most of the parish, an ideal home for the many forms of wild life that have been driven here by the growth of towns and villages in this corner of Essex. It is indeed an enchanting place if you want to get away from the hustle of modern life. The church and Hall are about a mile south of the crossroads on the B1025 where we come out from Fingringhoe, and they are down a lane to the east. St. Mary's was almost totally destroyed by the earthquake and was made good in 1886, much of the material of the old church being used again, including the wooden doors.

On the other side of the crossroads we mentioned are the village of Abberton and the large reservoir that shares its name. The cottages of this place have gathered together round the fork in the road at the entrance to the village. Many interesting palæolithic implements have been found in the area, used perhaps on the rather wild pastures that stand above and below the village. Let us take the right-hand fork and run down the hill to the edge of the delightful wood that occupies one end of the rough pasture. Hidden by this wood is Abberton House, while on the other side of the road is the moated site of Abberton Hall. Ahead of us the road runs on to the Georgian Abberton Manor, and rounds the retaining embankment of the reservoir; but to find the church turn left down the narrow lane. This is St. Andrew's, which was originally built in the fourteenth century. However, little of the original now remains and the building you will see is sixteenth and nineteenth century. As you look at the tower, from which the reservoir can be clearly surveyed, you are standing on the line of a Roman road.

The reservoir is huge, holding 5,500,000 gallons, and is now the home of many waterfowl. From Abberton it reaches four miles south-west towards Wigborough, where it flows under the B1026 just north of that village. Before thinking of a walk round the reservoir, a word of warning—it is a twelve-mile trip!

Having been provided with a natural break, let us follow the reservoir and take up the rest of this chapter in the western half at Great Wigborough. It is very easy to find the village when travelling along the B1026 from the south, for the main road has a nasty right-angle turn, but we just leave it by going straight on at this point. To the south we look out over the saltings to Salcott Channel, while to the north the land rises and we follow a lane towards the church and the old houses. Half a mile along the lane a track goes east to the church of St. Stephen, the most interesting feature of which is a piece of Zeppelin. The Zeppelin was brought down in the area during World War I, and after setting fire to their ship the crew surrendered to the local bobby! The farmer in whose field it landed charged a fee to visitors and used the money to provide comforts for some of our soldiers.

Hyde Farm, which lies just north of the track to the church, dates from the fifteenth century and is part timber-framed. Just across

the road and a little south is the medieval manor house of Moul-
shams. From here we can scan the slightly rising fields that are all
around. The church that stands out to the east is at Peldon and we
shall visit it after seeing Little Wigborough.

This village is out on the saltings and is reached by a road to the
right, a mile east of its Great neighbour. Little Wigborough is a tiny
place, with its few cottages lining the approach to the small church
of St. Nicholas. The fresh winds off the sea beat on to the south side
of the church as they have done for the last 500 years. While inside,
protected from the blast, the iron rails that date from the Victorian
age must be seen. A plaque on the tower commemorates its rebuilding after the great earthquake in 1884.

And so to Peldon, which sits right in the centre of this region, and
from where a road runs south to Mersea. The place occupies a
triangle of roads and a drive round all three is called for to do justice
to it. In the middle of the southern side is the Peldon Rose inn. This
is reputed to be one of the oldest inns in the country and was once
the haunt of smugglers coming in from the surrounding coast. After
the earthquake the inn was greatly damaged, but is now restored
again. At the western corner is Harvey's Farm, which is timber-
framed and dates from the sixteenth century. At the northern apex
is the church, dedicated to St. Mary, the stone nave of which dates
from 1600. The oldest possession of the church is the Norman font,
but the most impressive is the great hammerbeam roof of the nave.
Near the church you will see a timber-framed house which is all that
remains of a much larger medieval building.

FRINTON AND WALTON

TWENTY years ago the *Essex Chronicle* produced *King Cole's
Essex*, a scarce little paperback today, as a souvenir for returning Americans. It says "Whether or not you like the word 'exclu-
sive' it does apply to Frinton, even in these democratic days.
Here is the Deauville of Britain." This is praise indeed, and well
merited, for Frinton and Walton Urban District Council has carefully kept the atmosphere in which Frinton was planned by Sir
Richard Powell Cooper at the beginning of the century. Its regular
tree-lined avenues have been preserved so that even in the shopping
centre the trees break the line of buildings in an interesting and
relaxing way—and you *can* relax here.

The avenues run down to the sea front, where parking is allowed all along the edge of the broad greensward which runs like a local green belt between the road and the edge of the low cliffs, with pathways down through cliffside gardens to a fine sandy beach. Hotels and guest houses stand in pleasant grounds, all neat and clean and inviting in the lovely air which Essex enjoys, and evidence of the popularity of this place with holidaying families from all over the country and abroad.

There is a golf course running along the cliffs to the south, and pleasant walks take in beach and cliff in both directions as well as inland to the " broad, fertile fields with silvery backwaters and rivers stretching away into Suffolk."

As for history, Frinton's past has been washed away, quite literally. Before the stout sea wall was built the Hall was already half a mile out to sea, victim of erosion. The church of St. Mary is the sole surviving building to represent the old village before erosion and then development altered its identity. It dates from the fourteenth century, and up to its restoration in 1879 had the reputation of being the second smallest church in the country, seating just thirty souls. This was brought about by the severe storm of 1703 which blew down the chancel and reduced the accommodation. There is modern treasure in the stained glass in the east window, made at the Morris works and designed by Burne-Jones.

The new church of St. Mary in Old Road was built to the design of Sir Charles Nicholson in 1929, but as a landmark it is being superseded by the blocks of flats which turn their faces to the sun and sea.

It is a bright and breezy walk along the cliffs to Walton, but by car we must go inland, cross the railway and slant back to the seaside on the B1336. Here lies the twin town of the urban district, on the narrow neck of the promontory, ness or naze which reaches up to Pennyhole Bay and the wild creeks and marshes of the witch country of Tendring hundred. It has been given a testimonial as a " bright and inviting little seaside resort, clean and well built, with many charming residences, and holiday attractions of refined character," and it certainly lives up to this description.

Do not look for history here though—the sea swallowed it in massive bites at the end of the eighteenth century. Even the pier, complete with modern amusements and said to be the second longest in the country, does not reach out to the site of the village of old, where the church rests beneath the waves. Those very waves have been the cause of the siting of the life-boat station at the end of the pier—a focal point for a stroll or a ride on the miniature railway.

The Walton of today springs from the determined development of this naturally favoured site as a sea-bathing resort around 1830, when Marine Parade, then called The Crescent, was built. The church of All Saints is less than 100 years old, but in the fields behind it, looking over the magnificent boating lake on the other side of the Naze, is the martello tower which takes us back to 1810 and preparations against Napoleon's projected invasion.

Drive north as far as you can and the Naze takes on its natural guise. The cliffs loom higher, the place becomes almost deserted. You cannot drive beyond Walton Hall. Look seaward there and you will see on the edge of the cliff the eighty-foot-high brick tower, crowned with battlements, which was specially built about 1720 by Trinity House to be a landmark to shipping.

Anyone who pushes up to the point of the Naze will be well rewarded in a curious way, for here the usual London Clay gives way to a layer of " crag " deposit of shelly sand in which fossils abound; witness the collection in the Chelmsford and Essex Museum, made in just one day's excursion to the Naze. You may come across anything from the bones of an elephant to the teeth of a shark, all preserved for ever in stone-like permanence—rich reward for the souvenir hunter! There is just about everything for everybody in Frinton and Walton.

HARWICH AND DOVERCOURT

IN a country as rich in naval history as England a town has to have something outstanding to make one think twice about it. We believe that Harwich is one of the few such towns. From the days of the glorious tall ships to the present time of sleek black submarines this town has its name entered on the roll of honour. Let us review some of these events. Many of the crew selected by Drake and by Cavendish for their round-the-world voyages came from Harwich. The registers of the parish church of St. Nicholas record the birth of Christopher Newport, who helped Raleigh to settle Virginia, and the marriage of Christopher Jones, master of the *Mayflower*. During the many storms that raged in the Nort'

Sea Nelson often brought his tired and weatherbeaten fleet into the shelter of Landguard Point, to lie, sails furled, until it was calm enough to return to the attack on his country's foes.

Bringing our story up to modern times, we must pay tribute to Captain Fryatt, who was shot by the Germans for sinking a submarine while captain of a civilian ship, and to the members of the Harwich mine-sweeping flotilla who so gallantly gave their lives to keep the vital sea lanes clear. During World War I they held the record for the number of mines destroyed, and this covered any group in the world. The maritime history of Harwich is not confined to war, for it has grown from being a small Royal Mail packet station in 1661 to become one of the largest ferry and goods ports in England.

Let us now look round the town and sample its delights. We must not expect anything very ancient, but the narrow streets round the quay at the northernmost point of the town have great charm. An attractive place to start is the Cliff Gardens, just off the main road, for from here you can round Beacon Hill on its seaward side. This comes out near Harbour Crescent, at the end of which is the green, where a seventeenth-century treadmill crane can be viewed. Now in a weatherboarded housing, the crane was used for many years in the dockyard and was driven by men walking inside a drum. From this point you can look across to the west and see the high lighthouse, which is ninety feet high and was built in 1818. Ahead are the narrow streets leading to the quay, each offering Georgian houses in plenty.

The church of St. Nicholas, whose registers have already been mentioned, stands at the foot of Church Street, the two-tone brick of its tower standing out against the nearby houses. Opposite the church, near the end of West Street, stands a row of almshouses built in 1785 and still making an attractive sight for the visitor. Just beyond the church is the Three Cups hotel, built in the sixteenth century and used by Nelson on his visits to the town. Nearby is the Guildhall, built in 1769 in red brick, three stories high, and styled like a merchants' house. At the quay end of King's Head Street is the house where Christopher Jones of the *Mayflower* lived.

Running along the seafront, the quay offers an ever-changing pattern of sea life. To the east are the rolling waters of the North Sea, while to the west lie the river Stour and the way to Parkeston quay and the " big " ships. On the Harwich quay you can join a boat for a trip over to Felixstowe or down-river to Parkeston (you book at the oddly named Halfpenny Pier) or you can sit and watch the silver cascade of sprats as they pour out from the fishing boats. The more energetic can fish for sole, which are reputed to be as tasty as any caught at Dover.

While much traffic still comes into the old Navyard Wharf, the main port lies two and a half miles down the river Stour at Parkeston. The visitor can only go on to Parkeston quay between 2 and 4 p.m. on Mondays to Fridays, and permission should be obtained from the marine superintendent's office. The quay is at the end of the A604 and the road runs off from the main road through Dovercourt to Harwich.

Parkeston was built so far upstream because of a difference between Harwich and the old Great Eastern Railway, so Harwich lost this large port and in 1883 Parkeston was opened for public use—it was named after the head of the railway at the time. A sight worth seeing is the arrival of the rail ferry; it glides up the Stour only to turn at right-angles and disappear backwards into a huge girder structure. With only a couple of feet clearance, the ship's captain deserves all praise for not hitting the sides of the berth.

And so to the seaside town of Dovercourt, so involved with Harwich but so different from that town. Dovercourt has grown during the last 100 years from a tiny village round the High Street into a modern town, with the added attraction of having two miles of sandy beaches, backed by a strong sea wall. The High Street remains as the shopping centre, but for the visitor a walk down Marine Parade and on to the recreation ground is certainly called for. On this walk you can discover the variety of pleasures that the town can offer, from the pavilion to the model yacht pool and the sea-water swimming pool.

The country village atmosphere is preserved at Upper Dovercourt, where the parish church of All Saints overlooks the green at the junction of the roads into the place. Although much restored, the church is still recognizable as a Norman structure, and a blocked window confirms this. The lich-gate at the church was presented by Queen Victoria in memory of those who died as a result of the Walcheren expedition in the Napoleonic war. A window given by Kaiser Wilhelm II commemorates the Germans who are buried in the churchyard and were on the same expedition.

INWORTH, MESSING and EASTHORPE

YOU can take the A12 and travel speedily round Kelvedon and on to Marks Tey, Colchester and the coast, but if you really want to see this part of the county there is a parallel route of great charm. Along the Kelvedon bypass look out for the slip road to the B1023. Your first destination is Inworth, a small village built on the three bases of church, Hall and inn.

All Saints is a Norman building, but additions and alterations run through the centuries to the building of the brick tower and porch in 1876. Above the chancel arch you will see all that remains of wall-paintings done in the thirteenth century.

The lane just to the north wanders round to the associated village of Messing, through fields which smell of the strawberries or the flowers (for seed-producing) for which this area is well known.

Strangely enough, the church at Messing has a tower of Victorian red brick like Inworth's, and the rest of the church is of the same period except for some of the furniture, which is the great reason for a visit. In the chancel you will see pannelling and stalls of oak, with typical Jacobean ornament, over 300 years old, and the stained glass in the east window is contemporary with it. Another item of furniture, an iron-bound chest, dates back to the thirteenth century.

Houses and cottages are grouped attractively about the road junction, while to the north-west by the Domsey Brook there is evidence of Roman occupation.

The lane out of the village runs almost parallel with the brook, just far enough away to escape the flood level, as evinced by Winterflood's Farm, which it passes on the way north to Easthorpe, gathering about the T junction.

No doubt the east-west Roman road out of Colchester forming the top of the T is responsible for the original settlement. Today the church, a charming little building with later amendments, gives evidence of the Norman's hand. The south window has sixteenth-century stained glass.

West of the church stands the Hall, in the close association so common in Essex. The present Hall is 500 years old, with a wing added in the seventeenth century. The attractive scene is completed by Well Cottage on the other side of the road, built about the same time as the Hall.

From Easthorpe you can go west and quickly be in the rush and roar of the A12. Eastwards a maze of lanes opens up to villages covered in other chapters, which you can find on the map at the end of our book.

LAWFORD, MISTLEY AND MANNINGTREE

THE A137, a spoke in the cartwheel of roads out of Colchester, will point us through Ardleigh (covered in another chapter) and on to Lawford. Pleasant views along the way culminate in glimpses of the Stour valley which invite closer inspection.

The main road through the village makes loitering difficult, so it is best to look for peace in and around the remarkable church of St. Mary, which stands, with the Hall, down a little lane north of the village. It is notable for its chancel, built around 1350 in what is known as the Decorative Gothic style. The windows are decorated with tracery and carving which have to be seen to be believed. Owls and squirrels hide in deliciously carved foliage round two windows and another shows a sort of human chain of men in merry attitudes —dancing, playing instruments, even wrestling.

Other features of interest here include the seventeenth-century stone tower with renovations in brick, and the windows in the south porch, restored in memory of the Ogilvies, a couple who came to live at Lawford Place early in the century and stayed to be local benefactors, presenting the organ to the church and building a village club of the most advanced design. The Place itself dates from the early nineteenth century.

The Hall, in beautiful grounds, is of sixteenth-century origin, but what you see now is a brick front added in the latest fashion of the mid-eighteenth century, which hides the old timber and plaster construction. However, a couple of elegant eight-sided Tudor chimneys remain to confirm its true age.

Through the village look out for the B1352, which runs on to Harwich. Within a couple of miles Manningtree awaits us. The narrow approach roads all drop down a steep declivity carved out in the past by the flood waters of the Stour, and right-angle turns give tight corners.

The river nurtured Manningtree—the old sailing ships and barges plied up as far as Sudbury and the trade was good for this place. Today it dreams a bit of its past while the swan-flecked Stour rolls its days away. There are great mills here still, gaunt on the riverside, but the bustle is not so apparent and that old importance must be looked for in the Georgian façades in the High Street and at the junction with South Street. The church is now out of bounds to visitors. It was built in 1616 in pretty Jacobean style, but time and climate have worked their worst and rendered it unsafe. Repairs are beyond the means of the parish, so Manningtree's chief monument is doomed to demolition.Two of its treasures, an altar-piece said to have been painted by Constable and the organ, have been found a safer home in Feering church and Colchester grammar school respectively.

A brisk walk along the promenade by the river and the boundary is crossed into Mistley, where the road, still the B1352, bears away inland and the railway skirts the river. The old village was developed to take advantage of the lucrative river trade of the mid-eighteenth century. Known then as Mistley Thorn, it owed its existence to local landowner Richard Rigby, one of the few successful speculators in the South Sea Bubble. He planned the quayside, flanked by the tall malthouses which look out over the wide flats of the Stour, which here harbours the second biggest swannery in the country. It makes a wonderful sight.

Farther east New Mistley stands, though there is no division apparent to the eye. Rigby's son Richard, Member of Parliament, planned this new development in the last quarter of the eighteenth century, aiming at elegance rather than industry. He wanted the place to become a popular spa where people might take the waters, and actually started the famous Robert Adam on designs, but Rigby's defalcations as Paymaster General came to light and the scheme fell through. A square with a fountain crowned by a swan was laid out and can still be seen. The church of St. Mary, built in 1735 south of the village by the lane to Mistley Heath, was altered by Adam to suit the style of the proposed new village. The dashing addition of twin towers at north and south and porticoes with Tuscan columns gave an air of London pride to this humble village church. But in its turn it has fallen into disuse; the nave was pulled down and the towers stand as a monument to Rigby's vain ambition. Worship continues in the later, 100-year-old church of St. Mary.

MERSEA ISLAND

ANCIENT and modern is the phrase to describe this island. We reach it by crossing the surrounding marshlands on the old Roman road called the Strood (B1025), and on arrival we can look across the estuary to the gaunt shape of the modern nuclear power station at Bradwell-on-Sea. There is a local claim that since the building of this station the sea has been much warmer round Mersea!

Only in England could a small, oval-shaped island be administered by two authorities. Here it can, and does, happen. The western half of the island is an urban district in its own right (West Mersea), but the eastern half is part of Lexden and Winstree rural district. Rather neatly, the only approach road to Mersea divides upon reaching land, the left fork going east and the right going west. Most of the island's population live in West Mersea, and since this part of the island is also the chief attraction for visitors we will start here, where the B1025 passes the church and becomes the coast road.

Before heading towards the beach let us look at the buildings. The first of these is the church of St. Peter and St. Paul, which stands at the end of the High Street and is enclosed on three sides by tall old trees. The pathway leading to the embattled porch is lined by a row of well-kept small bushes. From this path you can see the full length of the church, which is dominated by its large square tower, parts of which date back to Saxon times, while the chancel is of Tudor origin.

Behind the church, in Beach Road, the visitor can see the remains of a wheel tomb. Now in the garden of a house, this tomb, dating from the Roman occupation, has a small hexagonal centre room from which six walls radiate outwards like the spokes of a wheel to join with the encircling outside wall. The outer wall has a diameter of sixty-five feet.

Across the road from the church is a site of a Benedictine priory, while on the corner of the coast road stands Yew Tree House, a good example of an eighteenth-century brick house.

Let us follow this coast road round the south-western corner of the island, for it gives the most attractive views of the many small boats that sail off the coast of Mersea. There are usually hundreds of boats of all shapes and sizes to be seen bobbing and dancing about on the gentle waters of the estuary.

At the end of this road The Lane runs back eastwards, and along this narrow road stand several fine old weatherboarded houses, mingling with groups of trees. This is typical of the island, for wherever you go a clump of fine trees is never far away.

Before looking at the eastern part of Mersea a word about the beaches—there are many of them round the coastline and most have at least a few yards of sand before you come to the shingle and mud that are left when the tide goes out. Quite often you will find a grassy edge to the beach where food can be eaten without getting too much sand in it!

On joining the East Mersea road (at the fork where you first cross to the island) look out on the left for the Mersea Mount. This is a hill some twenty feet high that covers a Romano-British burial mound. In the centre was found a tiny eighteen-inch-square chamber, built of Roman tiles, and inside was a casket containing the cremated remains of an adult. The mound has been dated as being of the first century.

East Mersea is the " country " part of the island, and to the north of the road lie the marshes that prove a rich source of wild-bird life. Here the enthusiast can spend hours watching waders and other waterfowl, or just walking across country that has seen the feet of Danes, Saxons and Romans. You may even cross a spot where Queen Boadicea once drove her chariot. Perhaps that stand of trees was once the camp of Norsemen pausing to rest before raiding the mainland; or perhaps some Roman farmer once tilled the land between the trees. Yes, all this is possible here in the quiet centre of the island.

South of the road, about a mile and a half from the Mount, stands the church of St. Edmund. The church was probably started in the twelfth century, although most of it is somewhat later. It has a large tower and stands within a moat that once surrounded a Danish camp. The site allows a wide-angle view over the parish and across to the Blackwater. Next to the church is the fifteenth-century manor house, which still has a well of fresh water.

Baring-Gould, the local author, who at one time preached at the church, has used Mersea as the setting for one of his novels. This is called *Mehalah* and has been described as " the *Lorna Doone* of Essex."

TENDRING, THE SOKENS and the witch-finder general

FROM the multitude of greens that sparkle in the small copses that abound round these parts to the dark richness of the soil you will find practically every aspect of the Essex country scene represented in this region. However, today you will be lucky to find any witches, for most of them seem to have been around in the mid-seventeenth century—and they all paid the price.

We have chosen this chapter to tell the story of the Essex witches not because Tendring and its neighbourhood was particularly rich in witches but because the world's first professional witch-finder made his debut here in 1644. This man was Matthew Hopkins, and, claiming a warrant from Parliament to search for witches, he started in Tendring and Thorpe-le-Soken.

Fear of the unknown is as old as man himself, and throughout history there have been those who for personal gain or religious zeal would try to profit by exploiting this basic human emotion. Hopkins was such a man. He recruited two assistants and the three of them embarked on their tour with the intention of hunting down any witch they could. Their charge for this service was twenty shillings per town, but for an added fee they would accuse almost anyone regardless of the evidence. Offers were soon flowing in and the credulous townsfolk listened to them as if they were oracles.

In every town they visited they asked if there were any reputed witches, always finding people willing to point the finger at an old enemy or some poor old crone. Zealous abettors took good care that Hopkins should have a clear run for his experiments to prove the guilt of these poor creatures.

Many and hideous were the lengths Hopkins went to in the investigations he made. Usually he started with carefully prepared questions designed to trick them into a confession. If this failed he had more persuasive methods. One of these was to place the accused, cross-legged and often bound, on a table in the middle of an empty room and keep them for anything up to two days without food. Should a mouse or other small animal enter the room during this time it was considered to be the witch's " imp " or evil agent, and she was convicted.

For those hardy souls who held out against all this there was always the water test. Here the victims were thrown into a pool with their thumbs and toes bound crosswise. If they floated it was taken as a sign of guilt, since it was well known that water, " being the symbol of admission into the Christian Church," would not receive an agent of the Devil into its bosom.

The fate of Hopkins was as might be expected at the hands of people recovering from their fear and seeing that they have been fooled. Dissatisfied with themselves for standing by and seeing one old woman after another put to death, they turned on the tormentor and " swam him for a witch." He floated, and the crowd drove him away " with hootings and revilings "—a fate richly deserved by one who preyed upon the weak.

We return to the twentieth century and take up our journey at the village of Tendring on the B1035, about eight miles east of Colchester. This village gave its name to the old hundred of Tendring and in more recent times to the modern rural district that replaced the hundred. All around the village are traces of the woods that once covered the region, but these are now represented by small outcrops amid the broad acres of agricultural land that now stretch away in every direction. The village street is distinguished by a thick holly hedge and its inhabitants are rightly proud of it. They are also proud of having what, with that of Westminster Hall, is probably the oldest hammerbeam roof in existence. This piece of glorious history can be found in the church of St. Edmund at the western end of the village. In the chancel of this church you can see an alabaster effigy which dates from 1615 and which clearly shows the fashion of that time.

To the north of the village, past Tendring green, can be seen a reminder of our not so glorious past. This is now the Heath Hospital but was once a Poor Law institution.

Let us now follow the B1035 south past the point where it becomes the B1033 and into the small township that was once the " capital of the Sokens." This, of course, is Thorpe-le-Soken, and you will find it where the A136 crosses the B1033. " Soken " is a Saxon word meaning " liberty," and this is just what the local villages had under the rule of the Danes. They were allowed special privileges with regard to ownership of land that were denied to other places.

As you enter this quite appealing place look out on the right for a large red-brick Georgian house. This is called Comarques and was at one time the home of Arnold Bennett, better known for his Staffordshire stories than for any set in Essex.

Among other things to see in the village are the old inn with its top story jutting out as it has done for the last four centuries; the Abbey House, which lies just east of the church, and which despite its pseudo look is genuine Tudor; and Thorpe Hall. The last-named is just outside the village to the south and stands in its grounds east of the A136. The original building is in white brick and was constructed in 1823; another wing was added early this century. Once the residence of Lord Byng, it is now a convalescent home and its grounds are often open to the public during the summer.

The village church of St. Michael stands near the crossroads, and all about are the old houses and shops of the place. St. Michael's was rebuilt in 1876, but its red-brick tower dates from the early sixteenth century. From high in this tower a peal of six bells rings out over this historic countryside calling the faithful to worship.

We now follow the B1033 across the level farmlands towards the coast. At Kirby Cross we turn left and head north to visit the other " soken " in this chapter, Kirby-le-Soken. On the nearby coast lie Frinton and Walton, but these have a special chapter elsewhere in this section. At the junction with the B1034 go left again and you are in the village of Kirby. From here you can look out over the crop-laden fields towards the marsh and streams that take up the northern aspect. Down there at the quay a solitary building puts man's mark on this outpost of wild nature. Here streams rise and fall with the tide between banks of rushes and moss, and the odd boat poking its way along disturbs the calm surface and sends ripples to lap at the banks and awaken some small creature. Out in the distance are dozens of small islands accessible only by boat.

As you pass through the village of Kirby look out on the left for the spacious churchyard that surrounds the church of St. Michael. Here tall trees cast their shadows over the mainly Victorian church, but none can reach the top of the embattled tower, whose solid form looks large even in such wide spaces.

Just outside the village we leave the B1034 by going straight ahead where it goes left. Our way lies on past the early-fifteenth-century Landermere Hall to the A136. At the main road we go right and on to Beaumont-cum-Moze.

The first part of this parish we see lies to the east and is Beaumont Quay. We mention this tiny place because it was built from the stones of the old London Bridge in 1813.

The Moze part of the name refers to a small place north of Beaumont, but there is little to see; even the church has gone. The only thing of interest stands east of the main road (A136) along a narrow lane. This is New Moze Hall, where some interesting remains of sixteenth-century brick architecture can be seen.

Beaumont village, however, is just off the main road, but before the village is reached look to the left for Beaumont Hall, a typical and pleasant example of Essex brick architecture of the late seventeenth century.

Beaumont village street runs up a gentle hillside, passing barns and timbered houses, before it reaches the diminutive church of St. Leonard. Parts of this rubble building date from Norman times, but most of it was built in 1854 with materials taken from the Moze church. Buried in the churchyard is Lord Byng, hero of Vimy Ridge in World War I. From the church his spirit can look out over the marshes towards the sea.

Past the church the lane goes south to join the B1035 Tendring road and our visit to the witch country is over.

THE TEYS AND ALDHAM

LET us go round in a square, as it were, starting at Marks Tey, a place which hits the headlines every summer with the traffic to the coast piling up at the roundabout on the A12 where it is met by the A120.

Life is hard for the village pedestrian, for the traffic flows like a river, fast and deep, which divides north from south. The age-old centre of the community, the church, keeps its serenity and peace down a mere track to the north of the A120 by the railway bridge.

The brick tower, damaged it is said in the siege of Colchester, is completed in its upper part with weatherboarding—even to the battlements! Lots of Roman tile and brick re-used by the Normans can be seen around windows and doors. The font is all of wood, a most unusual feature, with its eight sides carved in tracery and roses and a lead-lined bowl.

The Hall is now quite cut off from the church up a similar drive to the south off the A12, where the Saxons left a moat as evidence of their settlement.

Past the roundabout on the Colchester side there is a lane going north to Aldham, with many a twist and turn. Over the Roman River it passes Aldham Hall, sixteenth century and timber-framed, and goes on to the crossroads half a mile north, the centre of the village, a pleasant grouping of houses and cottages of all ages. The church is a 100-year-old imitation of early styles, but the fourteenth-century south porch is a remnant and reminder of an earlier church. The great Essex historian Philip Morant was rector here for a time, a commemorative tablet tells us.

Go on north and you come to Ford Street, an ancient settlement at the site of a crossing of the Colne, with pretty houses of medieval and Georgian pedigrees. From Aldham it is a straight run west to Great Tey, looping across the railway, turning sharply by Moor Farm and entering a clean-looking village where the little brook still runs across the street.

St. Barnabas was a great Norman church, but its importance is lost to us today. Its appearance shows that importance—a great battlemented tower, with Roman brick in it, is topped by the circular stair turret. The nave, of early-nineteenth-century build, looks small by comparison.

Straight down the road south you will pass Little Tey House and reach the village of that name, at the junction with the A120. It is one of the smallest parishes in Essex, with a tiny church of Norman origin. A fast run back east to Marks Tey completes the last side of our square journey.

The way to TOLLESBURY

THE way to Tollesbury passes through several pleasant villages, to say nothing of the fresh, clean Essex countryside. Across the route we shall take, the salt air from the Blackwater meets the country air from Tiptree Heath and they mingle to provide that bracing feeling that is special to these islands of ours.

Our point of departure is Goldhanger, a small village just east of the B1026. It stands on a creek leading to the wide waters of the Blackwater, and overlooks the island of Osea. Down on the shore-line you can see the duck-decoy ponds, no longer in use but still places to attract wild life. Also along the margin of the river you may come across the " red hills " that mark the site of ancient salt works, taken over and used again by the Romans. Bricks made by the Romans were preserved for us by the Normans, who built them into the walls of the local church. Since most of St. Peter's is built of flint the Roman bricks stand out clearly—touch them and you are holding something nearly 2,000 years old. Behind the church hundreds of fruit trees provide a foreground for the view down-river.

Passing the church, we travel up to join the B1026 again. Ahead of us on the rising ground over the crossroads is Falcons Hall, an attractive old farmhouse. We, however, go right for a while before turning left to see Tolleshunt Major. This Tolleshunt, the others we

I.S.E. 13

are visiting and Tollesbury all get their names from the same Anglo-Saxon source, which means Toll's spring.

Just before the road junction, walk right to see the historic part of the village; the pub and houses lie to the west at the top of the road. Concentrated into a small area are two fine old buildings, one the church of St. Nicholas and the other Beckingham Hall. Brick is the operative word here, for the church tower and much of the Hall are constructed of it, probably by the same builder under the orders of Stephen Beckingham in the mid-sixteenth century. The eye is carried up the tower to the low battlements by a pattern of blue bricks. From the top of the tower you can look out as far as Mersea in the distance, or down over the pond at the front of the church. To the south the blue ribbon of the Blackwater makes an attractive boundary to the parish. Down there at the water's edge it is possible to see the old salt pans once used to extract salt from the waters of the river.

Next to the church are the remains of Beckingham Hall. The two-storied gatehouse and the courtyard walls are the only remains of the Hall, but here the full beauty of well-executed brickwork still delights the present visitor. The Hall is now listed as an ancient monument.

Following the lane east, we pass through open farmland with verdant edges to the roadside before going up the rise and running into our next place—Tolleshunt D'Arcy. This village has grown up around the point where the B1026 and the B1023 meet, join and then go their own ways again.

Old cottages and houses open up off the narrow, tree-dotted roads that form the centre of the place. The history of the village is written in the church of St. Nicholas, which stands by the side of the main road. A fringe of battlements runs round the square tower and along the length of the church. A 500-year-old door welcomes you into the nave, from where you can look round at the many memorials to the D'Arcy family who gave their name to the village in medieval times. Among these memorials the brass of Anthony D'Arcy in Tudor armour and a mural to Sir Thomas D'Arcy should be noted.

Near to the church is the Hall of the D'Arcys, with its Elizabethan bridge crossing the remains of a clearly defined moat. The house dates from 1500 and has wood aplenty inside.

Before leaving the village let us remember a famous Essex doctor,

John Salter, who divided his life into serving his patients and country and building up a natural history collection that was second to none in the county. Much of this collection is now on view at the Chelmsford and Essex Museum in Oaklands Park at Chelmsford.

Tolleshunt Knights lies north along the B1023, and we follow this road for nearly two miles before turning right to run across country to the village centre. A bridge over a disused railway cutting marks the outskirts of the place, and shortly after a lane runs south to the church of All Saints. Inside this tree-surrounded building you can see the stone figure of a knight holding his heart in his hands. Reputed to be buried in the wall of this church is a watchman who had his heart torn out by the Devil. The story is that when digging a moat for a house in Devil's Wood they left a watchman on duty after the first day's work. During the night the Devil came and asked " Who is there? " The reply was " God and myself," and the Devil went away. For three nights the same thing happened and then the man answered " Myself and God," and the Devil struck out with his claws and tore out the poor man's heart for putting himself first. Then the Devil threw a beam up the hill and said " Where this beam shall fall, there shall ye build Barn Hall." He also said he would have the man's soul whether he was buried in church or churchyard; so they buried him in the church wall and cheated the Devil.

We now follow the road up to the village near Paternoster Heath and there go right and head down the hill towards the B1026 again. A mile along the way on the left you can see the Barn Hall of the legend—the Devil's beam is still in its cellar. Upon reaching the B1026 look left for the trees marking Devil's Wood, but go straight across for our next villages.

These are the villages of Virley and Salcott and they stand on either side of the navigable Salcott Creek. To the left is the tiny village of Virley with its ruined church, which is kept in a most attractive fashion. The walls, still upright, are covered in ivy, while pleasant borders line the nave.

Across the creek is Salcott, a most interesting old village. Picturesque old buildings line the street, some of them half-timbered and others thatched. This is just as many imagine a village, with its street running down to the river past a church that has stood since the days when smugglers used the river as their way into the village. Much of this church of St. Mary had to be rebuilt after the earthquake of 1884.

Rejoining the B1026, we travel south for a mile until a nasty bend is reached; here we leave by going left down the lane. Watch the bends down here. Just after the last bend we reach a lane running across in front of us. To the right lies Guisnes Court, which has a fine panelled room with a fireplace from Bourchier's Hall. This latter Hall lies to the left and we pass it on the way to Tollesbury. Hidden in the loft of Bourchier's Hall is the original fourteenth-century king-post roof.

Tollesbury is an attractive small town standing on the coast, with water lapping three of its sides. These waters have traditionally provided employment for the population, and the oysters, sprats and shrimps are rightly famous. In recent years a new trade has developed with America. This is the collection of a sea fern, which is dried and dyed and then exported for decoration. The village harbour is the home of many pleasure ships as well as of the fishing fleet.

The centre of the town is marked by a large square which is dominated by the massive squat tower of St. Mary's church. Inside the church you can see brasses dating from 1517 and 1654, but the inscription on the font is equally interesting. It reads " Good people all, I pray, take care that in ye church you do not sware, as this man did." The punishment of the man in question was to pay for the font! Just outside the church you can see the recently restored village lock-up.

South of the church is the timber-framed Tollesbury Hall, which dates from the fifteenth century. All about this part of the town you can see groups of cottages and houses that are well tended and pleasing to the eye.

From Tollesbury the B1023 runs west to meet the B1026 at Tolleshunt D'Arcy and our tour is over.

WIVENHOE and the east bank of the Colne

FOR this section of our book we ask you to join us in an exploration of the east bank of the Colne as it wends its way from Colchester to the sea. We leave on the A133 eastwards from Colchester, to turn down the B1028 and reach Wivenhoe Park, which borders the junction on the southern side.

Here John Constable, that most English of our painters, rendered in oils the glory of the pastoral scene. The house he showed far off beyond the grazing cattle by the lake was built 200 years ago, when the ornamental lakes were laid out, but its present ebullient style of imitation Tudor architecture is the result of extensive alterations 100 years ago.

What would Constable think of the park today? It is now given over to the University of Essex, and residential blocks are sprouting over the pasture—sorry, campus! The teaching block is a massive building made irregular in shape to mask its size and suit the site. It is inevitable, we suppose, that many a student will become a graduate without appreciating the beauty of the setting or the fact that Constable walked and worked here.

It is another mile down the B1028 before Wivenhoe proper comes into view, and as far again to the most picturesque place, the church and the quayside with its old houses. The church of St. Mary is a fourteenth-century building restored 100 years ago, and its tough-looking tower is a sixteenth-century survival, like some of the brasses to be seen inside. The quay is a pleasant place to stroll, taking in the sights and sniffing the tang of sea air which creeps up the Colne. From the opposite bank you can get a panoramic view—houses all of a jumble architecturally, with colour-washed plaster, clapboard walls and mellow tiles in pleasing combination, seen through a lattice-work of masts and spars, and overlooked by the strong church tower with its crowning cupola.

The quiet little port seems to dream of its palmy days, when it flourished as the port of Colchester. Development of road and rail has taken away that medieval importance, but Wivenhoe still functions as a place to buy a boat made with traditional craftsmanship. The old occupation of smuggling, indulged in by many a fisherman-citizen, has gone, and with it the excitement of escaping the ever-watchful eye of excise-men like Daniel Harvey, whose anti-smuggling exploits in the river became something of a legend. While you are on the quay think yourself back to 1884. The earthquake which brought churches tumbling in north Essex also damaged Quayside Cottage so badly that its back wall had to be rebuilt, and still carries the date.

The town itself, with narrow streets and varied architecture, is worth exploring. Garrison House in East Street has a reputation in the county for its pargeted plaster front of seventeenth-century origin. Another house of the same period is now Halsey and McKay's in the High Street, opposite the church. The bay windows are Victorian, but the timber-framing and plaster work are original and inside there are wall-paintings contemporary with them. All in all it is a place for a restful stay, where sky and land and water meet, making views which have inspired the brushes of gifted painters and humble amateurs alike.

To follow the Colne farther down we must bear away east and pass through Alresford. The older village lies about a triangle of lanes just west of the B1027, but it is on this road that the new building is developing. The Eastern Region of British Rail has a frequent service from London to Clacton which stops at the station at the western end of the village. The tiny lane running due north from the crossroads near the station is a " no through road " which gives access to all the history of the place.

On the right you will see the church of St. Peter, built by the Normans (and they used all the *Roman* bricks they could find!), which later generations have lovingly restored, even to the wooden belfry and the shingled spire above it. The gallery at the west end inside has lovely eighteenth-century wooden balusters.

The 200-year-old Hall on the other side of the road is delightfully isolated in its wooded park, the subject of a Constable painting. After the road crosses a brook there is an entrance on the right to Alresford Lodge, important not for itself but because it stands on the site of a Roman villa probably connected with the Roman fort that existed on the opposite bank of the river. Our lane ends abruptly at the edge of a creek which takes the waters of the Tenpenny or Frating Brook into the Colne. For those who like a walk it is possible to get across past Plumpton's Farm and over the creek to the B1029 and so to Brightlingsea or Thorrington.

To reach Thorrington by car, however, it is necessary to run back to the village and on to the B1027. The road runs south-east to the crossroads at Tenpenny Heath and straight across to Thorrington. Here the old Red Lion has been attractively restored to offer refreshment in pleasant surroundings to travellers of the petrol age. Hall and church are off the main road past the inn on the right-hand side, backed by woodland.

Note the tower of St. Mary's, which, built of knapped flint, is a slightly smaller version of that of its sister church of Brightlingsea, seen standing high across the fields. The interesting thing is that the date of the tower is known because a brass in the floor below it records the death of its provider, John Deth, in 1477. The exterior, all made of pebbles, has been likened to "a cobble pavement put up vertically," a word-picture that cannot be bettered. The church looks charming, also, through its setting in a beautifully kept churchyard.

The village street, the B1027, runs on past St. Osyth to Clacton (both places are indexed), but to get back to the banks of the Colne we must go back north-west on that same road to Tenpenny Heath crossroads, where we diverge south-west on the B1029. Less than a mile down this road, at the head of Alresford Creek, stands a dilapidated old tidal mill, dated 1831 on a stone inset. It is one of the very few tidal mills left in this county. Cross the brook past the bend in the road and we are in Brightlingsea.

Only the church and Hall at the next bend in the road give an indication of the waterside town that lies more than a mile farther down the twisting road. The motorist who pauses by the church is richly rewarded. The peace of the place is a dividend in itself. It stands proud and high, a fine example of the East Anglian Perpendicular style, with a big, strong tower, pinnacled and battlemented, which is a welcome landmark for sailors far out to sea. The Beriffe family, a merchant family of the fifteenth and sixteenth centuries, is commemorated in a number of interesting brasses in the north chapel

The monument which really hits the eye, however, is that in the chancel to Nicholas Magens, who died in 1764 after making a fortune in insurance. This splendid testament to his worldly success is said to have cost £6,000 in the money of his day! Yet the importance of this one man's monument is overshadowed by the tiny plaques set waist high around the church—each one recording the loss of a ship and its crew or some other fatality at sea. What a record of the fury of the elements it is; and a reminder too of Brightlingsea's long-continuing connection with sea and ships.

This connection is apparent when the little town is reached. There are no great buildings here, except for Jacobes, a fourteenth-century house in the High Street with an unusual sixteenth-century stair turret added on. The place has slowly developed, so that even today, with the incursions of modern traffic, it wears the air of a seaside town in the early part of the century, faintly surprised by modern goings-on.

An annual ceremony in the belfry of the old church marks the town's connection with the Cinque Port of Sandwich, to which town allegiance is sworn.

For years the oyster beds about the creeks were a profitable employment for many fishermen. A recent heavy frost wiped out the beds, but now they are gradually being restocked. For the visitor there are good fishing and boating, bathing and wildfowling, and all the holiday sports.

WIX and the north-eastern margins of Essex

PLUMB in the middle of this group of villages and astride the A604, Wix is probably the only place on this tour where you cannot see one of the water barriers that mark the limit of our county. These boundaries are the North Sea to the east and the broad waters of the River Stour to the north.

It is strange to think that Wix, a village whose recorded history goes beyond the Domesday survey, should be cut by a modern continental highway. However, a place that has seen the rise and fall of a priory, a nunnery, its church and its annual fairs can take the modern intruder in its stride. An old inn and the village church of St. Mary are at the western end of the village. The inn dates from the seventeenth century; much of the church is a century later. Hidden in the much-changed church is a blocked thirteenth-century arcade. The peal of bells for this parish stands in an ivy-covered cage in the churchyard. Just north of the village crossroads stands the new Abbey Farm. This is built on the site of the old priory, founded in the twelfth century, but nothing remains of this early building except a few of its fishponds. The present building has one main feature of interest—a porch dating from 1570, which is crowned by a stepped gable.

Taking the A604, head east for three-quarters of a mile, then branch right down the lane that cuts across country to the Oakleys. Great Oakley is the first we see, and it is reached by turning left when you meet the A136. To see the church, however, go right and walk down the tree-bordered lane. All Saints stands apart from the village and its partly weatherboarded tower overlooks the pyramid roof of the church. Inside, look for the font, which is of Purbeck marble and has been poised on its five shafts since Norman times. In the north wall another reminder of the Normans can be seen, this time a window.

As we pass through the village proper, look out for some of the old houses that occasionally peep out on to the busy roadway.

Two miles away is the sister village of Little Oakley. On the way there see if you can spot Great Oakley Hall, on the left opposite the orchard, and Little Oakley Hall, which is on the right about half a mile farther on. Along this road look across to the right over the farmland and marsh to the dancing waters of the sea.

Little Oakley clusters round the road to Harwich (see the separate chapter), and some of its cottages go back 300 years in the history of our county. In this village the unusual has to be looked for down a little trackway. At the end, protected by a group of trees, is the church of St. Mary. We have come here not just to see the fine old wooden doors but to pass through them and look for the very small priest's doorway cut through a buttress that widens like a porch to take it.

Leaving the village, follow the main road on towards Harwich, but after a mile go left and find the village of Ramsey. We are now going along the northern boundary of our county. At the head of the lane where we come out on to the A604 stands the church of St. Michael, which has a nave and tower dating back to the time of Agincourt. The south doorway is 500 years old and around it is a carving of the coronation of the Madonna. Going west, we turn right to join the B1352 and go down the dip and past the houses of the village. Down a road to the left is a windmill. Built in 1842, it was used until recent years to grind the local corn for a biscuit-maker.

Taking our leave of the village, we follow the B1352, which at this point takes what is one of the most attractive routes in Essex. Running level with the Stour and offering glimpses into the county across the water, the road runs through some beautifully wooded countryside. The largest of these woods is Stour Wood, and at the end of it we turn right and head for the ness or promontory that gives the village of Wrabness its name.

Scattered round the village are old barns and cottages with thatched roofs, while the church lies across the railway lines on the river side of the village. The church of All Saints has two things of interest. The first lies within, and is the hammerbeam roof of the nave. Having lost its tower, the bell is now housed in a most attractive weatherboarded bell-cage in the churchyard, and this is the second item of interest. Beyond the church is a tiny beach from where the ever-moving waters of the river can be viewed.

Journeying south, we rejoin the B1352 and follow the river west to visit the orchard village of Bradfield, which stands on some of the highest ground in this part of the county. Some of the most impressive things hereabouts are on the skyline. Across the river is the tall tower of the Holbrook naval school set in the fields of Suffolk, while in Essex the B.B.C. booster station at Manningtree pokes its mast skywards. Down by the river a pleasant lane runs under the railway and follows the river towards Jacques Hall and its swan-bedecked pond.

The church of St. Lawrence stands near the crossroads and is a plastered brick cruciform building with several brasses, one dating from 1598.

Just past the church the lane runs south towards Bradfield Heath and passes an area of fruit trees. Away to the right is Bradfield Hall, which has a Tudor brick gable. From here we run down to the A604 and find ourselves back at the beginning of our tour.

WORMINGFORD

TUCKED away from the busy world, the historic village of Wormingford lies along a hillside lane just north of the A133 about six miles from Colchester. As you might expect by its proximity to so famous a Roman settlement as Colchester, the area we are now visiting is rich in Roman remains and many of the churches have bricks of the period included in their structure.

The tree-lined lane that is Wormingford tumbles from the high ground near the main road to reach the waters of the Stour, passing on the way many fine old houses and cottages. At the middle point of the lane is the church of St. Andrew, which has marked the focal point for village life since Norman times. Under the Norman tower can be seen some interesting civilian brasses dating from 1450—the detail is still quite clear. Across the road is the sixteenth-century Church House, with its gabled front, while on towards the river you can see the plastered and timber-framed Church Hall of the same period.

Leaving the village, we join the A133 by turning right and in a few hundred yards leave it behind again by going down the lane on the left towards Fordham. This is a journey full of interest, and the first thing of note is three-quarters of a mile along the lane on the left. It is Jenkins Farm and is dated around 1583. What a splendid sight it is with its exposed timberwork and projecting gable. A little farther on Rotchfords lies to the right, its timber frame covered with plaster. Scattered all around are other farmhouses, many of a beauty rare in these days of quick concrete building.

The lane on to the village centre passes by orchards and a small copse before it reaches the fork in the road that marks the middle of the place. Going left brings us to the old pubs and the fourteenth-century church of All Saints. In this church, too, we can find traces of Roman bricks, although most of the building is fourteenth century, while the aisle windows were rebuilt in 1500, as the line of bricks shows. The Congregational chapel is also interesting, for it is weatherboarded and was constructed around 1789.

The late Georgian manor house, Fordham Hall, lies down the right hand of the fork and is a good example of this period, having a fine bow window. To the east of the house lies a large weatherboarded barn built in the seventeenth century.

We continue our journey, leaving Fordham by passing the church and travelling down the hill towards the River Colne. After crossing the river the road passes a large wood, bends round and goes through Fordham Heath before it starts the climb north to recross the Colne and enter West Bergholt.

This is a growing township and is the largest place we shall visit in this chapter. Although much of the village is relatively modern, it has connections with our history dating back to the Stone Age men, whose implements have been brought to light in many parts of the place. There is little to see in the main village, but by turning left just before we reach the A133 we can follow the lane round to visit the old parish church and the Hall that stands nearby. The church is 600 years old, and boasts a huge chest of equal age, but is no longer used for worship. Next door is West Bergholt Hall, a Georgian house built in the style of the town houses of that date. Constructed in red brick, it stands three stories high and seven bays long. Round this corner of the village lie several fine stands of trees fitting perfectly into the rolling landscape.

Straight across the A133 and we are heading for Great Horkesley. About a mile along this road you will see a large group of trees to the right, and hidden away among them is an Early Iron Age encampment. It is well worth the walk to see the Pitchbury Ramparts, for you will find an unusual double rampart. Only the north end remains, but the line can be clearly seen—ramparts ten feet high, separated by a sixty-yard-wide ditch.

From Pitchbury the road crosses the plateau before arriving at the approaches to Great Horkesley. We turn right to find the Roman road known as the Causeway (A134) and upon joining it turn left to see the village. Great Horkesley lies to the left and right of the wide main road and has many old houses to show the traveller, some of which are timber-framed. Worthy of note is the Chapel Cottage, now a home but once a chapel-cum-priest's house. The steep gables and projecting upper story cover a small room with a most interesting rose in it. This is a piscina in the shape of a Tudor rose and is so designed that the water runs away through the petals. Half a mile north of the main village, just off a bend in the A134, lie the village church and green. All Saints dates from the twelfth and fifteenth centuries and contains three real treasures, one in stone, two in wood. The first is a Norman pillar piscina, which is quite rare; the others are the octagonal pulpit and a delicately carved chair, both dating from the 1700s.

To find our last village, Little Horkesley, we leave the A134 almost on the county border and turn left down a side road. This lane climbs the hill towards Little Horkesley and in doing so gives views over countryside that is the quintessence of rural England.

The first group of picturesque dwellings we meet is not the village proper, but it is worth a halt to look away to the right to see the splendid timber-framed house called Joselyns. Built in the fifteenth century and lovingly restored in present times, it remains the pleasure and attraction it was to its original owners.

Round the bends in the lane lies the village proper; the church and most of the cottages stand round the corner of the crossroads to the right. From one or two places the visitor can look out from the hilltop on which the village stands and see the River Stour marking the limit of our county. Inside the church of St. Peter and St. Paul a treasure of great beauty can be seen in the form of figures carved from solid oak. Yes, these figures do date from the thirteenth century in spite of the rather recent look of the church building. This in itself is a story of endeavour, for the original church was destroyed in 1940 by bombing, to rise again in 1958 after public subscription.

We end our tour where the lane from Little Horkesley joins the A133 on the way again to Wormingford; here on the left is Wood Hall, a moated residence.

SECTION SIX

LONDON IN ESSEX

LONDON IN ESSEX—an introduction

FOR many centuries the towns recorded in this section of our book have played a glorious part in the history of Essex. In 1965 they were taken away from us and metropolitan Essex became part of Greater London. However, a sudden severance like this cannot, overnight, break the social and historical links that have existed between Essex and these places, so, although no longer a part of this county of ours, we thought it only right that mention should be made of them before any book on Essex could be called complete.

In keeping with the modern approach that we hope has been a feature of the previous sections of our book, we are treating the old towns under their new " super borough " names. That is to say there are five chapters, called Barking, Havering, Newham, Redbridge and Waltham Forest.

BARKING

THE new borough of Barking consists of the old towns of Barking and Dagenham, though both have lost bits to other London boroughs in the great rearrangement. The boundaries on three sides are rivers: the Thames to the south, the Roding to the west and the Beam to the east. The Roding gave old Barking a character from early days, for it was navigable right up to the town, where smacks were built for the big fishing fleet which sailed out into the Thames. At this time, too, down to our grandfathers' day, there were extensive market gardens here which catered for the London trade.

Those days are gone, but for those interested there are signs remaining of Barking's history. Barking abbey, founded by St. Erkenwald in 666, was in fact a nunnery, the richest and most powerful, it is said, in the whole country—great and mightly families provided its abbesses. But the abbey fell at the dissolution, demolished in 1541 to provide material for the royal palaces at Deptford and Greenwich. Today only the fire bell or curfew tower remains as a fifteenth-century reminder of earlier glory. It became known as the Town Gate; maybe affection for its familiar bulk spared it from destruction, and so it stands serenely still, astride the path to the church from the east, with its little chapel over the gateway.

The church, dedicated to St. Margaret, goes back in its fabric to the twelfth century. Some features, like the fifteenth-century tower, are later additions. It is aptly described by one expert as " a happy, rambling town church that has never been tidied up." Captain Cook walked down the aisle in 1762 to bring his bride, Elizabeth (Batts), out through the porch and into the sunlight where today the building of the new Town Hall (opened at the end of 1958) has been combined with the preservation of an open space around the old church, that it might be the better appreciated.

One of the oldest houses left in the town is Eastbury House, a mile or so east of the church on the south side of Ripple Road. It dates from about 1580 and is three stories high in mellow brick, with mullioned windows and big gables beneath the fine Tudor chimney-stacks. Its history has been most chequered in recent years, when one last-ditch stand after another was made to prevent its demolition or spoliation. The uses to which it has been put since it was bought by the National Trust in 1920 must have made its dormers blink in astonishment, but it has survived and now finds suitable occupation as a centre for the physically handicapped.

Of the modern buildings the railway station must be given praise for its functional yet attractive design. But there is one disappointment for the visitor: the river, the very reason for Barking's existence and development, cannot now be seen. It is completely shut in by the industries and factories that line its banks.

If the old town of Barking could be likened to a ball, Dagenham is the bat, with its broad blade running up from its tip in the Thames to its handle through Chadwell Heath and Marks Gate, where Whalebone Lane North (B196) runs on to Hainault and the forest. Let us start at the river and work northwards.

Dagenham dock fronts the Thames between the Barking and Halfway reaches. The factory buildings, the railway complex and the general industrialization of the marshy border of the old river hide a history which was frightening in its happening and romantic in its development. In 1707 a great tide broke the river bank at this point and through the gap thousands of acres of land were inundated. Soil washed back into the Thames threatened the passage of ships. By charging a toll to river traffic, and by thirteen years of unremitting labour under that great water engineer Captain John Perry, the breach was repaired, trapping a vast lake on the landward side.

This lake exists today, still known as the Dagenham Breach after nearly 300 years. It was a great novelty in its day. A fashionable club was formed at the Breach House, where members fished, ate and drank in noisy conviviality, originating the whitebait dinners for which Greenwich later became famous. It is interesting to know that the place was bought by Joseph Fry and his wife, the well-known Elizabeth, Quaker and prisoners' friend, who lies at rest in the Friends' burial ground in North Street.

Today this area has another importance. As the recent very useful Barking guide says, " Ford and Dagenham are as one in most people's minds—and with some degree of justification, for Fords have an extensive frontage on the Thames and a total site of 600 acres. Since its foundation here in 1928 the factory has grown enormously and has its own road and rail access, its own jetty on the Thames, and its own gas and power plants. Fords is self-reliant (it owns its own car body and wheel firms) and with recent expenditure of tens of millions of pounds it is one of the largest and most ambitious car plants in the world—certainly in this country." Sixty thousand people find their living here.

North-east of Fords, down Church Elm Lane, which runs east from the Heathway (A1112) to the Rainham Road (B178), stands the reminder of that other Dagenham, the ancient Essex village, the church of St. Peter and St. Paul. In 1887 Miller Christy said it " has been almost wholly rebuilt in a very unsightly style," but fashions change, and Pevsner in 1965 finds it a " true village church in a village street," an agreeable surprise in this area. The answer is to see for yourself and enjoy the features that take your eye—the fifteenth-century north chapel perhaps, or the " curly battlements " of the recent restoration. There is an interesting old tomb chest inside, on which large brass figures commemorate Sir Thomas Urswyck, Chief Baron of the Exchequer and Recorder of London, who died in 1479, and his family.

Opposite the church the Cross Keys inn furthers the village atmosphere, for it was built around 1500 and its timber-and-plaster gables give it a real period flavour. The sign of the Cross Keys ties up with the dedication of the church to St. Peter, keeper of the heavenly keys.

From here the Rainham road runs into Becontree Heath, a place visited by architects and planners from all over the world because of its housing estate, the largest in the world when it was built, between 1921 and 1935, in virgin countryside. Its 25,000 homes in this borough are supplemented by many more now over the border. Their siting and the amenities provided were a kind of anticipation of the post-war new towns. Valence Park, off Becontree Avenue, surrounds Valence House, a seventeenth-century manor house much altered and extended which has been taken over by the library service but also accommodates a small museum, to which admission is free.

Out of this vast estate the A1112 runs north, called over this stretch Whalebone Lane, after Whalebone House at Chadwell Heath, where the jawbones of a whale washed up by the Thames in the great storm the night before Cromwell died were set up as an archway.

London swallowed Barking like another whale swallowed Jonah, but, unlike that fortunate man, this busy borough can never be returned to its old position in the Essex countryside.

HAVERING

THE wheel has turned full circle here at Havering, for the principal towns of Romford and Hornchurch that grew to surpass the old royal liberty of Havering-atte-Bower must bow once again to the old town. So let us pay our respects to the old place by starting our review of the area at Havering-atte-Bower in the northern part of the borough on the B175.

The place will be a shock for those who think that anywhere within a dozen miles of Charing Cross must be overcrowded by people and buildings. Here acres of parkland surround the church, which stands on part of the site of Havering palace, once the home of kings and queens. The present church of St. John is less than 100 years old, but it has a pleasant setting on the village green, where the old stocks can still be seen. North-east of the green is Pyrgo Park. The house has long since gone, but remains of the terraced gardens can still be discovered. South-east of the church the most interesting house can be seen. This is Bower House, which was built in 1729 of red brick.

A walk across Pyrgo Park comes out at Noak Hill and the church of St. Thomas, where Flemish stained glass fills the place with rich colour. To the south lie Harold Wood and Harold Hill, residential districts, but with Dagenham Park to preserve a touch of the countryside.

I.S.E. 14

South of Havering-atte-Bower is the ancient market town of Romford. Here on Main Road (A118) the famous market, which dates from 1247, is still held every Wednesday, Friday and Saturday. Also in the market place is the large church of St. Edward, its tall spire throwing shadows across the square towards the Town Hall at certain times of the day. Farther along in Main Road are the beautiful Raphael Park with its lake, golf course and county cricket ground. Three-quarters of a mile south of the market place, along South Street (A125), is the Brentwood road, where the most interesting of Romford's mansions can be seen. Hare Hall (part of the Royal Liberty School) was built in 1768 and has a rustic ground floor, but it is enlivened by the Adam-like columns above this.

The A125 leads us down into Hornchurch, whose ancient leather tanners were the reason for Romford getting its market, as a place to sell their goods. In fact Main Road was once called Pelt Street because of the many leather workers who occupied it. The present High Street marks the centre of the old village and several cottages have lasted to the present time; these are near the church of St. Andrew, which dates from the thirteenth century and has brasses from 1500. While in the High Street notice particularly Wykeham Cottage and Appleton almshouses, which date from the 1800s. Up Billet Lane stands Langtons, built in 1760, now the council offices. What a glorious place it remains, with gardens and a lake to entrance the eye.

Going east we reach Upminster, a place with so much to offer that descriptions must be brief. We enter from the west along the A124, and the first thing of note is Ingrebourne Cottages, lying to the left near the railway and built in 1750 as a poorhouse. Still on the left you cannot fail to see the wonderful 150-year-old windmill, preserved in splendid condition. From the top you can look south and over the Thames into Kent. Opposite is Hill Place, built in 1871. As we approach the crossroads interest moves to the right to see the parsonage, built in 1765, and the church of St. Laurence. The latter has an imposing tower of the thirteenth century, and hidden in the Victorian nave is a Norman arcade.

From the crossroads go north to see timber-framed Upminster Hall, now the golf club house; across the road is the neo-Georgian villa Upminster Court, which houses the education offices. Again north, Bird Lane goes off to the right and down it a fifteenth-century yeoman's house, called Great Tomkins, still shows its timbers to the world. Nearby is the famous tithe barn; it is over 400 years old and probably the oldest building in the town.

South of the crossroads we can run down into Corbets Tey, a place with plenty of parks and space, and right, past the Huntsman inn, is Harwood Hall, a bow-fronted, castellated house built in 1782. Across the road is a great lake in a large park.

Continuing east from Upminster along the B187 we soon reach Cranham, a Saxon village which has recently seen much modern building. The best part of the village lies south down the Chase near Wantz Bridge. Down here in the midst of fertile farmland stands the church of All Saints, rebuilt in 1874 in the fourteenth-century style. It stands on a small hill and houses a large marble monument to General Oglethorpe, who owned the nearby Hall and in 1732 led an expedition which included John and Charles Wesley and which founded the American colony of Georgia.

Back on the B187, we continue until the B186 goes south and we follow it down to North Ockenden, which lies west along the B1421 and then down a lane which goes south. This is an attractive village surrounded by prosperous farmland. The parish church of St. Mary Magdalene, which suffered damage during World War II, is down a lane lined by fine old trees. The doorway and parts of the tower and nave are Norman, while the sun enters via a medieval glass window. A memorial to Sir Gabriel Poyntz, twice Lord-Lieutenant of Essex, is beneath the richly painted oak canopy. Nearby is a spring claimed to have been used by St. Cedd for baptism.

West along the B1421 is Stubbers, a three-story, seven-bay house of the eighteenth century. In the large grounds the botanist William Coys grew the first flowering yucca in England.

South-west, by way of country lanes, we reach the busy A13 to visit the last two places. The first of these is Wennington, which stands on the B1335 just across the A13. The land around here is shared among the market gardeners, the many small woods, and the gravel diggers. The latter excavate huge pits in their search for sand and gravel, but they refill the holes and restore the scene. St. Mary's is the much-restored parish church, but the doorway of the original Norman building remains. Inside are an old font with an ornate wooden cover and a Jacobean pulpit with an hour-glass fixed to it.

And so on to Rainham, an historic place that is fast growing these days. Many objects have been discovered in the parish and are now housed in the British Museum. The delights of Rainham are in the Broadway. St. Helen and St. Giles, the parish church, is the first of these. Built by the Normans in 1160-70, it is of flint and remains almost unaltered to this day, being one of the few churches able to claim this distinction. Inside, look for the narrow priest's door and the old chest of the fourteenth century. Nearby is Rainham Hall, a fine early-eighteenth-century structure. The splendid doorway is set in the red brick of the walls, which have stone quoins.

South of the town, across the marshlands, is the Thames, and down there at the edge of Havering and Essex is a picturesque riverside scene with jetties and islands forming a foreground to the view across to Kent.

NEWHAM

LONG before the Romans built their London to Colchester road, where the modern Romford road runs to this day, ancient pathways cut their way across the northern part of this borough, so these " hams " are not so new. Looking round the densely populated area today, with its tall modern buildings replacing those devastated during the war years, it is surprising to learn that until late in the nineteenth century the whole region was given over to agriculture. With the building of the royal group of docks, and with the outward spread of industry from London, the character changed dramatically and open fields gave way to open slums. It has been a major problem for the local authority to correct this early building, but things are now coming under control and even in deepest dockland modern building is pushing out the old.

Travelling round the present Newham one sees little trace of things old, but tucked away among the crowded streets and the broad main roads are pointers to the past. In Church Street at West Ham the church of All Saints has traces of Norman work in its now blocked clerestory windows, and its walls still show fifteenth-century wall-paintings. You can also see fragments from Stratford Langthorne abbey, which lay south-west of the church where Abbey Lane now runs. This abbey was founded in 1135 by William de Montfichet, lord of Ham, and at its peak it owned almost all of the present Newham area.

Not far from Abbey Lane you can see the three mills of Stratford. These lie on the lane along the Channelsea river at the end of Bisson

Road. The mills are contemporary with the abbey and since 1730 they have been the home of the famous Nicholson's distillery.

Farther west is the famous Bow Bridge, which gave its name to the well-known Bow porcelain. The works were built near to the bridge in 1748. A collection of this ware can be seen in the Passmore Edwards museum in Romford Road. This museum also houses the collection of the Essex Field Club.

North of All Saints' church is the beautiful West Ham Park. Once the grounds of Ham House, the park is now a green jewel in the midst of suburban London. Here fine cedar trees and colourful shrubs vie for attention, while the site of an ornamental canal is crossed by a small bridge that is hemmed in on every side by colourful bushes. Just north of this park is another that is known nationally. This is Upton Park, home of West Ham United soccer club.

Nearby in Upton Lane the Spotted Dog pub is a converted sixteenth-century cottage that is partly weatherboarded. Not far down the road is Upton House, built in 1731 and the birthplace of the surgeon Joseph Lister, founder of antiseptic surgery.

Crossing to the north-east of the borough we visit Manor Park, whose most famous son was John Travers Cornwell, the posthumous V.C. winner in the battle of Jutland in 1916. This boy, who stayed by his gun long after the rest of the gun crew had been killed by a German shell, lies buried in the Manor Park cemetery.

On the way south down the A117 we pass through Plashet. This place also has a famous figure associated with it. Elizabeth Fry, whose indomitable faith led to the reform of our prison system, lived here for twenty years.

Farther south on High Street South is the parish church of East Ham. This is St. Mary Magdalene, and here tucked away amid the bustle of busy highways is an almost unique specimen of twelfth-century Norman architecture. Although a little extended over the years, the basic ground plan remains unchanged from the days when the Normans built it on the site of an earlier Saxon building.

Passing through Beckton, we head for the southernmost part of the borough. The road, Manor Way (A117), cuts across the end of the docks and you may well be held up, for this section of road swings aside to allow large ships to pass into the Thames. The docks cover an area of over 1,000 acres, of which 230 are water. Here you get an opportunity to see a concentration of ocean-going ships that is unrivalled anywhere in the world.

Finally we reach North Woolwich, where a new shopping precinct has replaced some of the old buildings that abound here. The interesting thing here is at the water's edge, where the famous Woolwich free ferry continues taking people and their cars from Essex into Kent. Sad to record, the broad old paddle ferry has recently been retired and now a modern screw-driven boat gets you there more efficiently, if less romantically. The more energetic can walk under the Thames along the tunnel that goes from near the ferry over to the Kent side.

REDBRIDGE

IN the bustle of this London borough there is a retreat to peace and contemplation which includes the oldest building in existence in all these 14,000 acres. It is the hospital and chapel of St. Mary and St. Thomas of Canterbury, in the High Road on the south of Ilford Hill. It was founded back in the twelfth century by the abbess of a foundation already 500 years old to house " thirteen lepers of the king's servants." Though leprosy diminished and all abbeys were done away with this foundation survived. The chapel is still the original building, but the almshouses were rebuilt in 1927.

From this placid backwater, and with the aid of the excellent guide issued by the borough, we can overlook the interesting features of the constituent communities of Ilford, Wanstead and Woodford. Parking meters and one-way systems are almost natural hazards in Ilford today as in the other nuclei of the borough. The old town is known all over the world for the great range of photographic equipment which took the town's name as its brand and started life in the basement of Alfred Harman's house in Cranbrook Road in 1897.

The oldest mansion in Ilford is Valentines, in the park of the same name, also off Cranbrook Road. It was built at the end of the seventeenth century. Now its master and mistress are gone and its servants have disappeared, but it houses another kind of servant; the local government officers who run the housing service have their headquarters here. Creeper-bedecked, it stands in a 130-acre park which is as well cared for today as ever it was. Few people know that the Hampton Court vine started life as a cutting from a vine set here seven years previously in 1758 but the Valentines vine was destroyed by an over-zealous head gardener in 1875.

The A118 runs on south into Newham, while eastward Seven Kings and Chadwell are sandwiched between this road and the A12

(Eastern Avenue). Seven Kings remembers in its name the meeting here, long before the Normans, of seven great Saxon kings. Chadwell represents the miraculous flow of water dedicated to St. Chad. To the north, along the Hainault road through Aldborough, it is possible to drive through the last few acres of farmland left to reach the estates in Hainault ward which verge on the old forest we have described elsewhere. Here the park with its lake and refreshment pavilion and the municipal golf course act as one of the many " lungs " through which residents can breathe good Essex air, whatever boundaries mere men may make.

Immediately north of Ilford is Barkingside, which has a place in Britain's story because here Dr. Barnardo's " village home for destitute girls " was set up in 1873, the second in a long line of these wonderful homes. Thirty homes, each for twenty or so girls, forming their own village, lie along the Cranbrook road north of the Gants Hill roundabout. Farther north again at the edge of the borough another Barnardo village borders the grounds of Claybury hospital.

Between the River Roding and the western boundary lie the denser districts of Wanstead, Snaresbrook and Woodford. Wanstead's church of St. Mary was rebuilt in the eighteenth century, though you can still see in the churchyard a line of flat tombstones which marks the aisle of the earlier building. In the chancel, look for the monument to Sir Josiah Child, father of Sir Richard, builder in 1715 of the fabulous Wanstead House.

In its building there came to light a Roman tessellated pavement, proof of the long history of this place, where much of the past has had to be destroyed in the interest of modern development. Lord Rich, owner of Wanstead manor in the sixteenth century, built the first house, but Sir Richard's replaced and eclipsed it, to become the miracle of the age, costing around £360,000 even in the coin of the times! The splendour of the gardens brought an endless stream of spectators. Today these gardens are perpetuated in Wanstead Park, where the Roding runs to feed the decorative pools, the boating lake and the waterways, but the only remains of the house are the gateposts of the main entrance on either side of Overton Drive at the Blake Hall Road junction, for a spendthrift inheritor brought the house to demolition and its contents to the sale room in 1825. The golf club in the park still uses part of the old stables, though they have had their share of damage from fire in the recent past.

Another open space, Wanstead Flats, was originally planted with trees in 1886 as a project to give relief to the unemployed.

Snaresbrook bestrides the A11, the Woodford road, just to the north. Much built up now, it can still boast an early Georgian inn, the Eagle. At Woodford, where the same A11 forms its High Road, there is nothing left to remind us of the wells which were once much patronized for the cures they were reputed to effect, except the name of the inn nearby, the Horse and Well. In modern times Wanstead and Woodford became famous as the constituency, from 1924 to 1964, of Sir Winston Churchill. His statue stands on Woodford green at Salway Hill, cast in bronze by David McFall and eight and a half feet high—a kind of symbol of the way Sir Winston stood that much taller than his contemporaries.

WALTHAM FOREST

WE reach the end of our search for the beauty and attractions of Essex here at Waltham Forest, a long, slender borough right on the western boundary of the London boroughs of Essex. This is a fitting place to complete our series of journeys, for here is a microcosm of the whole. In the north at Chingford you can look over the great Epping Forest, all that remains of the Forest of Essex that centuries ago covered this county like a frozen army; away to the west at Walthamstow, where the reservoirs on the River Lea catch the reflections of the sun and remind us of the many stretches of water and sea that are so much a part of Essex; and finally down to Leyton and the modern Essex of crowded streets and large shops.

Any inspection of this borough must start in the north at the edge of the forest, for here near Forest Avenue on the A1069 stands the famous Queen Elizabeth's Hunting Lodge. Three stories high, this glorious Tudor building proudly shows its timbers to the modern world. The present visitor can still enjoy the view that was once reserved for royalty, for the lodge is now a museum of natural history and is open each Thursday, Friday and Sunday from 2 to 5 p.m., free of charge. This is a unique sixteenth-century building and should not be missed. Nearby is the timber-framed Royal Forest hotel, but this is an imitation of the lodge built in 1933.

To the west the land climbs to become Pole Hill, and on this hill in 1824 a granite obelisk was erected to mark north from Greenwich observatory. It is a fine place from which to look to the forest.

Havering-atte-Bower : ". . . a shock for those who think that anywhere within a dozen miles of Charing Cross must be overcrowded."

L/E

Barking.
" Today only
the fire bell or
curfew tower
remains as a
fifteenth-centu
reminder of
earlier glory."

Tilbury Fort. "You can still see in all its impressive majesty the main gateway built by Inigo Jones."

The Tilbury hailing station looking out across the River Thames at Tilbury. "On a sunny day it is a pleasing sight to . . . watch a host of ships from all corners of the world."

A little south, the A110 cuts its path across the borough, but it leaves behind a small green. Close by is the new parish church of Chingford, St. Peter and St. Paul, built in 1844 in the Gothic style. Inside is the Norman font from the old church of All Saints. This latter church is in Old Church Road, south-west of our present position and near the reservoirs. For many years the church was roofless and the haunt of artists, and was so overgrown that it was locally called the " green church." In 1929 this was changed with a rebuilding that restored the church to some of its former beauty.

East from All Saints, the A1009 (New Road) carries us past the modern Larkswood swimming pool and the large park behind it to Larkshall Road. Here we go north again to see the remains at Pimp Hall. The farmhouse is now demolished, but the great barn and dovecote still remain from the seventeenth century. To the east, down Simmons Lane, is Friday House, a country house of early Victorian building.

Let us retrace our steps a little and go south into Walthamstow along the A112 (Chingford Road). Described by White in 1848 as one of the " handsomest suburban villages near the metropolis," Walthamstow has grown from 5,000 people to a town of over 100,000. It would be impossible within the space available to guide you in detail round all the scattered things of interest, so we must content ourselves by picking out some typical of the rest.

We leave the A112 by turning right at the junction with Bretten-ham Road, and then left down Carr Road. On the left is the large Lloyd Park, most of which was donated by Frank Lloyd. At the end of the park, in Forest Road, is Water House, an imposing house of yellow brick built in 1762. It was here that William Morris spent much of his childhood. The house is now the William Morris gallery and is open, free of charge, from 10 a.m. to 5 p.m. every weekday, with later extensions during the summer on Tuesdays and Thursdays. It is also open on the first Sunday of each month from 10 a.m. to 12 noon and 2 to 5 p.m. Exhibitions show the contribution of Morris to art and printing, and loan exhibitions are also shown.

West along Forest Road, where it crosses the River Lea, and close by the six miles of reservoirs that provide such a happy home for a multitude of wild animals, is the unspoilt eighteenth-century Ferry Boat inn. This inn has a long connection with the history of Walthamstow, for until the nineteenth century the manorial court of Walthamstow Toni was held here on Whit-Tuesday.

From Forest Road run south to the High Street, where on Fridays and Saturdays you can walk down the longest market in London. At the eastern end you can find houses from 1700 hiding away behind the shop fronts.

Continuing east, we cross Hoe Street into Church Hill and arrive at the parish church of St. Mary. There is little of the original Norman building to see since the thoroughgoing rebuilding of the sixteenth century, but you can still see many old brasses and some notable monuments, including one to Sir George Monoux. The Monoux name appears all over the borough, and it dates from 1507, when Sir George left Bristol and settled here. He was master of the Drapers' Company and mayor of London in 1514-5. Across from the church are the Monoux almshouses, founded in 1527. They were much and well restored in 1955 after war damage.

South of the church in Vestry Road is one of Walthamstow's proudest houses—Vestry House, built in 1730 as the workhouse and now combined with the Old Armoury to form a museum of local history. It is open from 10 a.m. to 12 noon and 1 to 5 p.m. on weekdays, with an extension to 8 p.m. on Mondays and Wednesdays; admission is free.

Finally, let us have a glimpse of the old Walthamstow. We can do this out on the eastern edge of town at the southern end of Woodford New Road. Here, gathered round the common, are groups of Georgian houses preserved from more leisurely days. The Forest School incorporates a row of these Georgian buildings and provides a most pleasant setting for feeding the mind.

We enter Leytonstone by going " round the corner " and leaving Woodford New Road to join Lea Bridge Road and then Whipps Cross Road. To the left lie 200 acres of trees and glades, with a giant lake shaded by a variety of foliage. This is a corner of the forest trapped at the edge of a busy town. There are many paths through the forest, and one leads up to the open-air swimming pool, an ideal place to spend a warm afternoon. Across the road is the hospital, and this includes an eleven-bay seventeenth-century house (Forest House) among its buildings.

Just north of the junction of Whipps Cross and High Road is a Roman milestone counting the distance from London.

On the right, along the High Road, is the parish church of St. John, which was built in 1843 through the efforts of William Cotton, one-time governor of the Bank of England. Its other claim to fame is the connection of its third vicar, Mr. Waller, with David Livingstone. Waller gave Livingstone his last communion before he left England.

Let us travel the length of Leytonstone's High Road and see the variety of shops and dwellings that line it before we go west along Crownfield Road to join another High Road. This one runs up through Leyton and passes the Orient football ground before we bear left to visit the church of St. Mary. This is a block-like building in the Perpendicular style, parts of it dating from 1658. Among many memorials the one to the famous historian John Strype stands out, for he was vicar here for sixty-eight years.

Nearby in Church Road is Etloe House, once the residence of Cardinal Wiseman and now a home for destitute girls. The house was built in 1760 and has a Tudor-like appearance.

So we end our book about Essex, but it would be unfair to leave you in the midst of buildings, for essentially Essex is still a place of grass, trees, light and space. So let us journey a short distance up Leyton's High Road to find the Coronation Park right in the centre of this shopping street. Here we will take our leave of you on a park bench, with birds singing in trees and the sun's rays falling through leaves to make an ever-changing pattern on the rich green of the grass.

BOOK LIST

A selection of books for further reading

Brimble, J. A.: *London's Epping Forest*

B.M.C.: *Guide to Essex*

Christy, M.: *Handbook on Essex*

Coller, D. W.: *People's History of Essex*

Cox, J. C.: *Essex* (" Little Guide " series)

Edwards, A. C.: *History of Essex*

Essex Countryside 1952 to date

Essex Record Office: exhibition catalogues, map reproductions and other useful publications

Essex Review 1892 to 1956

Grieve, H.: *Great Tide*

Kelly's Essex directory of 1937

Mee, A.: *Essex* (" King's England " series)

Morant, P.: *History of Essex*

Ordnance Survey: one-inch series sheets 148, 149, 160, 161, 162

Pevsner, N.: *Essex* (" Buildings of England " series)

Royal Commission: *Historic Monuments of Essex*, four volumes

Town guides: available on application to local council offices

Victoria County History of Essex (in progress)

Warren, C. H.: *Essex* (" County Books " series)

Wright, T.: *History and Topography of Essex*

INDEX

223